VISUALS FOR INFORMATION
RESEARCH AND PRACTICE

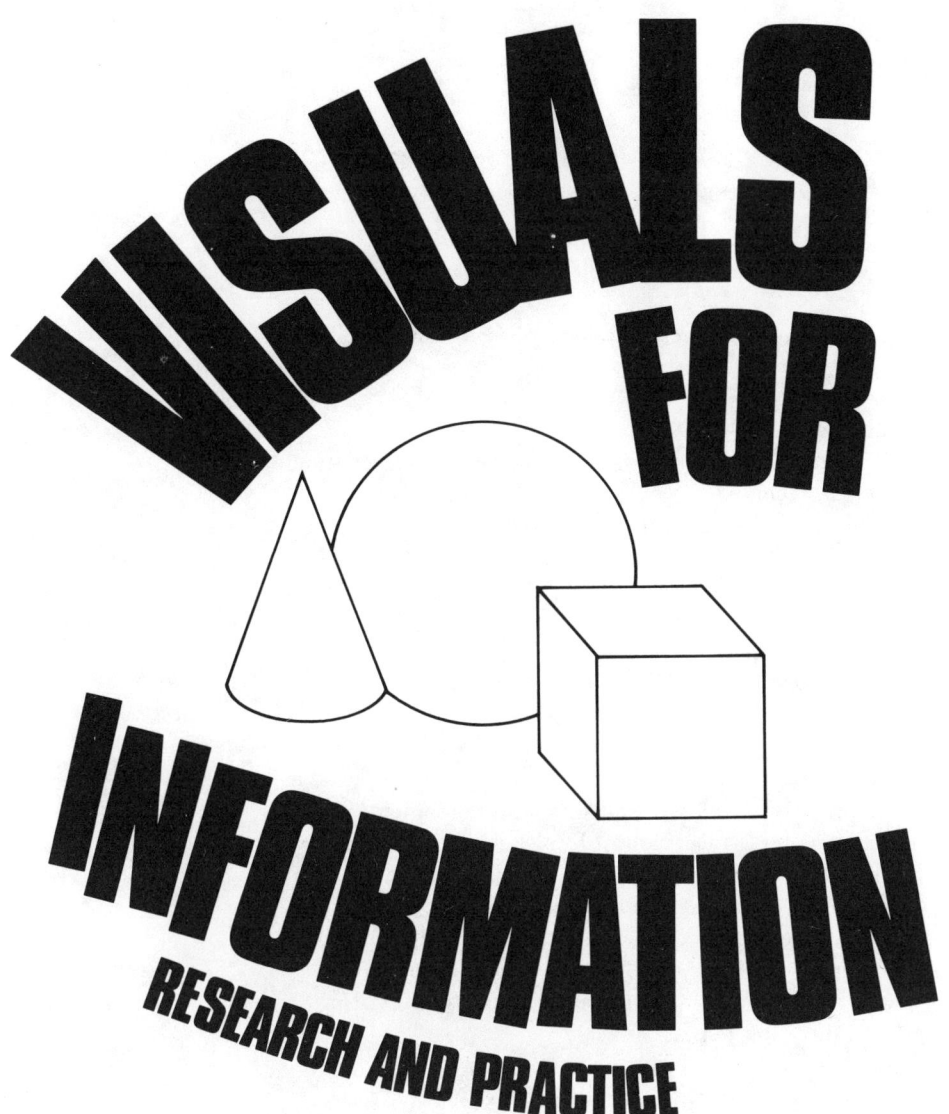

RUNE PETTERSSON

**Educational Technology Publications
Englewood Cliffs, New Jersey 07632**

Library of Congress Cataloging-in-Publication Data

Pettersson, Rune, 1943-
    Visuals for information : research and practice / Rune Pettersson.
      p. cm.
    Includes bibliographies and index.
    ISBN 0-87778-218-0
    1. Visual communication. 2. Communication—Audio-visual aids.
I. Title.
P93.5.P48   1989
302.23—dc20   89-7809
                                                                                                                        CIP

Copyright © 1989 by Educational Technology Publications, Inc., Englewood Cliffs, New Jersey 07632. All rights reserved. No part of this book may be reproduced or transmitted, in any form or by any means, electronic or mechanical, including photocopying, recording, or by any information storage and retrieval system, without permission in writing from the Publisher.

Printed in the United States of America.

Library of Congress Catalog Card Number: 89-7809.

International Standard Book Number: 0-87778-218-0.

First Printing: July, 1989.

PREFACE

The past few decades have witnessed dramatic developments in technology. One example from each decade can serve to illustrate the major changes, especially those occurring in the media field.

In 1946, ENIAC, the world's first electronic computer, made its debut. It weighed 30 tons, contained 18,000 tubes and had a memory capable of storing only 20 numbers. Pocket calculators of today have a much greater capacity, and personal computers can easily store the contents of a book in internal memory.

In 1956, the first regularly scheduled TV transmissions began in Sweden. The American Ampex company introduced the first video tape recorder. It was a large, expensive machine with an insatiable appetite for 2-inch, open-reel tape. 1988, one-third of all Swedish households (33 %) have small, handy video cassette recorders, usually employing 1/2 inch tape. The corresponding figures for the United States and Japan are 46 % and 62 % respectively.

In 1962, the first communications satellite, Telstar, was launched into orbit. In 1988, 600,000 Swedish households (8 %) can view satellite TV transmissions via local cable TV networks. At some locations in the United States, viewers have a choice of 50–60 programs. Many channels also broadcast around the clock.

In 1973, the Dutch company Philips launched its optical video disc system. This medium permits the storage of truly vast amounts of information. CD-ROM discs of today are only 12 cm in diameter but can store 600 mega-bytes of information. All the text in several encyclopedias can be made easily accessible in a database stored in CD-ROM.

In 1985, the Japanese company Sony presented the world's largest video screen, 40 x 25 meters, i.e. 1,000 m^2 (10,764 ft^2), at EXPO 85 in the Tsukuba research village outside Tokyo. This "Jumbotron" image was more than two million times larger than a similar TV image on a wrist-watch TV. Flat, high-resolution video displays emitting virtually no harmful radiation are currently under development.

Now systems for desktop publishing are common. Easy to handle software gives the layman the opportunity to combine verbal and visual messages. Unfortunately most desktop publishers know little about visual information.

So technical developments have moved at a very rapid pace. Everything suggests that the pace of developments is likely to increase rather than decrease. So *visual messages* in different forms *will become increasingly important*. However, only limited knowledge is available on visual communications, pictures as a means of linguistic communications and the interplay between verbal and visual messages. So attention must be devoted to issues concerning the production, transmission and perception of verbo-visual messages.

This book is useful to practitioners as well as to researchers. In fact the book might be interesting for everyone interested in verbo-visual messages. I hope that it is possible to narrow the gap between research and practice.

The author acknowledges his dept to a large number of researchers and practitioners in the field of verbo-visual literacy.

Rune Pettersson
Stockholm, Sweden
1989

INTRODUCTION

The word "information" is derived from the Latin noun informatio which means a "conception" or "idea". "Information" has therefore long been synonymous with "data", "details" or "facts" (1). The word ultimately acquired three additional meanings. Nowadays, it may even refer to the import ascribed to specific data (2). Then information does not arise until the received data, e.g. a text or a picture, are interpreted by the receiver. The term "information" is also sometimes used for data processed in a computer (3). "An internal structure which regulates processes" is yet another meaning (4). The latter meaning is used in computer science and in genetics. The verb "inform" means to supply or convey information or provide knowledge of and is therefore an unidirectional process, e.g from one person to another. However, to "communicate" entails an interplay between two or more persons.

Information is a richly varied concept covering many important disciplines and areas of knowledge plus different kinds of information. Most people are involved with communications and communications systems in one way or another. Some of these systems have "soft", human or linguistic dimensions, whereas others possess "hard", technological dimensions. Some subject fields have been well-established for many years. Others are relatively new. These fields can be regarded as independent scientific disciplines. In several instances, there is some overlapping because certain sub-issues are addressed in different disciplines, even if approaches may vary.

Information science
Information science, or *informatics*, is a scientific discipline comprising information in general and storage of information with areas like classification, indexing, cataloguing, bibliographic and other databases. Other important areas are seeking, retrieval and transmission of information. Information science also comprises various library information service activities like administration, collections, circulation as well as scientific communication, use of information and information resources management..

The task of an *informatic, i.e. documentalist,* is to collect and tabulate scientific information. This information is often sought in national and international databases.

Information processing
Information processing is a scientific discipline comprising e.g. mathematical and numerical analysis plus methods and technics for administrative data processing. The discipline also comprises the study of information searches in databases, information systems, computer aided translation, computer aided education, computer aided problem solving and design etc.

The term "information processing" is often used as a synonym for data processing, i.e. the execution of a systematic series of operations on data. The term is also sometimes used for studies of the way people process information mentally (see "Psychological information theory" below).

Information theory
Information theory is a scientific discipline which comprises measurement of transmitted information and comparison of various communications systems, especially in telecommunications.

In information theory, the information's contents lack inherent interest. Information theory is based on a mathematical theory presented in 1948 by the American mathematician Claude E. Shannon. It subsequently came to be known as Shannon's and Weaver's mathematical communications model. In this kind of communications system, a sender (e.g. a telex unit) communi-

Introduction

cates with one or more receivers (other telex units) via a channel. The sender codes the transmitted signal, and the receiver decodes the received signal. Information theory utilizes the *bit* as the smallest unit of information. A bit can either be a one or a zero, representing e.g. "yes"/"no" or "on"/ "off".

Shannon's and Weaver's communications theory was originally developed for studies of telecommunications and other technical systems. But it has also been used for communications between people.

Psychological information theory
Psychological information theory is the designation for one of the main branches of cognitive psychology. It refers to the study of Man's mental processing of information, i.e. mental information processing. A major principle in cognitive psychology is that Man organizes impressions and knowledge into meaningful units. This process starts at the perception stage.

Psychological information theory describes the brain's work as a process in which the flow of information between different types of memory functions determines whether or not we are able to solve different intellectual problems, such as learning something.

Semantic information theory
In philosophy, semantic information theory refers to the information supplied by a proposition in terms of the proposition's probability and specifies the principles for measuring information. One basic concept is: the greater a proposition's information content, the less probable the proposition.

Information technology
Information technology (IT) is a science dealing with the technical systems used for making production, distribution, storage and other information handling more efficient. This includes e.g. computer technology and electronics.

The term *information society* is sometimes used in information technology. This is a designation for the society which follows an industrial society and in which Man's thinking power is supported by information processing computer systems and telecommunications technics. The information society is dominated by the resource "information" instead of energy, raw materials, labour and capital.

Social information
Social information, i.e. the result of all information measures whose aim is to make it easier for citizens to know what their rights, privileges and obligations are, is studied in social science subjects. Good social information should be readily accessible, tailored to local requirements, readily grasped, adapted to individual needs and capable of creating a state of preparedness in the receiver. The information must be closely integrated with the activities of the respective authorities, professionally planned and designed and disseminated through efficient media.

Information ergonomics
Information ergonomics comprises research and development of the ergonomic design of Man-machine systems. The design of an information system must be based on studies of the information user's aims, knowledge, experience and way of working.
 Tasks making particularly heavy information demands occur in work at computer terminals, work at complex information panels and signal systems (e.g. for the monitoring of industrial processes etc.) Information ergonomics include lighting, the design of chairs, terminal tables, instrument panels, video display units, characters, symbols, signals etc.

Infology
Infology is the science of verbo-visual presentation of information. On the basis of Man's prerequisites, infology encompasses studies of the way a verbo-visual representation should be designed in order to achieve optimum communications between sender and receiver. Some studies concentrate on the sender, others on the receiver, representation or communications process as such.
 Infology is interdisciplinary and encompasses many aspects from "established fields" such as art, cinema, computer science, esthetics, film, graphic design, information science, information ergonomics, information technology, information theory,

Introduction

journalism, linguistics, mass communications, pedagogics, physiology, psychological information theory, semiology, sociology, trade language, visual arts etc. As far as various aspects of verbo-visual messages are concerned, it is necessary to work from a holistic point of view in which the individual receiver is at the centre.

Points in common
As the above presentations of the different research fields shows, many of these fields will be seen to have points in common.

Data processing is studied in information science, information processing and information technology. *Information searches in databases* are conducted in both information science and information processing. The concept *communications* is studied in information science, information theory and infology. The *measurement* of information occurs in information theory, semantic information theory and infology. *Perception* and *cognition* are studied in psychological information theory, information ergonomics and infology. *Social developments* are studied in information technology and social information. Information *design* is a subject of interest in information ergonomics, infology and social information. The *development of new media* is a subject of interest in information technology, social information and infology.

This book deals mainly with the "visual" part of verbo-visual presentations.

CONTENTS

Preface *v*

Introduction *vii*

Chapter 1-Communication 1
  Media and representations 1
      Communication models 2
      Medium and message 5
      Production of need-oriented information 9
  Media consumption 10
      Media market size 12
      Media-industry mapping 14
  New media 22
      Electronic Publishing 24
      Video 25
      Teletext 26
      Videotex 27
      Cable TV 29
      Databases 30
      Mediateques 31
  The information society 33
      From writers to readers 34
      Consequences of electronic publishing 35
      Changes in media consumption 39

The introduction of new media 40
   Users' viewpoints 40, Producers' viewpoints 41, Originators' viewpoints 43, Viewpoints of the society 43
Screen Communication 43
   Visual Displays 45
   Color Description Systems 47
   The message on the screen 50
      Text 50, Numeric Data 53, Visuals 55
   Computer Print-Outs 55
References 58

Chapter 2-Perception, learning and memory 61
Our senses 61
   Hearing 61
   Vision 63
      Eye movements 64, Movement and change 69
Listening and looking 70
   Perception "laws 70
   Choice of information 72
   The brain 75
   Picture perception 78
      Assignments 79, Approaches to picture perception 89, Message design 92
   A cognitive model 93
Learning and memory 97
   Learning 98
   Memory 101
   Inner images 107
   Development 108
   Illusions 113
References 117

Chapter 3-Literacy 127
Language 127
Verbal languages 132
   Spoken languages 132
   Written languages 135
      A printed message 137

Introduction *xv*

   Characteristics of verbal languages 140
  Visual languages 141
   Functions 142
   Levels of meaning 146
   Structure 153
    Ratings of variables 155
   Properties 157
   Picture readability 162
   Picture quality 165
   Measuring picture properties 167
    Before the original 167, Before technical production 167, After publication 171
   Classifications of visuals 174
    The picture circle 174, Symbols 178, Computer pictures 180, Picture archives 183, Picture databases 186
   Picture dimensions 191
   Characteristics of visual languages 200
  Linguistic combinations 201
   Lexi-visual representations 204
    Interplay of text and graphic design 204, Interplay of text and pictures 205, Interplay of text, picture and graphic design 205, Cartography 206, Infography 206
   Audio-visual representations 210
    Speech and visuals 210
     Speech and body language 211, Speech and demonstrations 211, Speech and stills 212, Speech and moving pictures 213
    Recorded representations 213
     Linear use 213, Interactive use 213
  Current research 213
  References 218

Chapter 4-Designing visuals for information 223
  Content 223
   Structure 224
    Realism 225, Degree of detail 226
   Factual content 227

Objects 227, Time 228, Place 228, Statistics 228
Events 230
   Motion 231, Sound 232, Humour and satire 232, Relationships 232,
Emotions 232
Credibility 233
Viewer completion 234
Execution 235
   Graphical elements 239
   Type of visual 243
   Subject 243
   Light 244
      Outer orientation functions 244, Inner orientation functions 245, Lighting 245
   Shape 246
      External shape 246, External contour 246
   Size 247
      Size of visual 248, Size of subjects 248, Size and depth 250
   Color 250
      Color preferences 251, Color visibility 251, Attentional use of color 251, Affective use of color 251, Cognitive use of color 252, Color coding 252, Decorative use of color 252, Color psychology 253
   Contrast 253
   Emphasis 253
   Composition 254
      Organization 254, Centers of interest 255, Balance 256
   Perspective 256
      Depth 257, Depth of field 258, Picture angle 258, Picture height 258
   Technical quality 259
   Symbols and explanatory words, lettering 259
   Mixing and zoom 260
   Picture editing 260
      Selection 260, Changes of image content 260, The picture in context 262
   Copyright 263
      Terms of delivery 264, Ethical rules 265
Context 265
   Interplay of words and visuals 266

Introduction xvii

           Text 268, Legends 270, Image framing 273
      Interplay of visuals 273
      Layout 274
  Format 277
      Image morphology 278
      Analogue and digital coding 284
      Perception of pixels 285
      Image format categories 286
  References 288

Index 311

Chapter 1

COMMUNICATION

Technical developments have moved at a very rapid pace. Everything suggests that the pace of developments is likely to increase rather than decrease. New media like video, teletext, videotex, databases and hyper-media all indicate that visual messages in different forms will become increasingly important in all kinds of communication.

Today computer-based interactive systems are used for training and learning in schools as well as in industry. The information society is already here. Attention must be devoted to issues concerning the production, transmission, presentation, and perception of verbo-visual information.

MEDIA AND REPRESENTATIONS

Communications between people have always been important. Aspects of our society are becoming increasingly intertwined, and the need for communications between people is increasing at a fast pace. We need to communicate in order to establish contacts with one another, to maintain and improve those contacts, to exchange information and views and to develop ourselves and the society. If communication is to be possible at all, signals in some form must be transmitted, received and deciphered. Both animals and people communicate with the aid of simple signals. The signals may be aural or visual. They can also consist of odors or tactile contacts and therefore act on our sense of smell and touch rather than on our hearing and vision. There is often an interplay between different signals or stimuli which coalesce into a unified whole. Simple signals usually elicit simple responses in the message recipient whose responses elicit responses from the original message transmitter etc. Information systems of considerable complexity can arise in this way.

Communication models

Many information and communications theorists have devised models to explain the way the communications process operates. As early as 1948 Laswell put it this way: communications are WHO says WHAT to WHOM via which CHANNEL and to what EFFECT. Then Shannon and Weaver (1949) proposed the following model which illustrates the way information is passed from a sender to a receiver: A message is selected by an Information Source and incorporated by the Transmitter into a signal which is received by a Receiver and transformed into the message reaching the Destination. The signal can be influenced by noise.

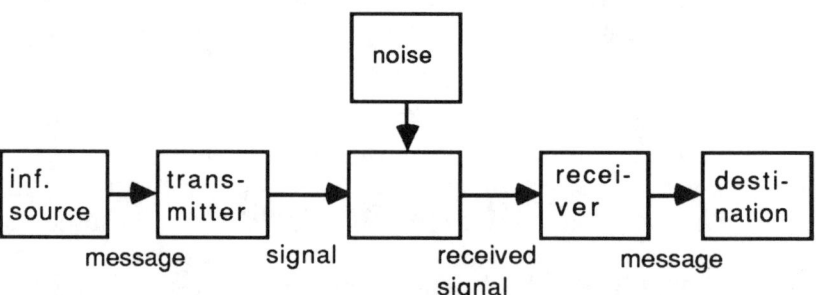

The Shannon and Weaver communications model.

We can be sure that people do not derive the same information from things they read, hear or see. The meaning of any language, verbal or visual, is not only resident in words, lines, colors etc but in ourselves to a large degree. We have to learn to assign meaning to language symbols used. We have to learn the codes, and they differ in different societies and in different cultures. Schramm (1954) used a model to show that there must also be some overlapping in the fields of experience of the sender and of the receiver for communication to take place.

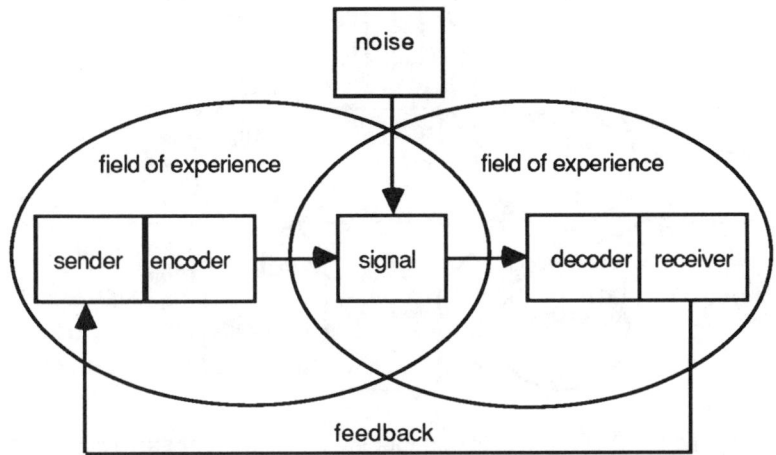

Schramm's adopting of the Shannon and Weaver communications model.

Designers often produce instructional material for their own counterparts, not for the people who need the information. This is because many designers lack basic knowledge about communication possibilities. Subsequent models have incorporated an increasing number of variables but often fail, in my view, in their treatment of perception processes.

In the production of information, a sender conveys information on a part of reality via a representation to an information receiver who, via sensory impressions, is able to obtain some perception of that reality. This perception may then evoke some response which affects the reality and/or creates some feedback to the original sender. The receiver's perception varies as a result of a number of factors, e.g. his current cultural and social status, the time and stage of his development, his mood, experience, memory and other cognitive processes, such as creativity. Perception is divorced from the representation which, in turn is divorced from the reality ($P \neq Rp \neq R$). Some of our sensory impressions give rise to "garbage" and some to learning. Learning is transferred to the memory by cognitive means. The cognitive variables exert an influence on subsequent perceptions and may also evoke inner perceptions and inner imagery.

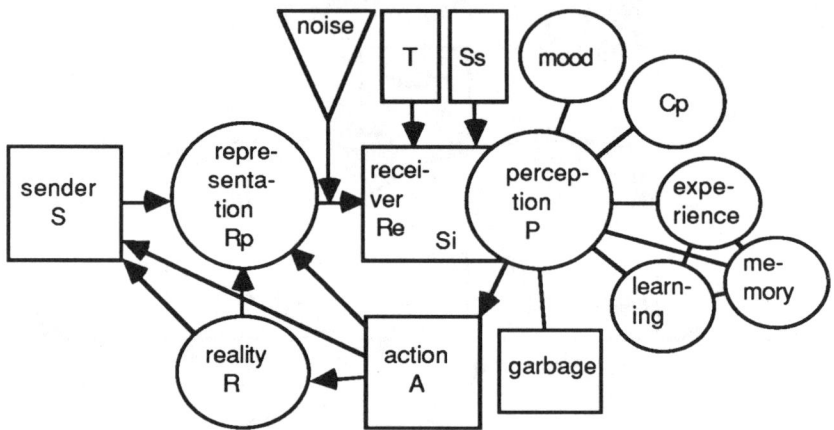

Pettersson's 1982 communications model. T = Time and stages of development. Ss = Cultural and social status. Si = Sensory impression. Cp = Cognitive processes such as intelligence and creativity.

"Noise" may intrude on various occasions and interfere with this process. Every "perception", such as a visual sensation, is actually composed of a large number of different sub-components which are aggregated into a single holistic impression. A representation, e.g. a visual, which is to be used to convey certain information, has a sender, one or more receivers and even a content, of course, a structure, a context and a format. The visual is produced in a certain way with respect to various variables. The model shows that perception is different and never twice the same: $P \neq R_p \neq R$, $P_1 \neq P_2 \neq P_3$, $P_{Re1} \neq P_{Re2} \neq P_{Re3}$, $A_1 \neq A_2 \neq A_3$.

The content, the structure, the context and the format influence the viewer's ability to perceive the picture. There is every reason to assume that the various picture variables play a very important role in our ability to read and understand pictures. A picture which is easy to comprehend provides good learning and memory retention. This makes it a better representation than a picture which the viewer finds difficult to comprehend.

So the task of the information producer is to select a representation in such a way that perception of the representation is optimized. This is a task with many different dimensions. Communications are successful when a receiver comprehends the message a sender has wished to convey to him or her.

People are being exposed to an increasing volume of "messages" from many different senders. The messages are transmitted from senders to receivers with the aid of different media. In all communications (even in masscommunications), *many individuals are the recipients of the messages.*

Medium and message

In the 60's the famous media expert professor Marshall MacLuhan coined the expression "The Medium is the Message". This expression has given rise to considerable confusion. Now, in the 80's, it is often said "The Message is the Medium". Technology is the servant, and the message, the idea, is the matter. This is said to be demonstrated by the fact that in 1980, for every dollar spent on A-V equipment, there were nearly three dollars spent on A-V software. However, the medium is not the message. A medium is an aid used in the transfer of information from a sender to a receiver.

The term aid is used here as a collective designation for the channel, or information carrier, and the processor/equipment required for encoding and decoding the information.

An information carrier is the material which carries the information, such as paper, plastic, film, electromagnetic waves, magnetic tape etc.

The term information refers to content, message, knowledge etc. Information can be moved from one place to another and stored in analog or digital form.

There are different types of media. Each has its own particular properties, advantages and disadvantages.

Our existing media may be classified according to several different criteria. (See Media-industry mapping.)

A general principle of human communication is that the likelihood of successful communication increases when a concrete reference is present. In the absence of the actual thing, the next best reference is a visual representation of the thing. A visual is more pertinent reference for meaning than the spoken or written word. Visuals are iconic. They normally resemble the thing they represent.

A medium plus its contents is a representation (or even a re-presentation) of reality. Representations of reality can display varying structures, consist of a number of different components and be related to one another in different ways. Words and visuals, sound and visuals or sound, words and visuals are examples of components which can interact.

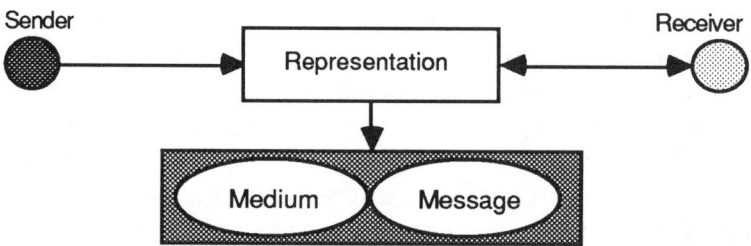

A representation or (re-presentation) is a medium plus its message/content.

A message/content with a given design/form is conveyed by the sender to the receiver with the aid of a medium. The various media are undergoing comprehensive (technical) changes, changes in terms of production, duplication, stock-keeping, distribution or presentation of contents. Some of these developments are proceeding in the same direction and working together. Others are on separate paths. Some are even counter-acting one another.

Visuals used in instructional message design are usually representations of our external reality. However, fine arts are sometimes representations of our inner reality, such as thoughts and dreams.

In a *redundant relationship*, the same information is conveyed via e.g. words, sound and visuals and is therefore "superfluous". For example, subtitles can be added to a TV program so the action displayed on the screen is described by the words. This greatly enhances the educational impact of the program. A redundant relationship should be used in instructional message design.

In a *relevant relationship*, the information presented via e.g. a text or sound supplements the information supplied in the visual. Visuals with a relevant relationship to a spoken or printed text can greatly enhance the text's informative effect and vice-versa.

In an *irrelevant relationship*, the information presented in various channels is completely independent of one another. In TV programs, for example, the picture sometimes deals with one aspect, the text with another and the sound with a third. This makes it harder for viewers to make the most out of the programme. Conflicts readily arise between a concrete visual event and abstract verbal information. When this happens, the concrete, readily accessible information assumes priority over the abstract information.

A *contradictory relationship* exists when the information in various channels conflicts. This is disastrous for an informative programme.

Different media are capable of representing reality with varying facility owing to differences in their structure, the kind of representation involved and the content. The text (both spoken and written) is an example of a "one-dimensional" representation. It "flows" in a relatively fixed and often unambiguous form along a time axis. A still picture is "two-dimensional". Its interpretation is less constrained. A still picture can be interpreted in more than one way. We extract differing parts of the available information in it each time we view it. A stereo picture adds a third "dimension". Having a "one-dimensional" and "two-dimensional" representation at the same time, or even "one-dimensional", "two-dimensional" and "three-dimensional" representation, at the same time is possible, even commonplace. In the future media also might be capable of representing smell which would add still another dimension.

Different media are also related to one another as regards their level of structural complexity. The simplest form of a "one-dimensional" representation is a simple acoustic signal, such as a baby's cry. A higher degree of complexity is found in texts, interactive texts or dialogue, monophonic music, stereophonic music and stereophonic radio theatre with sound effects.

Tableau showing the relationship of various media to structural complexity and to different types of representation.

Level of complexity	Type of representation				
	1-dimensional	2-dimensional	simultan. 1- and 2-dimensional	3-dimensional	simultan. 1-,2-, 3-dimensional
low	acoustic signals (e.g. baby crying)	children's scribbling	teletext, (text & graphs) telefax	stereo-picture	mirror-image
	text, spoken & written (letters, telegrams, papers, books, telex)	still pictures, informative pictures, symbols)	comics (text + cartoons + graphical symbols	hologram	"living-visuals", sign-language body-language (clothing)
	dialogue, i.e. interactive text, spoken & written (telephone)	still pictures, realistic pictures	videotex, (interactive text & pictures	model	"living-visuals", ballet
	music, performed & written	still pictures, suggestive pictures maps	filmstrips, and slide series with sound	sculpture	"living-visuals", theatre, conference
	stereo music, performed & written	still pictures, true-to-life analytical picture	exhibition	exhibition	holograpic film & TV in stereo & color
	radio theatre in stereo	lexivision, complete co-ordination between text & image	film & TV programs	stereo picture & holograms with movement in image	
high					reality

If text is likened to a flow along a time axis, then music can be likened to a multitude of streams flowing along the same time axis at the same time. Music is always structurally more complex than text but can, of course, be very simple in content. The greater the degree of structural complexity, the closer the representation approaches reality at a given time, in a given place and in a given context. The table (p.8) is an attempt to describe my view of the interrelationships of various media in a twodimensional represen-tation of a multidimensional reality.

The sender, like the information receiver, can be a person, a group, a company, an organization or an authority. A distinction is often made between private media, group media and mass-media. Each medium has its own particular properties. The selection of a suitable medium is important when informative material is to be produced.

Production of need-oriented information

When producing information for instruction, education or any other reason we have to choose between different representations and between different media. Which representation would be best then? That question has many answers related to the needs and to the objectives. There are vast differences in a person's needs when s/he seeks information, general knowledge, diversion, entertainment or leisure.

For entertainment and leisure, representations close to reality might be good choices. For instance it could be exciting to "walk around" among the actors in a holographic film in stereo and realistic color. For information and education, too much realism in the representations would make it difficult or even impossible for the viewer or learner to identify the essential learning cues. On the other hand, too little realism would also be a poor choice. The information is inadequate. A moderate amount of carefully selected realism gives the best learning. Thus, a series of slides could be a better choice than a film in a specific learning situation. In addition a few slides cost only a fraction as much as an instructional film to produce.

When a need for information is identified, the need can be satisfied as listed below:
- Carry out a problem analysis and find out what the problem really is and to whom it is a problem. Identify the characteristics of the receivers of the information.
- Carry out an analysis of the information requirement and find out just what the information is to cover.
- Frame the objectives as specifically as possible and express them in measurable terms.
- Select a suitable method and determine in which way or ways the objective should be attained.
- Select a suitable medium or identify which media are to be used.
- Prepare an outline of the contents. This will clarify the structure. The information production can then begin. Select, modify or design new materials.
- Distribute the completed material to the users.
- When the users utilize materials, collect information on results and usefulness
- Test can result in the correction of the information, correction of the method and choice of medium and identification of new information needs. In the later instance, the entire cycle is repeated.

As far as the choice of medium is concerned, regard must be paid to the suitability of various media in every individual case. To be successful the sender has to know the medium and its unique possibilities. Advantages should be utilized and disadvantages should be avoided.

MEDIA CONSUMPTION

Our media consumption will vary considerably depending on several different factors such as:
- cultural differences
- socio-economic factors

- individual interests, which may cause large differences even between persons in the same family
- different needs of education, entertainment and information during various periods in a person's life
- different usage of the media at home, in school and at work
- costs
- technical developments
- ease of use
- competition with other activities, and
- competition with new media

In the industrialized, European cultural sphere, we are today living in mass-media societies. Every day we are bombarded with information via the media, at home, in school, on the job, and in the society in general. It is rather hard to avoid information and just as hard to obtain the "right" information, the information that we need at the right time. Audio, text and visuals compete for our attention. It is possible that we miss the information in which we are really interested. In addition to radio, TV, books, newspapers and magazines vast amounts of information are distributed in the form of letters, advertising throwaways, posters, placards, stencils, photocopies, photographs etc. We may "drown" in this "information flood".

Already well established media will meet a lot of competition. Will people read books in the future? Will people listen to radio? To follow the development the Swedish Broadcasting Corporation's Audience and Program Research Division (SR/PUB) conducts an annual survey on the way in which Swedes utilize different media on "an average day". As it turns out people spend an average of more than five hours a day on mass-media consumption in Sweden. However, there is probably some overlapping in the figures. Other studies have shown, for example, that radio listening is largely a passive occupation. People sometimes listen to the radio while simultaneously reading a paper, for example. There are also wide individual differences in people's consumption habits. Five hours a day for mass-media consumption is anyhow a considerable amount of time in view of the fact that most people also hold down jobs, entailing time-consuming travels back and forth to work and that they sleep anywhere from seven to ten hours a night. The average hours per day and night spent on major activities by the urban US population in 1975 were as follows: sleep 7.8; leisure time 5.5; work for pay 4.6; personal care 3.1; and family care 2.9 hours.

North American children may spend 11,500 hours in school during the period five to eighteen years of age. During the same time they watch TV at an average of 15,000 hours and listen to the radio, records and cassettes 5,000 hours. In the US people watch TV 31 hours a week and in Sweden 12 hours and 50 minutes a week. The corresponding figure for reading is six hours and six and a half respectively.

Media market size

We can hardly talk about or define one single media market. Instead there is a vast amount of specialized markets or market segments. These are dependent on factors such as:
- populations and demographic data
- geographical and political situations
- cultural and socio-economic factors
- languages
- trade and customs regulations
- the information economy
- technology trends
- different user groups and needs
- hardware, equipments and services, sales, rental
- software, production, distribution, sales, rental
- the chicken and egg problem.

A specific market may be considered very large for one medium but at the same time minor for another medium. Obviously the characteristics and the economics of different media are extremely different. It may be worthwhile to produce a newsletter as an on-line database-service for a few hundred subscribers but not possible to produce a spectacular superstar movie for less than millions of viewers.

The activities needed to enhance the possible net profit per copy are different for various groups. For private media a solution may be to get more customers. For mass-market media the producers should get better margins. It might be forecasted that the information economy takes an increasing part of the total economy in the future.

Finance and business markets are time critical. Such services demand "real-time" communication. They may be available on demand or include an alerting service. Typically these services will be concerned with financial matters such as stocks and shares, commodity trading, etc.

Non-time-critical services will include a series of browsing and alerting services similar in purpose to newsletter-type publications. They may be supplied by such media as videotex, teletex, electronic mail, audio tape and digital discs.

In-house publications such as manuals can be expected to be increasingly presented in electronic form, with greater interactivity and also quality of reproduction and presentation.

Professional markets have restricted and selective applications and specialized subject areas. Services are likely to grow out of existing requirements in answer to specific needs and will include provisions of specialist information and data, fast updating, current awareness, software packages, complex information retrieval and research dissemination. The services may be provided by commercial umbrella information providers, professional organizations, or commercial publishers, and are likely to be mounted on host computers accessible via telecommunication networks, or supplied on portable machine readable files such as tapes and discs.

Education markets have a number of features which are important to education markets. One of the most important is the degree of interactivity which is offered between the teaching material and the user. Others include the variety of media and the ability to deliver the material where and when it is required.

Electronic media must be expected to provide an increasingly important supporting role. Typical services and products will include books with machine-readable sections, modular material, audio tapes and discs, video tapes and discs, mixed media productions, personal computer software, authoring languages to enable teachers to prepare their own material, and on-line computer-based training.

In further education distance learning facilities are important. These will be provided by programmed learning and fault finding routines, computer-based learning, television programmes linked to other facilities such as software, simulation exercises and teleconferencing with tutors.

Consumer and leisure markets are expanding. One of the key marketing concepts in new media is to create products which will stimulate consumers into buying or renting the necessary hardware. The organization and networking facilities will differ from country to country.

Local or regional news and information services will emerge covering news stories, travel information, guidance on local authority services, advertising, entertainment, shopping etc. Relevant media are videotex and cable TV.

Magazine-type services will focus on a collection of related topics and include information, entertainment and advertising. Key features will be segmentation of the market, e.g. according to demographic or user needs; use of sound and moving pictures as well as text; creation of several products on the same theme but using different media; creation of multi-media products; co-production with several types of organizations and sponsors; new ways of handling advertisements. Appropriate media will be videotex, cable TV, video tape, video disc, and magnetic and optical media for use with personal computers.

Computer games can be regarded as the leading edge in consumer displays and consumer involvement. The media which will be used include audio cassettes, floppy discs, plug-in memory, video tape, video discs, optical disc and card, videotex and holograms.

Media-industry mapping

Several attempts have been made to make different kinds of "maps" or "models" of the media-industry. These maps might be useful as tools for strategic planning for the information business. It is by far not easy, or even possible, to make one single map that covers all aspects of the media-industry. Thus we have to work with a set of different maps at the same time. Such maps have been produced according to different criteria such as the needs of the users, time of delivery and number of receivers, growth of the information business, media evolution, and technical development (several other possibilities may still remain). A few systems will be briefly presented here.

We all have individual feelings towards media. Our media consumption is depending e.g. on factors like our interests and our *perceived need* for education, entertainment, information and news. Our need for education, entertainment, information and news can be visualized as areas partly covering each other. "Double" areas are the subject of special interest for publishers since these areas are most likely to attract more attention from consumers than other areas. Thus *edutainment* is education and entertainment. *Infotainment* is information and entertainment. *Infocation* is information and education. The BBC series about the life on earth by and with naturalist David Attenborough is an example of a television program with elements covering all these needs.

News is handled differently in different cultures. In the US news has got a good portion of entertainment. In Japan news is more related to education. In Sweden news is related to information.

We have "fast" and "slow" media. We have "personal", "group" and "mass-media". In direct broadcasting radio and television may reach large number of receivers. Books and magazines may also reach many individuals but much more time is needed. When Japanese researchers marked different media on a "time of delivery and number of receivers"-map they found new segments for development. Videotex and other new tele-communications media are developing fast to reach various market segments of say between one hundred and one thousand customers.

At the Harvard University Center for Information Policy Research "the information business map" has been developed. The map is a rectangle in which the left side ranges from basic products like paper and file cabinets to delivery services of parcels and mail. The bottom side of the map ranges from the plain paper to books. In the upper right corner we find financial and professional services. Thus all kinds of products and services related to the information business are placed on the map according to their conduit or content. The map is strikingly nice to look at. However, in my personal view, this model is not very easy to use in practical work.

Existing as well as future media may be mapped according to an evolutionary aspect. For many years the media situation was very stable, only expanding a little each year. In 1950 we had live media, sound media, film media, broadcast media, models and exhibitions, graphical media and telecommunications media (the "leaves in the mediaflower"). In the 1970's video developed into a competitive medium (between film media and broadcast media). At the same time the classical "borders" between the media groups begin to dissolve. In 1982 several new technologies, most based on computers, and completely new media began developing. Demarcations are even less pronounced today, and most media will interact and partly overlap each other in the future.

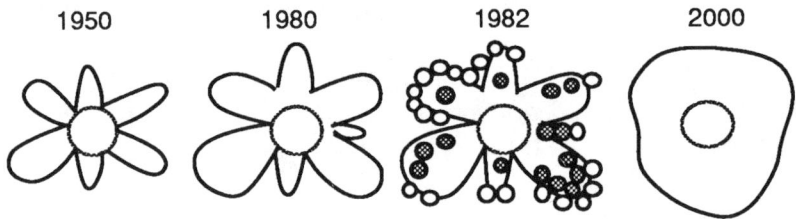

In 1950 we had live media (centre), sound media, film media, broadcast media, models and exhibitions, graphical media and telecommunications media (the "leaves in the mediaflower"). 1980 video was a competitive medium (between film media and broadcast media). In 1982 several new technologies (grey circles) and completely new media (white circles) began developing. 2000 most media will interact and partly overlap each other .

Live media include:

Personal communication personal body language, speech

Group communication social body language, ballet, pantomime, theatre, live music, conference, church, school

Communication 17

Sound media *can* be put into four groups based on the ways they can be used and the technology involved as shown below:

Products	Characteristics	Examples
1 Records	rotating disc with mechanical pickup	long playing record
	rotating disc with optical pickup	compact disc
	fixed disc with mechanical pickup	TAI-minidisc
2 Audio tape	soundwire	
	tape in open spool	
	compact cassette	Philips standard audio cassette
	mini cassette	
	cassette with endless loop	
3 Sound card	film base with magnetic layer	line reading
4 "Firm' memory	printed coding	EAN-coding
	computer (speech synthesis)	speaking toys speech output
	photographic audio disc	digital hi-fi

Film media may be two- or three-dimensional, still pictures or moving pictures.

Products	Characteristics	Examples
A Two-dimensional		
1 Still pictures	non-silver based	overhead transparency, slides, microfiche
	silver based	overhead transparency, slides, microfiche, panoramic, film strip, microfilm

2 Animated pictures	dynamic picture	overhead with overlay
	picture with movement	overhead with movement
	multi-projector show	multiple projectors
3 Semi-moving	programfilm	PiP (S-8), Bezeler (16)
4 Moving pictures	school and training films	single-concept, S-8, 16 mm
	movie theatre	16 mm, 35mm, widescreen
B Three-dimensional		
5 Still pictures		viewmaster, autostereo, chromatic stereo, polarized light
6 Moving pictures		chromatic film, polarized light

Broadcast media include both audio and television services. Examples are shown below:

Services	*Characteristics*	*Examples*
1 Radio	broadcast	national radio, local radio, narrow-casting, cellular radio
	communications radio	alarm, military, police, civil
2 Television	sound and picture	television, local TV, narrow-casting TV, interactive cable TV, closed circuit TV, direct broad-casting by satellite
	3D-TV	chromatic
3 Data		teletext, cable-text

Communication

Video media provide a high level of information content in a simple to understand form. Many of them include audio information. Because of the need to store a lot of information a major characteristic is compactness of storage. Major examples are shown below:

Products	Characteristics	Examples
A Still pictures		
1 Videotape		compact-cassette
2 Videosheet		Mavica
3 Video discs		optical pickup
4 "Firm' memory		pictures
B Moving pictures and sound		
1 Videotape	open spool	1/2 in, 1 in, 2 in
	video cassettes	angular search (U-matic, VHS, Beta, V-2000), Compact cassette (8) longitudinal search (BASF, Toshiba)
2 Video disc	long-play	mecanical (TeD)
		magnetic Disc (MDR)
		optical reflective disc (LaserDisc)
		optical transparent disc (Thomson CSF)
		capacitative disc without groove(VHD)
		capacitative disc with groove (SelectaVision)
	interactive	optical reading (Laser Disc, Thomson CSF)
3 "Firm' memory		video games
4 3D TV		polarized light

Models and exhibitions offer a means of expression which is more accurate than many other media. Increasingly these can be seen to provide a total 'experience'. Different types and applications are shown below:

Products	Characteristic	Examples
1 Models	three-dimensional	sculpture, modelled items, globe, diorama
	multi-dimensional	robot, happening & events, simulation
2 Exhibitions	*fixed:*	
	two-dimensional	exhibitions with pictures and text
	three-dimensional	pictures, text, sound, objects
	multi-dimensional	moving pictures
	moving:	
	two-dimensional	exhibitions with pictures and text
	three-dimensional	pictures, text and sound, objects
	multi-dimensional	moving pictures
3 Holograms	fixed hologram	transmission-, reflex-, dichromatic holograms and hologram with projected picture
	moving hologram	integral hologram, hologram film

Graphical media can be put into two groups: manually or personally produced; and manufactured media.

The *manually produced* graphical media include pictures, such as drawings, paintings, etchings, lithographs, signs, and text such as letters and handwritten manuscripts.

The *manufactured group* of graphical media has a wide range of products or services, as shown below.

Products	Characteristics	Examples
1 Serials	several times/week	morning papers, evening papers, business publications
	numerous times/year	weeklies, comics, journals, newsletters/bulletins

Communication

2 Books	periodical publications	year books, almanacs, catalogues
	reference	dictionaries, directories, tables, encyclopaedias, statistics, indexes
	non-fiction	handbooks, biographies, travel guides, monographs,
	school and college textbooks	teachers' manuals, textbooks, workbooks, programmed instruction
	fiction	novels, anthologies of essays, poems
	comics	comic books
	children's books	baby, infant, teenage
3 Printed music		sheet music
4 Maps		atlases, gazetteer, wall maps
5 Separate pictures	two-dimensional	reproductions, posters, postcards
	three-dimensional	autostereo, chromic stereo
6 Printed matter	for distribution	booklets, brochures, reports, lists, manuals, circulars, bags, printed articles
	for display	signs, menus, posters, decals, pamphlets,
7 Security print		bills, shares, bonds, lottery tickets, coupons
8 Copying		electrostatic, diazo, thermal
9 Computer media		computer printouts

Telecommunications media are able to transmit a wide variety of information, examples are:

Products
1 Sound

Examples
telephone conversation, teleconferencing, dial-up services, voice mail

2 Text
telegram, telex, teletex, facsimilie, mobitex

3 Pictures
video teleconferencing, facsimilie, TV-pictures

4 Data
datel, datex, telepak, teleshopping, telebanking, telesoftware, videotex

Computer media may be found as parts of the other groups, especially in the telecommunications group. Examples are: computer print-outs, computer programs, computer conferences, artificial intelligence, expert systems, computer games, hypertext, hypermedia, CD-ROM, CD-I and Laser cards.

At present we can see a tremendous amount of work being done in technical laboratories all around the world. In the coming decades this will result in new techniques to produce traditional media as well as in new media and in different kinds of new services. Especially interesting is the development of integrated digital tele-networks capable of transmitting sound, text, data and pictures at the same time and in the same system. Various "technical development maps" or "time-scales" exist in different parts of the world.

NEW MEDIA

The amount of information being disseminated is increasing with unparalleled rapidity. At the latest turn of the century there were about 10,000 technical and scientific journals in the world. By 1970 the number had grown to 100,000, and this number is expected to increase tenfold by the year 2,000. By now no signs indicate a paper-less society, maybe a "less paper" society. Video discs, cable TV, satellite transmissions, videotex, computers and other new media are due to increase the flow of information to even greater levels.

For several years now, digital storage of more than 50 TV images has been possible on an ordinary compact audio-cassette. Other systems are much more efficient. Fifty color pictures can be stored with very good quality on one A6-size microfiche (10.5 x 14.7 cm). A stack of microfiche, 1 cm thick, can store more than 1,000 frames. However, a video disc with optical reading is capable of storing the text contents of 500,000 A4-size pages (21 x 29.5 cm; 10,000 million bits of information). Data are recorded by a laser beam which burns microscopically small holes in a disc. The disc is then read by a semiconductor laser and the information is on demand displayed on a CRT tube. Other optical video discs can store 90,000-100,000 stills for the TV-screen.

In the future, digital techniques will be employed in the recording as well as the editing and distribution of TV-programs. When digital techniques are introduced, a common world standard will be possible. Then the problems caused by the different TV-systems in use today, NTSC, PAL and SECAM, will disappear. This will indeed facilitate international distribution of programs. However, in 1986 there were about 600 million TV-receivers in use in the world and the electronics industry is set up to manufacture conventional TV-sets. That means that it will take some time before the new technique will be in common use.

TV-screens might become the "spiders in the communication webs of the future". Some years ago there was only conventional broadcast television. Since then, however, a dozen different functions have been or are being introduced. So the TV-set will play a major role in the "pushbutton society" or rather the "voice recognition society" of the future and will only be employed to a limited degree for displaying traditional broadcast programs in the 1990's. This will heighten demands for more TV-sets and for large, flat color-TV-screens with stereo sound (Also see Format).

Current laser techniques make it possible to create three-dimensional images, holograms, enabling viewers to see "behind" image objects. These techniques are at about the same stage of development as photography was at the beginning of the century.

Many people are aware of the dramatic developments in photographic and film techniques since that time. The development of holography will be equally dramatic, although more rapid in coming decades.

Studies in Japan have shown that the ratio between "utilized" and "available" information has fallen from about 40% in 1960 to about 10% in 1975. So 90% of available information was "wasted" from the sender's point of view. Today, the figure for "wastage" is probably even higher. We are rapidly heading for an information oriented society characterized by a need for selectivity in information consumption tailored to our individual needs instead of to the availability of large amounts of general, mass-produced/copied information. Computers with routines for intelligent searches of large amounts of information can be very useful and are probably essential.

Electronic Publishing

At the end of the 1960's the "electronic revolution" was announced. The book was said to disappear and would very soon be replaced by new electronic media like video cassettes. During the first years of the 1970's publishing houses throughout the world were hit by severe crises followed by necessary re-organizations. At that time some people saw only threats. Others could see that the development of new media also could mean new opportunities as well as new risks. After more than 500 years the printed word is still alive and will certainly be so for a long time but together with other carriers of information and partly in other formats. We will experience "on-demand-publishing" when only the information needed at one specific occasion is copied or printed, for example by a laser printer linked to a computer. Most of the information needed can be read on the screen and might never be printed as a hard-copy.

In recent years, the concept "electronic publishing" has come into increasing use. However, the concept is not really very good. Like "traditional publishing", "electronic publishing" is far too vague, comprehensive and ambiguous. Traditional publishing comprises publication of e.g. books, newspapers, magazines,

maps, films and AV material. Electronic publishing comprises the following media/forms of distribution:
1. Traditional ether media. Local, neighbourhood and network radio and TV.
2. Special transmissions. Cable TV, pay-cable TV, coin-operated TV, satellite TV, viewdata, home fax.
3. Videograms and phonograms. Video cassettes, Video discs, audio cassettes, phonograph records.
4. On-line databases and distributed databases, e.g. on CD-ROM.
5. Future media. "Electronic holograms" etc.

So publishing can comprise many different media with different properties and requirements. We should therefore try to express ourselves with greater stringency when discussing the subject of electronic publishing.

Video

Videogram is a collective designation for video cassettes and videodiscs, i.e. media for the storage and replay of TV programs at an optional time and place. The utilization of video cassettes can be said to comprise three main fields:
1. The recording of transmitted programs for subsequent replay.
2. Distribution and rental or sale of pre-recorded programs, such as movies for entertainment and education, and
3. Program production.

In the beginning of the 1970's expectations were high, especially in the electronic industry and from many producers of programmes. However, changes in patterns of behaviour are often slow. It takes time to develop a new medium.

For a number of years video developments progressed very slowly because of factors such as the multiplicity of incompatible technical systems, i.e. a cassette recorded according to one system could not be played on a VCR using another. Nor were the earliest VCR's particularly reliable. Playing time was also limited, in general no more than one hour. Modern cassettes have playing times of several hours. One critical requirement was a need for 90 min of uninterrupted playing time so a whole movie could be run with no need to turn the cassette.

In 1980, there were no fewer than 70 different companies world-wide which manufactured 195 different kinds of video cassette recorders (VCR). There were about 50 different systems for video discs. Most of these systems lack any real practical significance. But the numerous "major" and widely distributed systems often create practical problems for users since these systems are not compatible and the incorrect type of cassette or disc could be purchased.

Videodiscs offer new possibilities. As mentioned earlier an optical video disc can store 90-100,000 stills to be presented at random on a TV-screen. It is possible to retrieve and display any one of these stills in a matter of seconds. Interactive videodiscs offer great possibilities for e.g. education and information. The possibilities to produce adapted and individualized programming is almost unlimited. The possibility to have e.g. all the paintings from the most famous collections in the world in all museums and all libraries is thrilling.

Teletext

For the past 15 years, experiments have been conducted in different parts of the world in which certain information stored in computer systems can be accessed from the home, company, agency, school etc. The simplest of these experiments is teletext, sometimes called broadcast or one-way videotex. It is a one-way system for transmitting data from a data-base to TV sets with built-in decoders A TV set with a teletext capability costs only about 1,000 Skr more than the corresponding unit without a decoder. The disseminator of information is able to reach several million sets with a limited number of messages (i.e. a few hundred "pages"), but these messages can be updated continually.

Teletext pages are transmitted by broadcasting or cable and viewed at any time. The digital data signals are stored on lines not utilized to form the ordinary TV image. An accessory with push-buttons is used to "browse" until the desired information e.g. a news summary, weather forecasts or sports results is found.

Waiting time in a teletext system comprising one hundred pages varies from a tenth of a second to 15 seconds with a mean of seven and a half seconds. When an entire channel is committed to teletext - which is easy in a cable TV network covering a total of 100 channels, the data base could hold up to 50,000 pages. Waiting time would then not exceed 30 s. Separate channels for teletext are currently being considered in countries like Japan. Such channels could be used for educational purposes.

Teletext might develop into the TV-newspaper of the future with news as most important programming. The role of daily newspapers and disseminators of news could be taken over by teletext to a large extent. A number of national systems have been devised for teletext. Experiments and services are carried out in several countries. Britain was first of the mark with Ceefax from the BBC (1976) and ORACLE from ITV. The latter is a commercial radio and TV company.

Teletext is sometimes confused with "teletex" - minus a "t" at the end. "Teletex" is an interactive word processor linked to the Swedish data network and introduced by the National Telecommunications Administration in November 1981. Teletex, sometimes referred to as "supertelex", consists of terminal hardware, a teletex network, a number plan and a teletex catalogue.

Videotex

In contrast to our established media, videotex has no natural or clear cut niche. Many standard products and/or services are threatened or can be augmented by videotex. One important application is in the distribution of messages, i.e. electronic mail. So postal authorities in many countries are interested in it. Videotex can be regarded as a data traffic via telephone lines, so telecommunications and computer companies are equally interested. It is excellent for supplying various kinds of economic information. So banks are looking at it closely.

Videotex can currently be used to book tickets or make direct purchases of all kinds of goods and/or service in many countries. In the future, wholesalers may be able to eliminate retailers in a number of different trades. Videotex can also be viewed as a kind of electronic newspaper and/or book, so the medium has also attracted the attention of newspapers and book publishers. However, videotex can also be described as a kind of newspaperlike TV-service offering animation and attractive image quality. So TV companies are looking into it. Electronic games have proved to be the most popular videotex feature, so video game companies are interested. These are only a few of the fields covered by videotex. There are more. Videotex allows numerous information suppliers to store anything from a few "pages" to tens of thousands of "pages" containing information in one or more computers. Many different users are able to conduct simultaneous searches for information of interest to them on any occasion. So salespersons in the field can always have access to absolutely fresh information on stocks, prices, delivery terms etc. A person with specialist knowledge in a particular field can offer consultancy service, newsletter, reports etc. - all delivered via videotex systems to customers in different countries. National boundaries are no longer obstacles to the flow of information as was previously the case. By means of appropriate search routines, users can gain access to information in one or more data bases.

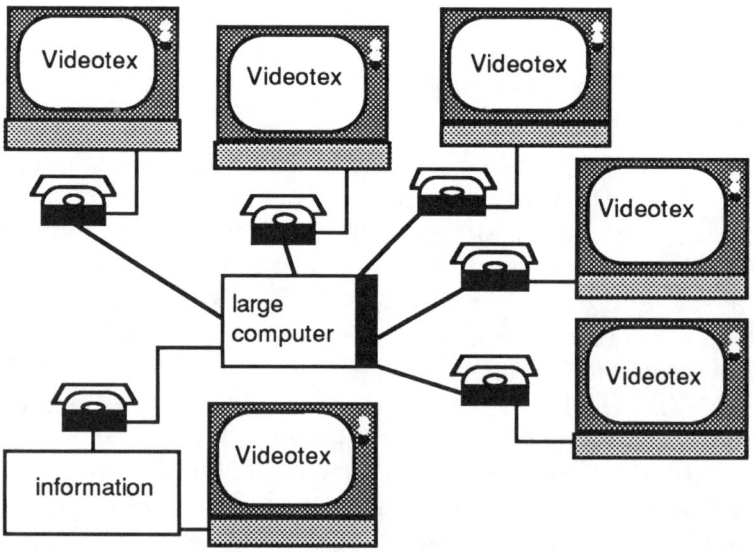

In a videotex system the signals are transmitted via ordinary telephone cables.

Since the signals are transmitted via ordinary telephone cables, the resolution of "pages" is necessarily limited. There are a number of different technical systems. Most of these systems can transmit text and very simple pictures. This works fine in the case of brief texts and various kinds of tabular information. A "page" on a TV screen has only 24 lines with 40 characters/line. This is a major limitation in many contexts. Compared to traditional graphical reproduction methods, text is difficult to read in all videotex systems.

The Swedish DataVision, like Prestel in England, Bildschirmtext in Germany, Telset in Finland, Teledata in Norway etc., is a version of the same basic system and only the first step towards more sophisticated systems in the future. Both the Telidon system in Canada and U.S. and the Captain system in Japan are examples of systems which already offer a wider range of options than the Prestel systems. Digital telecommunications networks and digital TV sets will make it possible to use videotex in education. In my opinion, future videotex systems should display the following properties: excellent image quality, animation, intelligent search systems, sound and user friendly man-machine interaction

An alternative to videotex is *audiotex* commercially introduced by Dow Jones News/Retrieval in January 1984. With a digital telephone is it possible to communicate with the computer and have messages delivered by synthetic speech.

Cable TV

Radio and TV reception at many locations in North America, Canada in particular, is often difficult because of the terrain. So companies began erecting television distribution aerials (often on mountain tops) in the 1950's. There were no serious copyright problems or difficulties since the TV programs were largely financed by advertising and regarded as a "natural right" by the public. TV distribution systems were ultimately improved. Since the TV programs were distributed via cable, the system was referred to as "cable TV". The first cables were only able to carry a single TV channel. But 6 to 12 channels were normal by 1970.

Modern systems can now accommodate more than 100 TV channels.

The new systems offer channels only showing movies, sports, news, weather reports etc. in addition to the programs, financed by advertising, transmitted by ordinary TV stations. This development has become possible, thanks to new distribution technology. A distribution chain may comprise the following:

A "wholesaler" who owns program rights, such as Time Inc.'s Home Box Office (HBO) which broadcasts on two movie channels (24 hours a day, 365 days a year, on Eastern Standard Time and Pacific Standard Time) from its studio in Manhattan. Programs are transmitted by cable to the roof of a skyscraper. The programs are then beamed by microwaves to Long Island where they are relayed to a TV satellite. The signals are reflected by the satellite and picked up by thousands of parabolic antennas all over the U.S. and Canada. Local cable TV networks then operate as "retailers", decode and "clean up" the signals and deliver them to households subscribing to HBO. The "retailers" often offer several different entertainment channels without any advertising. Every movie is broadcast up to ten times every six months.

In the future, cable TV systems will offer two-way communications in the next generation of videotex systems. Since image quality will be superior to the quality of present TV systems, the limitations imposed by the "mosaic images" in the present videotex systems when goods, services and even information are ordered will be eliminated. Future cable TV systems will also offer extensive technical opportunities for advanced "remote education" programs.

Databases

Optical media are being developed at a rapid pace. This is especially true of 12 cm optical *compact discs*. They can be viewed as "distributed databases." In the future they will probably capture a major share of the market from *on-line data-bases*, particularly in fields whose information does not require frequent updates. Compact discs are likely to attain widespread use in schools, universities and other educational institutions as well as for inhouse job training. A number of different systems with different characteristics are available. A few will be mentioned here.

CD-ROM, Compact Disc Read Only Memory, a CD disc for the storage of data (540 - 600 MB.) It was announced in August 1983 and went on sale in the U.S. in 1985. One CD-ROM is capable of storing the text in several large encyclopedias, making this information available as a free-text database. Its capacity is equivalent to about 250,000 pages of typewritten text. One CD-ROM is capable of accommodating up to 15,000 simple line drawings while simultaneously storing all the requisite text information and procedures required for database searches. Today CD-ROM is a viable technology attracting interest and investment worldwide. A variety of commercial products are already out on the market and more are coming at a steady pace.

CD-I, Compact Disc Interactive, a CD disc capable of holding audio, images, text and data. CD-I can store 10,000 hours of "synthetic sound," 384 hours of natural speech, 40,000 line drawings, 4,000 "TV quality" color frames or various combinations thereof. CD-I was announced in February 1986. It should be on the market in 1989.

DVI, Digital Video Interactive, a "video version" of CD-I developed by the American company RCA. Since one hour of digital storage of video information occupies 65,000 megabytes, DVI operates with advanced computerized image compression. One prototype was shown in March 1987.

The development of different compact discs will open up fascinating, new opportunities to producers of e.g. teaching aids. They will make it possible to create "*the total teaching aid*" encompassing text, sound, pictures, numerical information *and* opportunities for various kinds of information processing in a single medium. A "total teaching aid" is a multimedia database (a hypermedium) offering the user complete freedom in moving back and forth between verbal, numerical, visual and audio information (Also see "Picture dimensions").

Mediateques

It is possible that our current libraries could be converted into mediateques in the future, i.e. places at which information can be sought. A mediateque could consist of a TV set/CRT display with decoders for teletext and videotex, a telephone plus a modem, a small computer with built-in memory, software for intelligent search routines and one or more optical video disc players (LV-ROM).

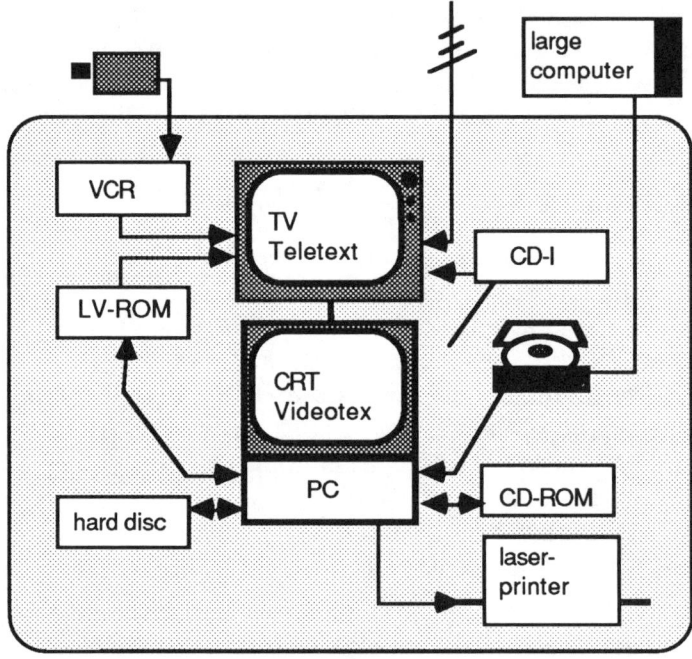

An example of a mediateque. It is possible to search for information in many different sources such as local data-bases on CD-ROM, CD-I or LV-ROM. It is also possible to use on-line services. Print-outs can be made with the laser-printer.

The computer makes it possible to "leaf" through 50,000 stills on one side of a single optical video disc. The same disc could also conceivably store more than two million videotex images. The system could offer an interesting combination of local and central storage of information. Absolutely up-to-date information in any of the world's various data bases could become accessible by means of a telephone link to the respective computer or by connection to a computer network. More stable and invariable information could be stored on optical video discs, magnetic discs or, to some extent, on magnetic tape. If a TV camera is added to the system, the user would be able to enter his/her own recordings of sound and moving pictures. Texts would be entered via the computer. A school could have a central mediateque with terminals in different classrooms.

THE INFORMATION SOCIETY

We live in a society in which the availability of and need for information as the basis for decision-making is continually increasing. We now learn a little about a great many subjects with the result that it is becoming easy to acquire comprehensive but very superficial knowledge. Our basic knowledge is also frequently inadequate.

The American media economist Parker has shown that the labour market's traditional subdivisions have changed strikingly in recent decades. The number of people employed in the information sector has risen from less than 5% of all the gainfully employed people in the U.S. in 1860 to more than 50% in 1980. The agricultural and industrial sectors have been the subject of extensive measures to improve efficiency measures. A number of measures aimed at making the service sector more efficient have also been implemented to some extent. For purely economic reasons, the same efficiency measures will also be introduced in the information sector. The number of people employed here will not continue to rise as quickly in the future. Nor will we be able to increase our information consumption very much in the future.

The information must be more effective. We must analyze the factors which are important to the way information is designed, distributed and perceived. Previously, information used to be produced by people who frequently only had a very vague idea about the objective and function of the information they were producing. In the future the production of information will probably be more objective-oriented.

The production of a message commences with an idea occurring to someone or with the need to convey information to a given target group. When an outline is ready, the generation of text, draft sketches, editing, graphical design, the production of originals, masters and, ultimately, a given quantity then begin. The sender produces a representation of reality. A representation is a medium with specific contents, i.e. a message. Other tasks for the sender are stock-keeping, distribution, marketing, advertising, selling, billing, bookkeeping etc.

From writers to readers

Cave paintings, rock inscriptions, clay tablets, rune stones, church paintings, letters and other hand-written material are all examples of unique documents conveying a direct message from the sender/writer/ picture creator to the receiver/reader. Although these messages were sometimes intended for gods and other higher powers, not for people.

Text and pictures have been produced, distributed, stored and utilized for thousands of years. The first "travel guides" were produced and sold as early as 2000 B.C. They were the Egyptian "Books of the Dead" which contained advice and information - in an integrated, lexivisual amalgam of text and pictures - on coping with the trip to the Kingdom of Death. They were completely hand-made rolls of papyrus and, thanks to their high price, only available to truly wealthy families. The trade in these books is reminiscent of the medieval Catholic Church's trade in letters of indulgence. Both phenomena are examples of what could be called profitable publishing. Duplicates were made in the most literal fashion imaginable by "middlemen", specially trained scribes and copiers who copied text and drawings, often repeatedly. The industrial production of books is a comparatively modern phenomenon. Despite the fact that books began to be printed more than 500 years ago, printing remained an exclusive and painstaking handicraft for many years. Gutenberg's 42-line bible was printed on 316 pages and took 3 years to make (1452 - 1455) in an edition comprising 200 copies. Some 170 of these copies were printed on paper and 30 on parchment. A total of 5,000 calf skins were required for the parchment versions. One goatskin was needed to cover each book.

Communication

Even at an early date, libraries of different kinds acquired major importance as "institutional middlemen" in the transmission of information From writers to readers. The first public library, Pisistratus, was founded more than 2,500 years ago (540 A.D.) in Athens. The first bookstore was opened, also in Athens, 160 years later (400 A.D.) Until the middle of the 19th century, bookstores often served as publishers too, producing as well as selling books and other graphic products.

A great many people in different occupational categories are required for transmitting a message from writers to readers. People such as text and picture editors, graphic designers, typesetters, repro technicians, printers, bookbinders, stockroom staff, salespersons, order takers, bookstore employees, librarians, buyers and administrators. The different steps involved in publishing are time-consuming and jointly represent a major expense. About ten percent of the price of a book, not including tax, usually goes to the author.

Electronic publishing could change this situation to some extent. It would reduce the distance between writers and readers. New opportunities for a dialogue could then develop in some instances.

Consequences of electronic publishing

There are a number of approaches to the field of electronic publishing. Depending on their frames of references, different people can interpret the same phenomenon in different ways.

The *user/reader* wants a fast, cheap, easy-to-use system. Disseminated information must also be presented in a clear and legible manner. A great deal of research and development is needed in this area. Poor legibility is currently fairly common in e.g. videotex, thanks to the erroneous use of colors, for example.

The volume of available information is constantly expanding. This may make it even harder for people to find desired information.

The information *supplier/writer* is offered new opportunities for presenting her/his message. In the future, factual information, training and entertainment will be processed in digital form throughout the entire production chain.

Writers and experts in different fields can generate their own texts and numerical tabulations in computers using programs for word processing, spreadsheets and graphics. Artists can create their illustrations with computer-aided image processing systems. Photographers can use a video camera for recording video frames, stored as individual pixels, on magnetic discs.

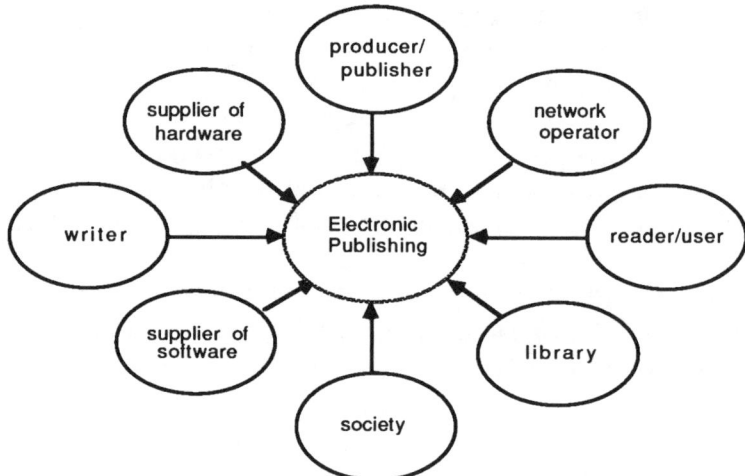

Different people see a phenomenon such as "Electronic Publishing" in different ways

The *producer/publisher* can "polish" basic material with typographical measures, editing and information verification. The results of her/his efforts can then be stored (sometimes in versions especially tailored to different user categories) for convenient user access. Like a database operator and supplier of hardware and software, the producer must market her/his services and find a sufficient number of buyers for those services. Increasingly flexible systems are making it easier to reach groups with special interests in different parts of the world. The development of new technology and new media present producers with exciting new options. An optically readable plastic card (about 3 x 2 inches) with 2 megabytes of onboard memory can store 800 pages of text, 2 hours of music or 200 computer graphics frames.

Communication

Once they get into large-scale production, the cards should only cost about $1.50 each. Optical compact discs offer interesting prospects for the storage of large volumes of information. In November 1985, the American publishing company Grolier issued all 20 volumes of the Academic American Encyclopedia, containing 9 million words, on a single compact disc (CD-ROM). A computer, a CD-ROM-drive and suitable software make it possible for disc buyers to browse at will in this vast database.

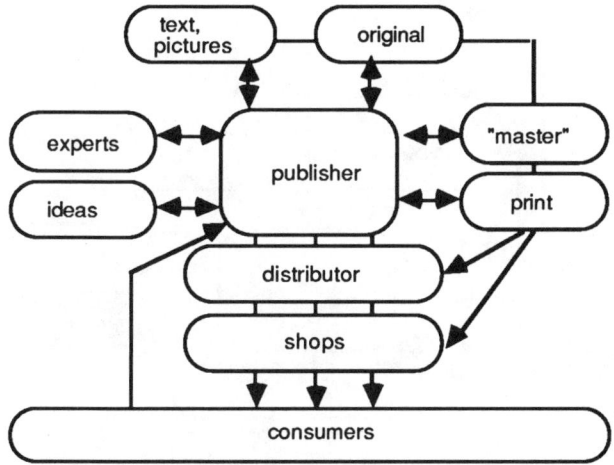

The traditional function of the information producer has been to coordinate people with ideas, experts on subject matters, writers, artists, designers, photographers and others in the production of original, masters and run. Traditional tasks have also been stock-keeping, marketing, distribution, accounting etc. Reactions from the consumers gives the information producer knowledge for new or revised editions, new runs and even new products. The information/content is delivered by means of the most suitable media.

Traditionally publishers and book-sellers have been working with books. Books are products. We can hold them in our hands. We can use them when we like and as often as we like. Regardless of the content, fiction or non-fiction, the book is still a product. Only a small part, say 10%, of what you have to pay for a book is the cost of the actual content. The rest is taxes, marketing and production costs. In the future, products are gradually going to be replaced by "content-services", that is, services to give people the information, the knowledge, the news or the entertainment they want to have in a specific situation.

When products gradually are replaced by "content-services" we will have a psychological type of problem. How much are people really willing to pay for something they cannot hold in their hands and keep in a physical representation? There is some experience from rental of video cassettes for entertainment. There are not yet much experience from the fields of information or education.

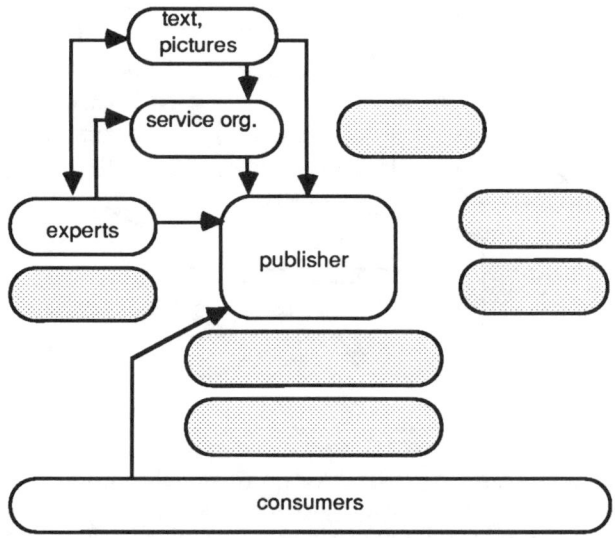

In the future information society with databases, cables and terminals installed it will be very easy for anyone with knowledge of a subject matter to "publish" certain kinds of information such as tables, manuals, reference books, dictionaries etc. The consumers, the users of the system, can easily access the information they need.

On-line databases are offered by different kinds of customers, such as the printing companies, publishing houses, computer manufacturers and libraries.

Libraries will gradually improve their range of service by offering new media. Phonograms and, to some extent, videograms and on-line database searches are already available.

The OCLC (Online Computer Library Center) is an interesting development. For example, the OCLC has a database holding more than ten and one-half million literature references and information on 166 million physical books, newspapers and magazines at 7,000 libraries. The OCLC is developing full-text databases, based on e.g. the aforementioned CD-ROM technique with facilities to permit local write-out of hard copy if, when and wherever needed.

Network operators must invest vast sums on the expansion and maintenance of their digital networks. In the future, networks will be capable of handling text, audio, video, pictures and data.

Governments are commissioning an increasing number of studies to examine the need for control systems, ethical rules and new sources of tax revenue. Copyright of and responsibility for factual information, i.e. data in constant need of change, processing and updating by many different people, are among the most difficult issues being addressed.

Changes in media consumption

It is unlikely that we will wish or be able to spend as much time on the media in the future as in the past. Economic trends suggest that there is unlikely to be any scope for major cost rises, in addition to inflation, for the mass-media in the next few years. So new media will have to compete with the media already in existence.

In the 90's people all over the world will be receiving far more audio-visual information than at any other time in history. And people working in audio-visual communications will be striving to help people communicate, educate, train, and inform.

Media likely to decline in relative importance are letters, advertising throwaways, posters, certain books, newspapers, magazines, traditional AV media, radio and television. Media likely to increase in relative importance are various telecom services, phonograms, videograms, teletext, videotex, cable TV and satellite TV.

Media likely to predominate in the future are telecom services, videotex, cable TV, satellite TV, telefax, teletext and various computer services. Most media will be under voice actuated or image-actuated control, making it unnecessary to have complicated routines to enter information via keyboards.

TV, videograms, cable TV, satellite TV, radio and phonograms will be our most important sources of *entertainment*.

Teletext, cable TV, TV and radio will be our most important sources of *news*.

Books, databases and videograms with computerized search systems will be our most important source of *knowledge and education*.

Videotex, databases, books and computerized reports, which are seldom printed in their entirety, will become our most important sources of *information*.

To summarize, I predict the following *long-range changes*:
1 A transition from products to services.
2 An increasing degree of segmentation.
3 Increasing flexibility.
4 Increasing competition for the individual consumer's time and money.
5 Gradual disappearance of demarcations between different media.
6 Development of new media and techniques through "hybridization".
7 Replacement of the different systems currently available by one international, integrated digital telecommunications system.
8 Development of a single world standard for TV.
9 Increasing copyright problems.

The introduction of new media

Before introducing new media it might be a good idea to consider viewpoints from users, producers, originators and also from society.

Users' viewpoints

Demand. Is there a demand for the new medium? Where? Why? For which categories? For which purpose is the new medium intended? Do other media offer the same or corresponding ser-

Communication

vices? Which are the unique advantages of this medium that other medium are lacking? How is the new medium adapted to reality?

Use. Is the medium easy enough to use? Does the user benefit in any way from using the new medium? How? Why? For how long will the medium serve its purpose? Will the media soon be "old-fashioned"? Is there a rapid technical development to be expected within the field that the medium represents?

Costs. Are the costs of the medium, when it is systematically used, higher than the costs of other media, which provide the corresponding information or experience? Is the cost a critical factor?

Producers' viewpoints

Demand. Is there a demand for the new medium? Where? Why? For which categories? For which purpose is the new medium intended? Do other media offer the same or corresponding services? Which are the unique advantages of this medium that other media are lacking?

Production. Can production be carried out within the frame of the present organization? By employees? By consultants? By "traditional" authors, drawers, photographers and others? Must new personnel (competence) be recruited? Who? Why? Are special skills needed for production of originals? Which skills? Which time-schedule? Costs? Are special skills needed for production of masters? Which skills? Time-schedule? Costs? Are special skills needed for production of editions? Which skills? Time-schedule? Costs at different editions? Could the supply of raw material be a critical factor? Are there any problems as to updating? Why? Time-schedule? Costs?

Stock. Is storage possible within the frame of the present organization? Is there a problem as to "perishables"? Costs?

Marketing. Can marketing be effected within the frame of the present organization? Is there any demand for special competence? Are there existing markets? Where? Which? How big? Can the users be reached through advertising? In which publications? Costs? Is it necessary to have an organization for direct selling? Is there a requirement for a special hardware? Is the necessary hardware available? Quality? Costs? Should the media be sold by the piece like certain products? Can you sell a "package" of hardware/software? Can you sell subscriptions? Is a high degree of price sensitivity to be expected? Are there "psychologically determined price levels" because of established price levels on similar services?

Distribution. Can distribution be carried out within the frame of the present organization? Costs?

Debiting. Can invoicing be made within the frame of the present organization? How do we charge? Costs?

Administration. Can the present organization be used for administration? Costs?

Investment/Financing. Does the new media claim special investments? By which means is the media financed? For how long will the media serve its purpose? Will the media soon be "old-fashioned"? Can you expect a rapid technical development within the field that the media represents?

Copyright. Is the product protected as to copyright? Can the products be protected from being copied? Are there any great risks with regard to copying? Why? To what extent?

Statement of accounts. Are fixed payments to different originators advisable? Is a royalty account system appropriate? Can statement of accounts be made out to the originators within the present organization and with the present routines? Costs?

Profitability. Which profitability can be achieved and when? Are there other alternatives with better profitability?

Originators' viewpoints

Demand. Is there a demand for the new medium? Where?Why? For which categories For which purpose is the new medium intended? Do other media offer the same or corresponding services? Which are the unique advantages of this medium that other media are lacking?

Income. What is the income? When is the money paid?

Production. Are there new creative possibilities? How will the working situation change? Do I actually need the producer? way? for what?

Copyright. Is the product protected as to copyright? Can the products be protected from being copied? Are there any great risks with regard to copying? Why? To what extent?

Viewpoints of the society

Value. What is the value with the new medium? To whom is it "good"? To whom is it "bad"? Why? Is the new medium likely to inflict any laws or ethical roles? Which? To what extent?

Tax. Is it possible to introduce new taxes? When? How much will it give?

Security. Will the new medium influence national security? Why? How much?

SCREEN COMMUNICATION

Today computer-based interactive systems are increasingly used for training and learning in schools as well as in industry. Graphics are combined with text. Videotapes and videodiscs may give high quality pictures. Voice input and output are also used. However, images used in most new media, like teletext, videotex, personal computers, and CAD/CAM systems, are often far too difficult to read and understand. Often combinations of colors are made in such a way that the actual information is more os less lost. Knowledge of traditional print design is usually not utilized.

Technical factors, programming factors, language factors and contextual factors all influence the viewer's ability of perception, learning and memory with respect to the function of the brain and the sensory organs. To achieve "good quality" man-machine interaction we have to consider all these factors in a kind of "wholeness-perspective". To learn we must be able to hear, see and also understand the message.

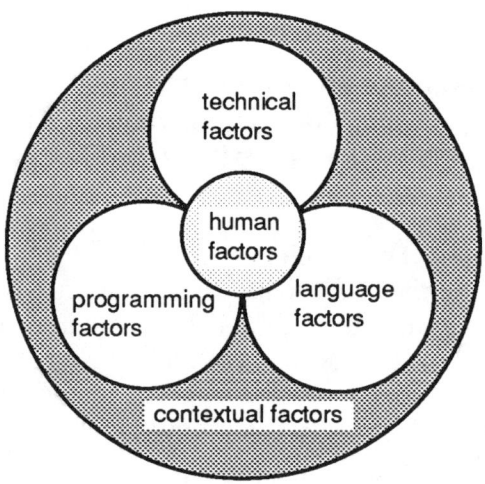

A model of man-machine interaction in a "wholeness-perspective".

In my view, it is no use to develop new, advanced systems and forget the aspects of the human factors. Such systems will never be successful in the long run.

In a printed material, such as a book, the table of contents and the index make it easier to find information according to one's wishes. When a person has read a page in a book, he or she may easily proceed to additional information by turning the page. Information stored in a computer system may be accessed in several different ways. The ease of use and the man-machine interaction are of vital importance. It is necessary to make the system as user friendly as possible by providing user support systems, standard function keys and for example a possibility of full text search. Instructions should always be clear, consistent, concise, and simple. It seem to be very important that the user has full control of the system, i.e. with respect to reading rate when text is presented.

Compared with traditional graphic presentations, a presentation of information on visual displays is *very limited.* Still, information may be presented in many different ways. Obviously the use of color is important. Different "rules of thumb" will apply to different types of presentation. Information, the "content", might be represented as text, as numeric data, or as visuals.

Visual Displays

Visual displays can be built in many ways. A color television set, an advanced color terminal, and a liquid crystal display all have very different characteristics. A television set is built to be watched at a distance of more than 120 centimetres. A computer terminal, however, is built to be used at a distance of 60 centimetres and has a much better picture quality. It also cost a lot more.

In discussions on technology, color is related to measurable amounts of light. In 1931 an international body called the Commission International de l'Eclairage (International Commission on Illumination), or CIE, defined standards of light and color. In this context color primaries are the basic color stimuli used for the synthesis of any color, by addition or subtraction. For color synthesis in a cathode ray tube (CRT) or a visual display unit (VDU), a range of colors can be produced by the additive combinations of a very limited amount of radiation. A color CRT is a vacuum tube, enclosing one or three electron guns for generating beams of electrons , a system for focusing the beam to produce a spot of visible light at the point of impact on the phosphorus screen, and for electric field deflection of the beam, suitable deflection electrodes. The thousands of small phosphorus dots are grouped into threes - called triads - with one dot emitting radiation that appears red, one dot emitting radiation appearing to be green, and the third emitting radiation appearing to be blue. Red, green, and blue are called the "three primaries", RGB. One lumen of white is given by 0,30 red + 0,59 green + 0,11 blue. Any two primary colors may be mixed to produce other colors. Red and green added can produce a range of hues around yellow. Green and blue produce a range centered on blue-green, while red and blue mixtures produce a red-blue range. The total number of colors that can be produced in a CRT depends upon the number of steps or grey levels obtainable for each phosphorus dot. Advanced systems are capable of producing up to 256 simultaneously visible color stimuli chosen from a palette of 16 million. However in most cases only a few color stimuli are needed at the same time.

The uncertainties in the co-ordinates of colors are rather large as a consequence of the heterogeneous distribution and efficiency of the phosphorus over the screen, the defects in electron beam convergence, and the departures of the relations between the values of the color signals and the digital counts.

One consequence of additive combinations in color television is that characters presented in white (the three-color-combination) is less sharp than yellow, blue-green, or red-blue (all two-color combinations). In a similar way the latter colors are less sharp than red, green, and blue (pure colors). Sometimes color rims may be seen at the characters with two- or three-color combinations.

The additive combination starts in dark adding light to produce color. Thus, another consequence of additive combinations is that secondary color stimuli will always appear brighter than the primaries.

Luminance is a photometric measure of the amount of light emitted by a surface (lumen/steradian/sq.m.). Radiance is a radiometric measure of light emitted by a surface (watt/steradian/sq.m.). It should be noted that neither luminance nor radiance is the equivalent of brightness, which is the experienced intensity of light (bright-dull). In color displays it is very difficult to distinguish brightness from lightness (white-black). When the signal to the display is increased, the brightness of the total screen is increased. If a signal to a specific part on the screen is increased, the lightness of the area is increased compared to the total screen.

It is usually possible in a CRT to adjust the luminance, the hue, and the saturation. Like brightness and lightness, hue and saturation are also psychological dimensions. Hue is the basic component of color corresponding to different wavelengths. Saturation is most closely related to the number of wavelengths contributing to a color sensation. We should always remember that the production of color, by additive or subtractive methods, have nothing to do with the actual perception of colors.

In a CRT some 8,000 to 20,000 volts of tension are required to form an image on the screen. Screens with several colors even requires up to 30,000 volts. The electrostatic field of the CRT is positively charged. Thus the person sitting in front of the screen is negatively charged and a strong field is created. The field affects the movement of dust particles in the air. Since the majority of the particles are positively charged they are attracted to the operator. The rate of deposit can reach 10,000 particles per square millimeter of skin an hour. Thus skin and eyes become irritated. People suffering from allergies can experience extreme discomfort. The electrostatic field can be eliminated with the help of a grounded filter, mounted on the screen.

The elctromagnetic field is created by the large magnets used to focus and direct the electron beam on the screen. The electromagnetic radiation consist of two components of which one can be shielded. It is not clear as to whether this radiation affects the adult human body unfavorably. However, it is known that this radiation might be injurious to unborn children when pregnant women work too many hours in front of the screen.

Color Description Systems

The relationship between hue, lightness, saturation, and brightness are very complicated. For practical use in art and in industry, several different systems providing numerical indexes for color have been developed. The most important ones will be 'mentioned here.

The Munsell System was introduced in 1905 and has been modified several times. The system consists of fixed arrays of samples which vary in hue, lightness (here called value) and saturation (here called chroma). The value scale ranges from white to black with nine steps of grey. Hue is represented by forty equal steps in a circle. The value and the hue is related to each other by a maximum of sixteen "saturation steps". The Munsell notations are defined by the color sample of the Munsell Book of Colors

There are many theories about how perception of colors actually works. In 1807, Young proposed a trichromatic color vision system. In 1924, Young's theory was formalized by von Helmholtz, who proposed hypothetical excitation curves for three kinds of cones in the retina, sensitive for red, green, and blue. In 1925 Hering based his "natural system" on man's natural perception of color that presupposes two pairs of chromatic colors block each other, red/green and blue/yellow. This model is the principle for the *Natural Color System NCS)*, developed during the 1970s in the Swedish Color Centre Foundation in Stockholm (Hård & Sivik, 1981).

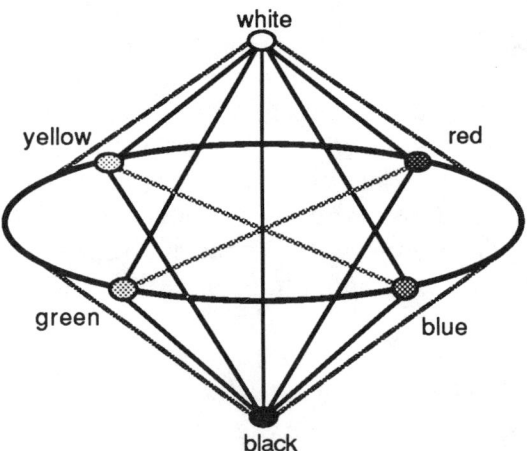

The NCS Color Solid with the six elementary colors. Yellow, red, blue, and green are all located on the circumference of the Color Circle. The color Triangle is any vertical sector through half of the NCS Color Solid, such as e.g. white - blue - black - white.

From a perceptual point of view, man perceives six colors as "pure". Black and white are achromatic colors. Yellow, red, blue, and green are chromatic colors. These six colors are called

Communication

elementary colors. All colors that are not pure elementary colors have a varying degree of resemblance to several elementary colors. Thus every possible color can be described with a specific location in a three-dimensional model, a twin cone, called the "NCS Color Solid".

The chromatic elementary colors yellow, red, blue, and green are all located on the circumference of the Color Circle. Each quadrant can be divided by one hundred steps, thus describing the hue of a color. The color Triangle is any vertical sector through half of the NCS Color Solid. It is used to describe the nuance of a color, i.e., its degree of resemblance to white, black, and the pure chromatic color of the hue concerned (chromaticness).

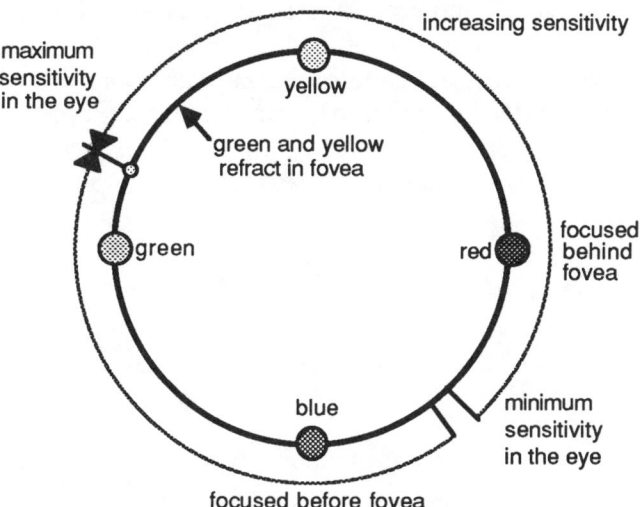

The NCS Color Circle combined with information on the eye's sensitivity.

When we want to describe a color using the color triangle and the color circle, it is done in the following sequence: blackness, chromaticness, and hue. For example, a color of 10 percent blackness, 80 percent chromaticness and with a hue of Y7OR will have the notation 1080-Y7OR.

The NCS places emphasis on qualitative variation in the color sensation whereas the Munsell System is based on equally spaced visual scales. Both systems are based on surface colors.

In the *hue-lightness-saturation system (HLS)* the hues are arranged as circles on the outside of a double cone resembling the NCS Color Solid (Murch, 1983). Hue specifications starts with blue at 0 ° and then follows the spectral order around the circle. Lightness and saturation are defined as percentages from 0 to 100. The HLS system is easy to use for colors on the surface of the model. However , colors inside the model are difficult to define. As in the Munsell- and NCS-systems, brightness creates problems.

The *hue-value-saturation system (HVS)* is a model that is rather similar to the NCS-system but utilizes another coding (Samit, 1983) Value is defined as the relative lightness. White has full value and black has no value at all. Also brightness creates problems.

In visual displays the color stimuli are specified by *red, green, blue (RGB)* values as discussed above. People who are specially trained can use the RGB proportions as a color description system. However, this is not possible for people in general.

The message on the screen

The message on the screen may consist of text, numeric data and visuals.

Text

A presentation of text on a visual display depends on the type of characters used, the design of the information, the background, and also the content.

The *characters* may vary with respect to font, size, lower-case and uppercase letters, color, and contrast to the background. Legibility of the text depends on the execution of the individual character and the possibility for each one to be distinguished from all others. A lot of work has been conducted to create legible characters. Knave (1983) has given guide-lines for the creation of characters. A minimum of ten to twelve raster lines per character is required. When characters are built by dots in a dot matrix, the characters will be round or square and not elongated. A dot matrix of seven by nine dots is often regarded as a minimum. The height of the characters should be a minimum of four millimetres for a viewing distance of sixty centimetres.

General *design rules* should be employed also in the design of screen displays. Thus material should be arranged and displayed so that it is easy to read, from top to bottom and from left to right.

A visual display design may vary with respect to spatial organization like headings, length of lines, justification, spacing, number of columns, number of colors at the same "page", and directive cues like color coding, twinkling characters or words, and scrolling text. Experiments (Pettersson et.al., 1984a) with 11,000 individual judgements of perceived reading efforts of text on visual displays were concluded as follows:

- Colors presented on color displays seem to be ranked in the same order as surface colors in traditional print media. Blue was most popular.
- When text is shown on a visual display, there is no easily read color combination. About thirty-five of one hundred and thirty-two combinations are acceptable. Most color combinations are bad.
- The best text color is black, which causes good contrast to most background colors.
- The best combination is black text on a white or yellow background.
- A text can be easy to read in any color, provided the background is carefully selected.
- The best background color is black, which has good contrast to most text colors.
- Reading efforts of color combinations are independent of the sex of the subjects.
- There was no difference between color blind (red-green) users and users with normal vision.

Inverse writing in various colors within a text may be used to achieve emphasis. Other possibilities may be a box around a paragraph or a change in font or size of letters.

Blank space in printed material increases cost, since more paper is required. Thus, it is not used often. However, color as well as blank space on a visual display is essentially free and might be used to increase readability. Full text screens in several colors are difficult to read and quite annoying. What about double spaced lines and/or spaces between columns? As stated above it is possible to make rather clear statements with respect to the use of colors. However, it is not as easy to give guide-lines for the other variables. Studies of attitudes to various variables (Pettersson et.al., 1984b) in the presentation of text on visual displays showed that subjects dislike fast scrolling text. Subjects seem to dislike more than three or four text colors on the same "page". They seem to consider color coding and/or twinkling text to be a good way to show that something is especially important. Subjects also seem to agree that text in upper case letters is harder to read than normal text. Attitudes are indifferent to a few design variables. Thus text on every second line only does not seem to make it easier to read than text on all lines. Higher characters do not seem to be easier to read than standard characters. Half lines do not seem to be better than full lines. A two-column layout does not seem to be better than a one-column layout. Other research suggest that margins should neither be narrow nor very wide. Old text that is not needed any more should be erased.

The *background* may vary with respect to color and brightness. Good combinations of text and background colors always have a good contrast. Optimum contrast is often found to be 8:1 to 10:1. Most subjects prefer a positive image i.e., dark text on light background with a minimum refresh rate of 70 Hz.

CLEA-research (Pettersson, 1984a) concerned with perceived reading efforts of text on visual displays and altering colors of the actual equipment found that the close *context* is really important for the perceived reading effort. The color of a terminal should be rather discrete. The best of ninety combinations were black text on a white screen with a dark grey terminal, closely followed by the context colors black, white, and light grey. It was also found that it is an advantage when the context color is the same as the color of either the color of the text or the background on the screen. The combination of context and text/background colors must match against each other. If they clash the reading effort increases.

Further experiments (op. cit.) with altering ambient light levels showed that this is of no or very limited importance for the perceived reading effort.

Numeric Data
Computer graphics hardware and software have become widely available. In advertisements it is often stated that business graphics communicate the information effectively, thus being very useful. However, in real life situations graphics often tend to be very poorly designed. Thus they may fail to improve the communication. Sometimes bad design might even make communication difficult or even impossible. Bertin (1967), Cossette (1981), McCleary (1983) and Pettersson (1983) all discuss the importance of individual design variables in visual language. However, these discussions are all based on research on traditional print media. Ehlers (1984) points out problems of legibility in business graphics. According to him direction and pattern or texture of graphic elements appear to be important factors as well as color and size.

In the CLEA-laboratory studies of *attitudes to different variables* in the presentation of information on visual displays (Pettersson et. al., 1984b) showed that subjects consider it easy to see the difference between vertical bars as well as between horizontal bars.

Further experiments by Fahlander & Zwierzak (1985) have shown that the greater the difference is between the color in a graphic presentation the more distinct is our *perception of the border between the color spaces*. On *white* background the following color combinations are suitable to use: Black combined with yellow, yellow-red, red, blue, green or the mixtures of red-blue (magenta), blue-green (cyan) and green-yellow. On *black* background the following color combinations are suitable to use: White combined with yellow-red, red, blue or the mixtures of red-blue. On white as well as on black background the following combinations are suitable to use: Yellow combined with red and blue, red combined with blue-green or green-yellow, red-blue combined with green or green-yellow.

Following this study Azoulay & Janson (1985) found that some colors used in business graphics have much higher *aesthetic values* than others. Blue, red and green are liked the most.

In an effort to find some more detailed knowledge about our perception of business graphics two comprehensive experiments were carried out with respect to *relationships between variables and parts of a whole* (Pettersson and Carlsson, 1985).

The findings, based on more than 2,300 individual assessments, were conclusive in the following points:
- Graphical information is very good in conveying a survey of a situation.
- When relationships between variables shall be presented, comparisons of lengths give the best results.
- When parts of a whole shall be presented, comparisons of areas can be used as well.
- Design of graphic elements is important to consider. Most available patterns are probably less good. Patterns should be discrete and not disturbing.
- Colors like blue, red and green are liked very much but they do not improve our possibility of reading the message accurately.
- Different parts in graphic figures should have about the same luminance and radiance. The true differences between areas can be hard to see when shaded differently.
- When accuracy is needed graphical information should be combined with actual figures.

In "Choosing The Right Chart" ISSCO (1981) supplies 21 practical guide-lines and pointers on effective chart design such as: "Make bars and columns wider than the space between them." In a study Ek & Frederiksen (1986) used the CLEA-equipment to find out about effective chart design. Forty subjects assessed the difference in size between two bars in a bar chart with six bars. The bars had one of three possible widths (1/60, 1/30 and 1/15 of the screen width.) The distance between the bars had one of six possible values, from zero to more than twice the bar width. The bar charts were produced and displayed at random and always presented with blue bars on black background. The findings, based on 3,600 individual assessments, showed:
- The bar width has no influence on our perception of size.

- The space between bars has no influence on our perception of size.

This study confirmed earlier findings (with the perception of vertical lines). It can be concluded that *we can make screen design according to aesthetic appeal.*
Finally, it may be stated that *it is extremely easy to convey misleading information about statistical relationships by using misleading illustrations.* Those who are serious in their work should avoid these mistakes.

Visuals
Our perception of visuals on visual displays are of course to a large degree dependent on the quality of the screen, especially when pie charts are used. European videotex terminals simply cannot reproduce a pie chart since the graphics resolution is only about 5,000 graphical elements. An ordinary television image consists today of about 250,000 image points or picture elements which vary with respect both to grey scale and color information.
Hayashi (1981) has reported on the development of High Definition Television (HDTV) in Japan. HDTV uses 1.125 scanning lines and can contain five or six times more information than the present NTSC standard color television system with 525 lines. HDTV developments of flat plasma screens will also give increased technical possibilities for better perception of the visual information.

Computer Print-Outs
In visual displays, the color image is produced by an additive mixture of red, green, and blue. However, in the production of hard-copies, computer print-outs as well as in painting, printing and also color photography a subtractive method of combining inks, dyes and pigments is used. Most colors can be generated in printing with the use of yellow, cyan (blue-green) and magenta (red-blue). Together these primaries produce black. However, pure black is often included as a fourth printing color because the

three primaries that produce the best chromatic colors usually do not produce the best black. Subtractive systems begin with a white surface. Colors darken as more wave-lengths are absorbed. (However, in some color hard copy printing, both additive and subtractive color combinations can occur.) The difference in the production of colors creates some problems. It should also be remembered that color codings will lose their meaning when monochrome printers, as well as displays, are used. There are many *hard copy systems* and possibilities to make computer print-outs for text as well as for pictures.

Photographs. The simplest way to make a hard copy documentation of a color display is to use a camera. Systems are available with hoods. Polaroid cameras give immediate results. In sophisticated systems analogue RGB signals from a color terminal are digitized and exposed to film.

Pen plotters. Pen plotters are the simplest of the non-photographic methods. They are best suited to simple line diagrams. In some systems the pen/s are fixed and the papers are moved. Usually, the print quality corresponds to a matrix printer with 2 - 4 dots per millimetre.

Color ribbons. Wire matrix printers can use color ribbons. The matrix head traverses the paper, printing a single color at the time. The quality is usually about 2 - 4 dots per millimetre but may be enhanced by the use of more print-heads. Matrix and daisy wheel printers are very good for text.

Ink jet printing. Small dots of ink are sprayed on to the paper through a number of nozzles. The resolution is determined by the ink drop size and the way it spreads on the paper. The quality range up to 20 dots per millimetre. It is possible to produce large size pictures.

Laser printing. A laser printer is an electrostatic device in which a laser beam is scanned across the surface of an electrically charged selenium coated drum. This is done with a rotating polygonal mirror. The charge of the drum surface is modulated according to the dot matrix character patterns. The text and images are transferred to a paper as in a conventional Xerographic printer.

Type-setting machine. Some computers may be linked up with professional type-setting machines. These "print-outs" obviously can have a superb quality and be used for originals in the printing process.

Electrophotography. With three toners being applied in the same way as in laser printers, color prints can be produced. The quality is 4 dots per millimetre. However, the dots fuse together. Thus, the quality appears to be better than it actually is.

Others. Also other methods exist such as thermal transfer, wire matrix printers using ink instead of ribbons and electrostatic methods.

In a study (Pettersson et. al., 1984c) print-outs from line, matrix, and daisy wheel printers were used. These eight samples were numbered and showed at random to 40 subjects who judged their perceived reading efforts of the different texts. The results showed that:
- Only the two daisy wheel print-outs and a normal font, normal mode matrix print-out cause little reading effort and thus are easy to read and quite acceptable.
- Reading efforts of print-outs are independent of the sex of the subjects

It was concluded from this study and the previous findings (Pettersson et. al.,1984a) that a text presented in a good color combination on a visual display was easier to read than print-outs from several printers used. Today, however good quality laser printers are often used.

REFERENCES

Azoulay, B., & Janson, H. (1985). *Estetiska upplevelser av färger på bildskärm*. (Undergraduate thesis) Stockholm: University of Stockholm, Department of Computer Science.

Bertin, J. (1967). *Semiologic graphique: Les Diagrammes, Les reseaux, Les cartes*. Paris:Moutin .

Cossette, C. (1982). *How Pictures Speak: A brief introduction to iconics.* Paper presented at the 32nd International Communication Association Conference, Boston, May 1-5. Translated from French by Vincent Ross, Quebec.

Ehlers, J. H. (1984). *Problems in Legibility in Presentation Graphics.* CAMP/84, Computer Graphics Applications For Management and Productivity, Berlin Sept. 25-28. Proceedings: AMK Berlin, 34-41.

Ek, G,. & Frederiksen, M. (1986). *Utformning av histogram.* (Undergraduate thesis). Stockholm: University of Stockholm, Department of Computer Science.

Fahlander, P . & Zwierzak, A. (1985). *Gränstydlighet mellan färger.* (Undergraduate thesis). Stockholm: University of Stockholm, Department of Computer Science.

Hayashi, K. (1983). Research and Development on High Definition Television. *SMPTE Journal,* 3, 178-186.

Helmholz, H., C., F. (1924). *Physiological Optics. Vol II.* (J. Southall Rochester, Trans.) N Y: Optical Society of America.

Hering, A. (1925). Grundzuge der Lehre vom Lichtsinn. Handbuch der gesamten Augenheilkunde. (2nd edition, 3rd volume). Berlin.

Hård, A., & Sivik, L. (1981). NCS - Natural Color System: A Swedish standard for Color-Notation, *Color research and application, 6, 3,* 129 - 138.

ISSCO (1981). *Choosing The Right Chart. A Comprehensive Guide for Computer Graphics Users.* San Diego.

Knave, B. (1983). *The Visual Display Unit.* In *Ergonomic Principles in Office Automation.* Uddevalla: Ericsson Information Systems AB, 1984.

Laswell, H. (1948). The Structure and Function of Communication in Society. In L.Bryson (Ed). *The Communication of Ideas.* New York: Harper & Brothers.

Lax, L, & Olson, M. (1983). NAPLPS Standard Graphics and the Microcomputer. *Byte 8, 7,* 82 - 92.

McCleary, G.F. (1983). An Effective Graphic "Vocabulary". *IEEE Computer. Graphics and Applications. 3, 2,* 46-53.

McLuhan, M. (1967). *Media. Människans utbyggnader.* Stockholm: Pan/Norstedts

Murch, G. M. (1983). Perceptual Considerations of color. *Computer Graphics World, 6, 7.* 32 - 40.

Parker, E.B. (1975). *Social implications of computer/telecommunications systems.* Program in information technology and telecommunications. Report No 16. Stanford University: Center for interdisciplinary research.
Pettersson, R. (1981). *Bilder Barn och Massmedia.* Stockholm: Akademilitteratur
Pettersson, R. (1983). *Visuals for instruction.* (CLEA-report No. 12). Stockholm: University of Stockholm, Department of Computer Science.
Pettersson, R. (1984a). *Visual Displays and Reading Effort.* (CLEA-report No. 20). Stockholm: University of Stockholm, Department of Computer Science.
Pettersson, R. (1984b). *Numeric Data, presentation in different formats.* Presentation at the 16th Annual Conference of the International Visual Literacy Association, Baltimore, Nov. 8-11.
Pettersson, R., & Carlsson, J. (1985). *Numeric data on visual displays.* (CLEA-report No. 30). Stockholm: University of Stockholm, Department of Computer Science.
Pettersson, R., Carlsson, J., Isacsson, A., Kollerbaur, A., and Randerz, K. (1984a). *Color Information Displays and Reading Efforts.* (CLEA-report No. 18). Stockholm: University of Stockholm, Department of Computer Science.
Pettersson, R., Carlsson, J., Isacsson, A., Kollerbaur, A., & Randerz, K. (1984b). *Attitudes to variables on visual displays.* (CLEA-report, No. 24). Stockholm: University of Stockholm, Department of Computer Science.
Pettersson, R., Carlsson, J., Isacsson, A., Kollerbaur, A., and Randerz, K. (1984c). *Reading Efforts on Prints-Outs.* (CLEA-report, No. 21). Stockholm: University of Stockholm, Department of Computer Science.
Samit, M. L. (1983). The Color Interface, Making the Most of Color. *Computer Graphics World, No. 7.* 42 - 50.
Schramm, W. (1954). Procedures and Effects of Mass Communication. In B.H. Nelson (Ed.), *Mass Media and Education. The Fifty-Third Yearbook of the National Society for the Study of Education. Part II.* Chicago: University of Chicago Press.
Shannon, C.E., & Weaver, W. (1949). *The Mathematical Theory of Communication.* Champaign, Ill: The University of Illinois Press

Chapter 2

PERCEPTION, LEARNING AND MEMORY

This chapter will examine some of the functions related to perception, learning and memory of pictorial information. Several experiments and studies concerning interpretation of image contents are presented.

OUR SENSES

How do we receive information about the outside world? We can smell, taste, feel, listen, see and examine our surroundings. We can also ask questions. Smell, taste and feeling are not as yet especially important factors to be considered in information production. So only aural and visual impressions will be the subject of a brief discussion here.

Hearing
Sound is a subjective sensation of hearing, i.e. the sensory cells in the inner ear's hearing apparatus are stimulated. In objective terms, sound consists of longitudinal wave motions capable of acting on our hearing apparatus and thereby eliciting sound sensations. Sound waves are picked up by the outer ear and conducted along the external auditory meatus to the eardrum. The

eardrum consists of an elastic membrane which resonates at the same frequency as the impinging sound waves. These vibrations are transmitted by the three ossicles of the middle ear, i.e. the malleus, incus and stapes, to the oval window, a membrane in the coiled cochlea of the inner ear. Thus, when the eardrum bulges inward, the oval window also bulges inward. This movement is transmitted to the fluid in the cochlea. Movements in this fluid excite auditory cells which, in turn, transmit signals to the hearing centre of the cerebrum. Another soft membrane, the round window, provides flexible closure of the other end of the cochlea. Thus, the round window bulges outward when the oval window bulges inward and vice-versa.

Man is normally capable of perceiving sound waves at frequencies from 16 to 20,000 Hz. Sound waves lower than 16 Hz are referred to as infrasound, and frequencies higher than 20,000 Hz are referred to as ultrasound.

Sound intensity, i.e. the average rate of sound energy transmitted per unit of time and unit area which passes a plane perpendicular to the transmission direction, is an objective measure of sound intensity. It is usually measured in w/m^2 (watts per square metre). However, a psychologically based concept is necessary in order to designate the strength of sound waves striking our ears. The hearing range is the interval between the lowest sound intensity we are capable of perceiving, i.e. the auditory threshold, and the highest level we are able to tolerate, i.e. the pain threshold. The range is very wide, so it is usually described as the logarithmic ratio N of two intensities, I_r and I_i, measured in decibels. $N=10^{10} \log I_r/I_i$. The auditory threshold and the pain threshold vary with the frequency. The auditory threshold for normal frequencies (1,000 Hz) is at 0.01 w/m^2. This value is used as a reference, 0 dB, when sound intensities are compared. Sound strength can also be measured in phons. A phon is a unit for measuring the apparent loudness of a sound. It is equal in number of a given sound to the intensity (in dB) of a sound having a frequency of 1,000 Hz when the two sounds are judged to be of equal intensity. A quiet whisper usually measures about ten phons whereas a compressed air hammer in action usually generates 110 phons.

Vision

In subjective terms vision is a complex process which elicits a sense of vision, i.e. awareness of the stimulation of the eye's vision perception cells. In objective terms, light consists of electromagnetic waves (light "rays") capable of acting on our eyes and creating sensations of light and images.

Human vision is sensitive within a wide wavelength range. Visible light ranges from wavelengths of 400 nm (0.0004 millimetre), that is violet, to 770 nm, that is dark red. In between these extremes are blue, green, yellow and orange. Green-orange (about 555 nm) lies in the region of the eye's greatest sensitivity. Sensitivity decreases markedly toward the red and violet ends of the spectrum.

Like sound waves light waves are propagated in straight lines from their source. They can also be reflected, refracted, bent and absorbed. The velocity of light in air is nearly 300,000 km/s. When light rays (usually parallel) from an object enter the eye, they are refracted in the cornea and lens and pass through the vitreous humour until they strike the retina. When the ambient light level is high, the light rays strike the macula lutea, the fovea, a small area of the retina which is rich in cones. Cones are the receptors which record colors. When the ambient light level is low, the receptors which record black and white are of greater importance to vision. The classical view is that each sensory organ picks up individual sensory impressions which are interpreted more or less individually. The retina's receptors are excited by light and respond by chemically converting a pigment, rhodopsin (visual purple). This conversion triggers impulses which are transmitted along the optic nerve to the brain's visual cortex. Here, the impulses are translated into a sensation of vision. The optic nerves cross on their way to the cortex. Information from each eye reaches both halves of the brain.

When light rays from an object are bent in the cornea and lens, an upside-down image of that object is formed on the retina. Very small children view the world as being up-side-down. After a time, however, the brain somehow learns to process retinal images so that they are perceived to be right-side-up. Since we have two eyes, both pointing forward and with partially overlapping visual fields, we can assess the distance, both forward and laterally, between objects. It takes a certain amount of time for the eye to record light rays from an object, such as a painting. And it also takes time before we are capable of perceiving that object as an image. The eye has inertia. This inertia enables us to perceive motion. When we look at a person who is walking or running, the eye records a series of stills which ultimately blend into one another and form a moving image. This inertia also enables us to see motion in the stills which comprise a movie film or a TV image.

Nowadays, however, sensory organs are often described as sensory systems and the total energy flux striking them viewed as information about the surrounding world and about ourselves. The individual sensory organs receiving this information are not merely passive receptors but jointly constitute an active, exploratory system in which all the senses intimately interact supplying us with an undergirded view of the world. So we are spared the task of having to consciously translate a myriad of individual sensory impressions into coherent perception.

According to Gibson (1966) the eye does not really operate like a camera. We are never conscious of the "stills" formed on the retina. We only perceive the external world they represent. The eye and head shift their attention constantly from one point to another in our surroundings or in a picture. Thus, our vision is an active, exploratory process. We usually concentrate our attention to interesting events within a narrow segment of our total field of vision.

Eye movements
Bergström (1974) noted that visual information on our surroundings is conveyed to the eye, a very imperfect optical system. Eyes never remain still. They tremble at a frequency of about 30-90 Hz. This serves to shift information of individual cells. The eye alters its fixation point constantly. It also makes constant small jumps, i.e. saccadic movements.

We constantly "scan" the things we look at. By using complex instrumentation that allows the researcher to record exactly where in a picture a person is looking at any given moment it is

Perception, learning and memory

possible to study the way in which the gaze wanders over a picture, pauses and fixes on certain points (Buswell 1935; Webb et al. 1963; Zuzne & Michaels 1964; Guba et al. 1964; Berlyne 1966; Leckart 1966; Gould 1967 and 1973; Yarbus 1967; Mackworth & Morandi 1967; Faw & Nunnaly 1967 and 1968; Fleming 1969; Wolf 1970; Noton & Stark 1971 a and b; Loftus 1972 and 1979; Hochberg & Brooks 1978; Baron 1980; Nesbit 1981; Pettersson 1983a). The gaze never fixes on most parts of a picture. Only certain image elements capture our attention.

Yarbus (1967) found that fixation usually lasts for two to eight tenths of a second and that eye movements between eye fixations took from one to eight-hundredths of a second. So we normally view a picture by means of a large number of eye movements and eye fixations in rapid succession. The location of each fixation influences how a picture is interpreted and later remembered (Nelson & Loftus, 1980).

The pattern of eye movements and fixations is entirely different when our objective is to search for something in a picture. The things we wish to see in a picture have a major impact on the location of eye fixations. Where we look and why we look there determines what we see.

A number of scientists have found that pictures which are hard to interpret require more eye fixations than "easy" pictures (Webb et al. 1963; Zusne & Michaels 1964; Berlyne 1966; Leckart 1966; Faw & Nunnaly 1967 and 1968; Mackworth & Morandi 1967; Hochberg & Brooks 1978).

Wolf (1970) determined that "difficult" pictures require more fixations up to a certain point. When a picture was extremely difficult, subjects tended to avoid looking at it or searching for a visual centre. However neither Baron (1980) nor Nesbit (1981) found any correlation between picture type and the number of fixations. But the two latter scientists did employ a different method in their studies than the authors mentioned previously.

Faw & Nunnaly (1967 and 1968) also found that new pictures required more fixations than pictures with which subjects were already familiar. Movement or change in a picture or event also attracts attention and therefore cause many fixations.

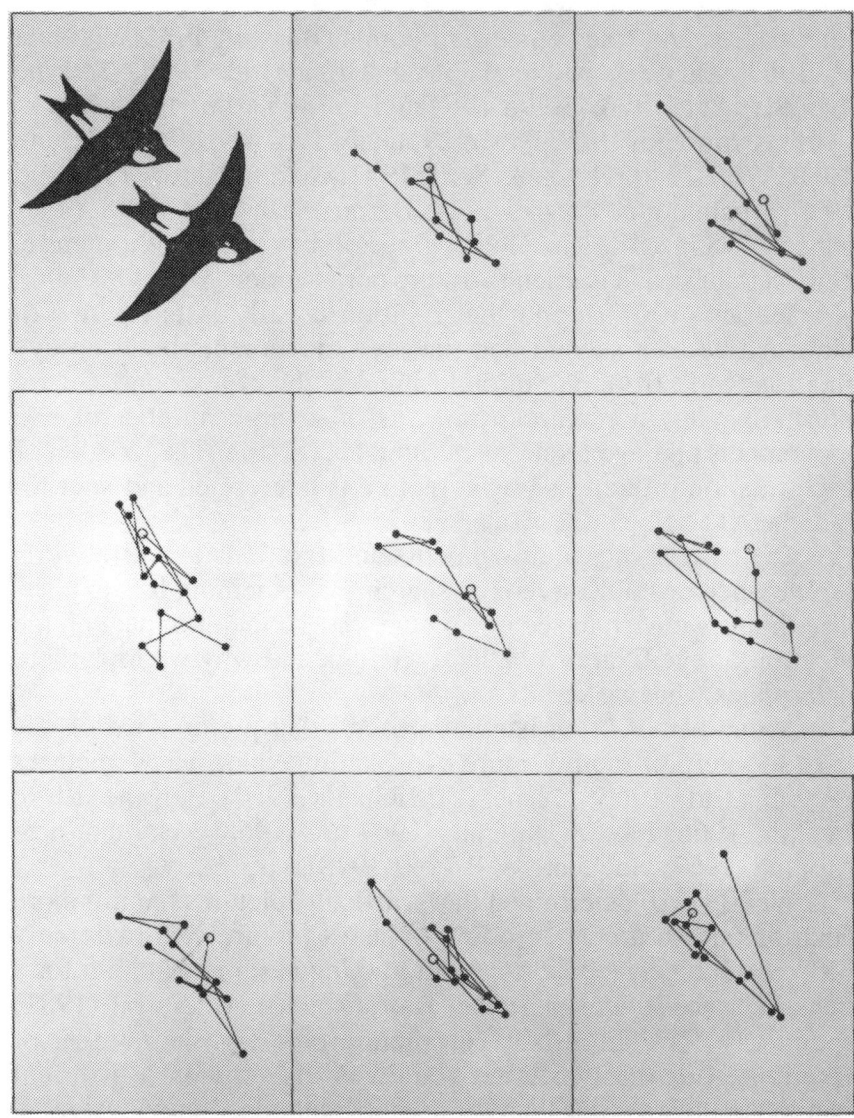

During experiments adult subjects looked at a drawing of two flying House Martins (1) as indicated in the above eight analyses of eye fixations and eye movements. Analyses 2 - 5 represent female subjects and 6 - 9 male subjects. In each case the first eye fixation is marked with an unfilled circle. Each fixation takes about 1/5 of a second. In this case subjects got the instruction: "Tell me what you see!" It takes only a few seconds for adult subjects to recognize "two birds".

Perception, learning and memory

A model of the "stills" formed on the retina during different eye fixations. Eye fixations are rapid, usually four to six per second. We are never aware of the stills on the retina.

Guba et. al. (1964), Gould (1973) and Nesbit (1981) found a positive correlation between eye movements and intelligence. Highly intelligent subjects utilized more fixations than less intelligent subjects. Wolf (1970) discovered that highly intelligent subjects displayed great flexibility in their "scanning patterns", irrespective of the stimuli, whereas subjects with low intelligence tended to display a static scanning pattern which was the same for different stimuli. Nesbit (1981) found a positive correlation between learning and the number of fixations.

Wolf (1970) suggested that eye movements can be employed as an index of visual learning. Eye movements supply information on where, how long and how often subjects look at different parts of a picture.

Looking at pictures is a "natural" way of free exploring. However *reading* a text needs to be very structured with several eye fixations on each line. The time for each fixation varies amongst individuals and different texts (Ekvall, 1977) with the average time for good readers between 1/4 to 1/6 of a second. It also takes from 1/25 to 1/30 of a second for the eye to move from one fixation to the next and sweep from the end of one line to the beginning of the next. In normal reading the text within foveal vision comprises an area of seven to ten letter spaces. At normal reading the angle of convergence is about 2°. This means a reading speed of five to ten words per second or 300-600 words per minute. Lawson (1968) has established the physiological limit of reading as being a maximum of 720 words per minute. Ekwall (1977) calculated the maximum reading speed of the most efficient reader as being 864 words per minute under ideal conditions.

The importance of eye movements can be summarized in the following five points:
1 Only certain image elements attract our interest.
2 The pattern for eye movements and fixations depends on what we wish to see or are told to see in a picture.
3 Informative parts of a picture attract more fixations than less informative parts.
4 Different kinds of pictures give rise to different kinds of fixations and intelligence and visual learning.

5 There is a positive correlation between the number of fixations and intelligence and visual learning.

Movement and change
Movement or change in a picture or an event attract our attention and therefore cause many fixations. Hubel & Wiesel (1962) found that many sensory cells in vision responded only very weakly to uniform light but very vigorously to changes in light intensity. This principle also applies to other sensory cells, i.e. the cells respond primarily to change. Sensory cells are also quickly exhausted. Acuity falls of rapidly outside of the fovea. However some information can be processed from peripheral vision The gist of a picture can be understood after only a few fixations.

Gibson (1966), Moray (1970) and many of their successors feel that movements detected in peripheral parts of our visual field automatically cause the eyeball to shift position to permit fixation of these movements. So even visual cells far from macula lutea are a major asset. Edwards & Goolkasian (1974) summarized a large part of the work carried out to determine the extent and importance of our peripheral vision. Not unexpectedly, they found that impact increases as stimuli approach the macula lutea, as they become larger, when they increase in brightness and when they have a low level of complexity.

It is possible for us to see the difference between several million color stimuli at simultaneous viewing. However, if not being seen simultaneously the number we can identify is much smaller, maybe 10,000 - 20,000. It has been assumed that our perception of colors is a two sided phenomenon. The discrimination capability represents our possibility to differentiate a figure from its background. It is strongly influenced by and dependent on contextual variables such as lighting conditions and other surrounding colors. The color identification capacity on the other hand makes us capable to interpret "the quality" of object we perceive. "Color constancy" is a tendency to judge objects as the same despite changes in illumination.

LISTENING AND LOOKING

Sensory organs jointly constitute a perceptual system which, in a natural environment, collects an enormous amount of superfluous information about this environment. In a natural environment, the sensory system normally supplies us with exhaustive, unambiguous intelligence about events occurring there. We are often unaware of the sensory channel(s) supplying us with information. We are merely aware of the external events, events which appear to be absolutely real and unambiguous. But in unnatural artificial surroundings, the brain often "translates" sensory stimuli in an attempt to relate them to its stored information about more familiar places, events and times.

We are capable of successfully hearing and seeing things at the same time. We are also capable of simultaneously hearing different stimuli in either ear. However, we are incapable of simultaneously perceiving different stimuli aimed at the right and left eye respectively. However, a stimulus may easily be perceived in different ways at different times.

Perception "laws"

The concept "perception" is a collective designation for the processes in which an organism obtains information on the outside world. We unconsciously make a constant effort to create some semblance of order in the impulses. Points, lines, areas, colors, tones, noise, heat, cold, touch, pressure, sound etc. are integrated in such a way that they can be interpreted as a meaningful whole. A number of psychologists view these attempts to establish order as an innate faculty carried out in accordance with certain "laws". According to the "similarity law", we tend to group impressions on the basis of their similarity. According to the "proximity law", we also group objects and events on the basis of their proximity to one another. According to the "continuity law", we perceive a slow and gradual change in a stimulus as a single stimulus. Events which have a natural relationship to one another also give the impression of being continuous. According to the "natural law", various stimuli form

Perception, learning and memory

meaningful patterns. According to the "contrast law", we tend to array impressions which form natural opposites, thereby reinforcing one another, in groups. Usually there is a constancy of size, shape, color and contrast in the perception of known objects. This is regardless of distance, angle and illumination.

■ ■   ■ ■   ■ ■   ■ ■

The "proximity law". We see four pairs of dots instead of just eight individual dots. Perception is organized.

● ● ● ● ● ○ ○ ○ ○ ○

The "similarity law". We tend to group elements that look alike. Here it is easy to see two sets of dots. Perception is organized.

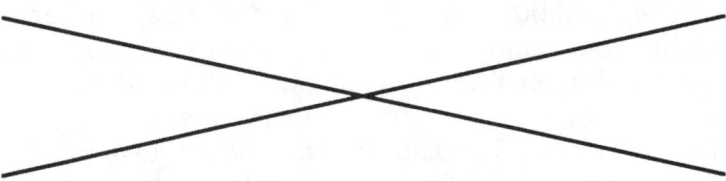

The "continuity law". We see this pattern as two lines crossing rather than as two angles joined together at their apexes. This is also referred to as "line of direction". Perception is selective.

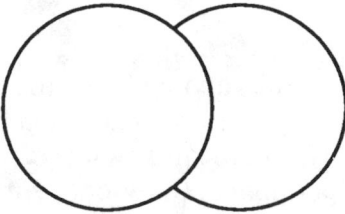

The "natural law" or closure. We see this pattern as one circle partially occluded by another. Even though there are many possibilities, this interpretation seems to be the natural one. Perception is influenced by expectations.

```
a _____
b _____
c _____
```

The "contrast law". A line (a) seems to be long when it is compared with a shorter line (b) but short when it is compared with a longer line (c). Perception is relative.

New impressions are dependent upon and interpreted against the background of our previous experience and learning, our attitudes and interests, our needs and feelings and the prevailing situation. We direct our attention to things which are large, have bright color, move, deviate from the surroundings or from familiar patterns, things which arouse feelings and needs and in which we happen to be interested in at the moment.

A torrent of information bombards us from the outside world. Each eye contains about 1 million afferent nerve fibers. Each ear has about 30,000. Thus, the eyes and ears are capable of receiving vast quantities of information. However, it is impossible (and undesirable) for us to be aware of everything happening around us. At any given moment, the eye may contain 2,500,000 bits of information. Laboratory studies have shown that a subject is able to perceive 3-6 different, simple graphical symbols per second when the subject's concentration is devoted solely to this task. It is easier to perceive large and clear symbols than small, blurred symbols.

Choice of information

The average person speaks about 135 words per minute (Judson, 1972) and the fastest professional television or radio announcers speak about 150 to 160 words per minute. Our top reading speed is some 720 words per minute (Lawson, 1968). Text, spoken and written, is always linear and must be processed sequentially, word by word. It takes a long time to convey a verbal message. Non-verbal information, however, seem to be processed very fast. It only took a few seconds for adult subjects to recognize "two birds" when shown a picture of two flying House Martins.

The perception process is often assumed to consist of two stages. Information processing is tentative, fast, rough and parallel in the first stage. It comprises all kinds of analysis, from physiological to cognitive processes. A number of different properties of a stimulus are identified simultaneously. In many instances, one such analysis is sufficient.

The second stage of the information analysis is conscious, demands attention, is detailed and sequential. Various hypotheses about a stimulus are weighed against one another and tested. Information processing is more definite on this level.

Color blindness, or better "Anomalies of color vision", is a condition in which certain color discriminations can not be made. It is much more commonly observed among men than among women, with estimates ranging as high as 8-10% of the male population. Only 1% of the female population has anomalous color vision. Most common is the problem to distinguish between red and green. Unfortunately, red and green are quite often used as discriminating symbols in our modern society.

In the torrent of information that bombards us we have to select the information we want. So one of the main problems in advertising today is to reach people with the "message". In view of our limited capacity for handling simultaneous information, it is important to find out which factors determine the parts of the available information that will be processed. Which stimuli do we select and why? When we first look at a visual we only see that which is necessary to perceive and identify objects and events in a reasonable and meaningful manner. This is Gibson's "principle of economy" (Gibson, 1966).

According to Brody (1982) preference for a particular visual format does not necessarily result in increased learning. Yet, in the absence of more substantial data, information based on student preference has a meaningful role to play in affecting learning.

Getting and keeping a reader's attention may be improved by using different design variables such as color, changes in brightness, varying the size of a particular pictorial subject. Attention getting techniques are used extensively in advertising. Vogel et. al. (1986) showed that it is undeniable that visual presentation support is persuasive. Presentations using visual aids were 43 percent more persuasive than unaided presentations.

The perception system strives to obtain clarity. If the system arrives at clarity then clarity serves as a reinforcement, a reward.

So our perception of an image depends on our previous experience, our mood, other pictures, text and sound, our personal interests etc.

When we look at a visual, we also "see" different details in the visual on different occasions. So highly "saturated", information-packed visuals may have something new to offer even after having been viewed tens of times.

We have to learn to read and comprehend the content of an image. According to Salomon (1979) the process of extracting information from messages that are presented in any symbolic format involves mental activities. In order to match between the symbols and their referents in the learner's cognitive schemata translation activities are needed. Such processes differ as a function of the symbolic systems used to convey the message. Tidhar (1987) studied children's understanding of the content in educational television programs. It was concluded that "Channel Dominancy", the degree to which either the visual or the auditory channel carries the brunt of information whereas the other channel provides compatible supportive information, was found to affect viewer's information processing in areas such as recall, comprehension, generalization and inferential activity. Equivalence in verbal and visual information was found significantly superior to verbal or visual dominancy in its effect on spontaneous recall. Presentations characterized by visual dominancy or equivalence in verbal and visual information were found significantly more comprehensible than presentations characterized by verbal dominancy. Visual dominancy was revealed to have the highest positive effect on generalizations, followed by equivalence, whereas verbal dominancy presentations achieved the lowest generalization scores. The effect of channel dominancy on inferential activity interacted with the viewing condition: when viewers were exposed to the visual channel only, visual dominancy elicited a higher degree of inferential activity than the presentations characterized by verbal dominancy or equivalence.

According to Lanners (1973) we only see the things that affect us emotionally. Everything else is ignored. When we look at a picture, we first discover the cues we already recognize. We probably become most easily familiar with simple patterns than with complex patterns. Closed shapes are preferred to open shapes and fields. Once we have identified a few well-known shapes, we sometimes feel that we have "seen everything" and could well miss some valuable information.

Thurstone and Carraher (1966) point out that some structures will be perceived as reversible when it is hard to choose between figure and background. Reality and what we see at any given moment will always be separated and different. We will see different things at different occasions both with respect to reality and pictures.

The brain

Verbal languages have digital codification with combinations of letters and/or numbers representing contents (Elkind, 1975). There is no direct correspondance between groups of letters, words, and reality. Each meaning is defined and must be learned. In contrast to this, non-verbal languages have analogical codification with combinations of basic graphical elements (dots, lines, areas and volumes) for likeness of a (concrete) reality (Pettersson, 1983 b). Usually there is a correspondence with reality. Visuals are iconic. They normally resemble the thing they represent. Meaning is apparent on a basic level but must be learned for deeper understanding. Gombrich (1969) argues that no pictorial image gains the status of a "statement" unless an explicit reference is made to what it is supposed to represent. Barthes (1977) uses the term "anchorage" to describe the relationship of pictures to legends or other accompanying verbal language. Most pictures are capable of several interpretations until anchored to one by a caption.

The modern era of brain research began in the mid-1960's, when Dr. Roger Sperry and his associates published their findings regarding patients who were operated on to control life-threatening epileptic seizures (see Gazzaniga and Le Doux, 1978; Wilson, Reeves and Gazzaniga, 1982; and Sinatra, 1986, for reviews). Several researchers have given a lot of thought to the function of the brain.

According to some theories, the two halves of the brain are apparently specialized and function independently of one another.

At the same time, however, either of the brain halves appears to be capable of assuming the functions of the other half. There is an immense communication between the two halves. It has been estimated at six billion pulses per second.

Each half of the brain has its sensory perceptions, thoughts, feelings and memories. Thus the left half of the brain is said to be mainly verbal, capable of speech, counting and writing. It seems to be specialized in abstract thought, is analytical, logical and working linearly, detailed and sequential. It is controlled, dominant, critical, has established symbols processing, facile recognition, positive emoting, goal-oriented and developmental learning. It performs convergent search, is time sensitive, aggressive and controls the right half of the body. The right half of the brain is said to be speechless but capable of concrete thought, perception of space and an understanding of complicated relationships. It is said to be knowing without words, holistic, spatial, intuitive, creative, minor and self-knowing. It is receptive, able to work with new symbols, will remember new faces, new data and is negative emoting. The right half of the brain is artistic, interprets auditory signals, emotional undertones and music. It is said to be immediate knowing. It is working with divergent search and is time-abhorrent. It can count only to twenty, is only capable of reading simple nouns and is unable to write. The right half of the brain is said to be completely superior to the left half of the brain in its perception of both two- and three- dimensional images. The right half of the brain also controls the left half of the body.

Most certainly there is a lot of cooperation between the two brain hemispheres rather than competition. Dual processing modes of the hemispheres are beneficial to the human being. Blood flow mapping during reading aloud has shown that seven cortical regions are active in each of the hemispheres (Lassen et. al., 1978).

According to Perfetti (1977) and Sinatra (1986) perception of linear representations, such as text, means a sequential, slow processing to compose and comprehend the content ("left brain activity"). Retrieval from verbal memory is a serial integration and sequential processing of auditory-motor perception systems (Sinatra, 1986).

According to Gazzaniga (1967) and Sperry (1973, 1982) perception of two- or three-dimensional representations means a parallel simultaneous, holistic and fast processing ("right brain activity"). Lodding (1983) concluded that the image memory and processing capabilities of the human mind are extremely powerful. Pirozzolo and Rayner (1977) suggested that *word identification* is a multi-stage process. Visual-featural analysis is carried out by the right brain hemisphere. Word naming and word meaning are processed by the left hemisphere. According to Sinatra (1986) the meaning of well-known phrase units may be accomplished without activating the auditory-motor speech system. This is said to be done by rapid interchange of information between the language centre in the left hemisphere and its non-verbal representation in the right hemisphere.

Western societies have long placed a premium on the properties represented by a well-developed left half of the brain. The design of our intelligence tests is usually such that residents of urban areas consistently record higher scores on the tests than residents of rural areas, middle-class people record higher scores than blue-collar workers and whites record higher scores than blacks. However, one study recently showed that Australian aborigines were dramatically superior to white Australians in solving test problems when these problems were designed so that the right half of the brain had to be brought into play in order to solve the problems. So intelligence is linked to culture and cannot be defined with numerical values. The right half of the brain is said to be more developed than the left half of the brain in boys. With girls it is the opposite. At school children receive a good training of the left part of the brain. After a few years boys catch up with girls with respect to the development of the left half of the brain and remain superior with respect to the right half of the brain. All children should be able to develop both parts of their brains at school. More right-brain activities like drawing, handiwork and rhythm exercises are needed.

Our Western society is dominated by the written word and extremely quadrangular. It is a society in which bureaucrats occupy quadrangular cells in such a way that creative and intellectually lively people are perceived as disturbing and disruptive features of the prevailing order. New ideas are effectively stifled.

This leads to stagnation, industrial crises and a breakdown of the social fabric.

It is conceivable that some of the fantastic success noted by the Japanese in the field of electronics and computer technology is due to the circumstance that the Japanese, since time immemorial, have lived in a "pictographic" society and therefore think differently than we do in Western cultures.

However, the development of new media will lead to a shift in our media consumption in the coming decades from "reading" and "listening" to "looking", i.e. in our consumption of "entertainment", "information", "education" and "news". Future generations are likely to grow up in a picture-dominated society, rather than in a text-dominated society. The unrestrained consumption of TV and video programs by children may lead to a drastic change in our cultural life and our perception of culture, human values and ethical norms. Even today we already know that the viewing of TV entertainment containing repetitious violence has an influence on our attitudes so that violence becomes more acceptable to us. This could lead in turn to antisocial attitudes and a-social or even criminal behaviour. We are faced by the prospect of major changes in our media consumption. Yet we still know relatively little about visual language. It is important for society to make resources available to facilitate our transition from text-orientation.

Picture perception

It is known from several experiments that images are perceived in many different ways by various subjects (Pettersson, 1985, 1986 b). Even simple line drawings evoke many associations. Vogel et. al. (1986) showed that image-enhancement intended to improve interpretation of image content sometimes got in the way of the message. They concluded that image-enhancement graphics should be used selectively and carefully. When in doubt, they recommended, plain text should be used. Limburg (1987) pointed out that receivers have even more ambiguity or semantic diversity with visual images than with most expressions of written language with its manifold meanings. Lodding (1983) reported on

Perception, learning and memory

the problems with misinterpretations of icons used in computer systems. However, he concluded that people find a naturalness in dealing with images either as an aid to or, in some circumstances, as the sole means of communicating.

When people turn on their TV-set they might not be interested in the programme. In Japan TV-viewing habits were recorded for participants in the Hi-OVIS project (Matsushita, 1988). During the first 30 seconds people sometimes switched between 15-20 different channels. Thus people only spent one to two seconds to view the TV-image and decide if the programme was interesting or not.

Assignments

In several experiments subjects have been given different assignments. Thus subjects have been asked to name image contents, to describe image contents, to index image contents, to write legends, to assess image contents, to create images, to complete a story, to illustrate a story, to produce informative materials, to produce information graphics and to describe picture context. Results from these experiments, based on more than 72,500 verbal and visual statements from 4,350 subjects, confirm the theory of a dual stage perception. It is suggested that different assignments cause perception and image interpretation on different cognitive levels.

To name image contents

When Snodgrass and Vanderwart (1980) asked 219 subjects to name 260 simple line drawings with concrete image contents such as "a doll", "a finger", and "a trumpet," they found that 80 per cent of the pictures were given the anticipated answers.

In one study (Pettersson, 1986b), 80 adult subjects were shown five illustrations. These concrete image subjects showed "two house martins in flight," "a young tadpole," "a squirrel with a nut between its front paws," "a gnawed spruce cone," and "a bird nesting box". In the following pages these drawings will be referred to as "the five illustrations". Subjects were asked to describe the content of each image. All subjects answered with very concrete and directly content-related, descriptive words. A total of

400 words were used. Usually two or three different words were used for each picture. The mean value was 2.8. The frequency for the most common word was high. The mean value was 60.5.

One of the five illustrations ("two house martins in flight") had been used in a previous study of eye-movements (Pettersson, 1983a). Within one or two seconds ("immediately") subjects recognized the concrete image content ("two birds" or "two flying birds") in the picture. This has also been true of other eye-movement experiments, for example Potter & Levy (1969).

These results all indicate that there is an *image interpretation mode* in which the "whole" and "immediate" concrete contents of an image are perceived.

To describe image contents
Subjects have been asked to make descriptions of the contents of images (Pettersson, 1985, 1986b). In one case, 80 subjects (other than those mentioned above) made brief descriptions of ten pictures, all intended to convey abstract image contents. Only some (12.5%) of these 800 descriptions contained the anticipated "key words". Each picture was described with several different descriptive words. The 80 subjects utilized 1406 words which can be regarded as "key words". For each picture the number of different key words ranged from 31 to 51 with a mean value of 37.6. The four most common key words for each picture accounted for half of all the key word designations (51%). Most of the designations were only mentioned once or a couple of times.

In subsequent experiments, 80 subjects have made detailed descriptions of "the five illustrations". These descriptions comprised 15 to 300 words. Here too, a large variety of descriptive words were used. Mean values were between 59 and 119 words.

To index image contents
Copies of "the five illustrations" were also subsequently given to 125 other subjects. Subjects were given the following task:"These five pictures are to be filed in a picture archive. Write one or more index words for each picture".

In this case, subjects answered with 40 to 51 different index words for each picture with a mean value of 43.6. A total of 1034 words were used. The words expressed in the first study were

Perception, learning and memory

always the most common in this test. On average they account for some 48 per cent of all the words used as index words for each picture. The three most common index designations for each picture accounted for half of all the index designations (52.5%). Most of the designations were only mentioned once (51.8%) or twice (17.4%). Concrete, descriptive designations dominated. Thus this study confirms the findings from the previous study with brief descriptions.

The suggested index words can be organized into various hierarchic structures with abstract and concrete words, as well as synonyms and near synonyms. Several of the words that were used clearly show that the images have been carefully studied.

These results all indicate that there is an *image interpretation mode* in which details and the abstract contents in an image are perceived. (Also see Picture databases.)

To write legends
Ten pictures were shown subsequently to some 80 students taking a course in visual communication. The students were asked to compose legends which were 1. positive and reinforced image contents, 2. negative and weakened image contents and 3. neutral and neither reinforced nor weakened image contents. Subsequent reviews of the legends (appr. 2,100) and also discussions in class showed that picture legends clearly have an ability to affect our perception of the image content. Actually *the legend has a very great impact on our image perception*. It might be said that *"to a large degree readers see what they are told to see in an image"*. This is also shown in eye-movement studies (Pettersson, 1986c).

To rank and rate images
Experiments with rankings and ratings of pictures (Pettersson, 1984) showed that picture readability is positively correlated with both aesthetic ratings and assessed usefulness in teaching.

To assess image contents
In one study (Pettersson, 1985) 46 "senders" as well as 80 "receivers" assessed image contents. Results showed that for seven out of ten pictures there was a significant difference between the intended and the perceived image content. The above

pictures were all mounted on cardboard paper in the A3 format (29.7 x 42.1 centimetres). In a follow-up study slides were made of the five drawings. These slides were then shown to and rated by 113 adult subjects at the UREX image laboratory in Finland.

In the first study, a semantic differential scale was used. The verbal ratings "very poor," "rather poor," "neither poor nor good," "rather good" and "very good" were supplemented with a numerical value from zero to one hundred. For practical reasons a Likert scale ("very poor," "rather poor," "rather good" and "very good") had to be used in the second study. Thus results from the two studies are not exactly and immediately comparable. However, these two studies show a remarkable similarity of results. In both cases pictures were rated very much the same. In this case it can be concluded that *content was more important than format.*

To create images
In four different experiments, art and design students in Sweden have been assigned the task of making pictures according to various instructions (Pettersson, 1984, 1985 and 1986b). These experiments resulted in a variety of pictures (almost 600). There is no doubt that an intended content can be expressed using many different images. It is also quite clear that different people perceive and depict a given text in widely differing ways. Content is more important than format.

In visual language, non-meaningful basic elements (dots, lines and areas) are put together into shapes which are combined into syntagms or sub-meanings (Pettersson, 1987). Syntagms can be part of complete meanings which in turn can be sub-meanings to other complete meanings. The basic elements can be put together in different ways, thus forming different images.

In an experiment, subjects were given three sets of basic elements. They were given the assignment "Combine the basic elements on each piece of paper into an image". The efforts resulted in 165 pictures. According to image contents the pictures were grouped in various categories. Contents comprised groups like eye, cat, bird, face, animal, person and also abstract ones. The basic elements had been produced by taking original pictures apart electronically. The elements were mixed in a new way and some got new orientations before they were printed out in hard-copy formats. It can be concluded that *a given set of basic elements can be combined to form various completely different images.*

The same subjects were also given a picture in which they were asked to use white ink and eliminate one hundred dots without changing the image contents. They all succeeded. Results fully confirmed earlier findings (Pettersson 1986d). We can delete, add or shift information in an image without drastically affecting perception of image contents

To complete a story
In comic strips the verbal information is carefully integrated into the visuals. Voice balloons indicate a dialogue and a sequence in time. Characters in a comic strip may be compared with actors in a movie or in a TV-program. The reader may get the impression that a story takes place while reading it.

During the summer of 1986 large Fanta bottles sold in Sweden had one of three different comic strips with popular Disney characters printed on the back of the labels. Each story consisted of four pictures and traditional balloons (in two cases). Soft drink buyers were asked to *complete each story* by writing a text in the balloon(s) in the fourth picture. The labels were sent to an advertising company. After a while some people were given T-shirts as gifts. However, the texts were not meant to be used for advertising. The texts should just end the stories. On request all 2,490 labels were donated to me for an analysis of the texts. The comic strips were grouped according to age groups and gender of the subjects. After this procedure names and addresses of the subjects were destroyed. All texts were then written into a computer system for subsequent analysis. The texts can be described as very simple. On average the LIX-value (see p. 269) is 15.6. The total number of sentences is 4,500 with an average of 6.4 words of four letters. On average only three percent of the words designating meaning are used more than ten times, and 91 percent are used less than five times. Thus the distribution of words with meaning is very similar to the average frequency of index words in the previous study "To index image contents". There is no difference between the texts created by female or male subjects with respect to statistical measurements. Results showed that *most subjects had their own ideas on how to finish the story* .

To illustrate a story

It is interesting to study the pictures in different editions of fairy-tale books (or movies). Different artists all have their individual styles of work. They also have their own ideas of what to select and how to emphasize interesting contents. It is an obvious fact that our perception of a story is very much depending on the illustrations that are selected.

To produce informative materials

In one experiment (Hellspong et. al. 1987) groups of students at the University of Stockholm were assigned the task of producing informative materials in different versions. After production senders as well as receivers assessed all the 29 versions of information materials according to the 0-100 semantic differential scale. Results showed that there were major differences between intended and perceived levels of quality for the four examined variables "text", "visuals", "graphic design" and "total impression". The average level of intended quality was higher than the perceived levels (m = 22.5), i.e. *the senders rated their material more favourably than the receivers*. Perceived quality was better than intended quality only in about 15 percent of all 116 group assessments.

To produce information graphics

IFRA Institute (in Darmstadt, West Germany) organized a workshop "Infographics" (Nov.29 - Dec.1, 1988). Twenty journalists, artists and graphic designers from different newspapers participated in the workshop. They worked in eight groups with two to three persons in each. All groups had computer equipment and they worked with the same theme.

The workshop was concluded with evaluations of the information graphics that had been produced. Copies of all graphics were distributed to all groups together with evaluation forms. Each graphic was assessed according to ten different criteria. A combined five grade numeric and verbal scale was used: 1 = not satisfactory, 2 = satisfactory, 3 = rather good, 4 = good, and 5 = very good. The ten criteria were: 1 = legibility of text, 2 = legibility of image, 3 = foreground (should be clear and distinct), 4 = background (should not be disturbing), 5 = text - image con-

Perception, learning and memory

nections (should be clear), 6 = location of places and/or events, 7 = documentation of facts and/or explanations, 8 = presentation of statistics, 9 = editorial comment/s, and 10 = overall aesthetic value.

Results showed that *all criteria were assessed in a subjective way*. In fact most of the grades were used for all criteria. This was true for all graphics. The eight graphics form three categories. One graphic has a concentration at the high end with 80 percent of ratings good and very good. The contrary is true for two graphics. They have a concentration at the low grades with 80 percent of ratings not satisfactory and satisfactory. The remaining five graphics have an even distribution of grades or a week concentration at the middle of the scale. It can be concluded that *subjects have different opinions about information graphics*.

Describing picture context
In communications, the sender is anxious for different receivers to perceive her/his message in the same or similar ways. But this is seldom the case. Major discrepancy between the sender's perception and the individual receiver's perception is very common. A picture always represents a choice, a "frozen" slice of time. Something is always going on *around, before* and *after* a depicted event.

In one experiment, adult subjects were asked to draw pictures depicting events in the enclosed field around a small, very simple illustration (test pictures 1-6). They were also asked to draw pictures depicting the events they considered to take place "before" and "after" each picture (test pictures 7-10).

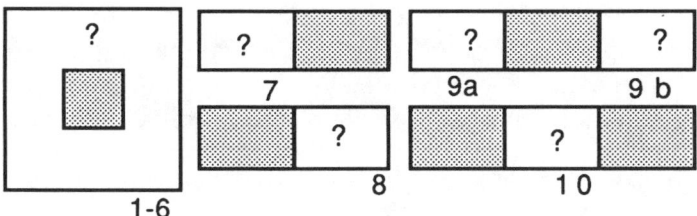

Each subject worked with a total of ten different tasks (and produced 11 pictures).

As expected, subjects had very definite and differing opinions about what was probably going on around particular pictures and about events prior to or after a depicted situation (designated above with a "?").

For the first assignment, 38 subjects drew an average of 22 different depictions of the picture's contextual events (228 pictures). On the average, seven different motifs were drawn by more than one subject. The most common motif was selected by an average of seven persons. Most subjects (82%) ignored the inner frame when depicting context. However, the inner frame was utilized as significant image element in the composition of 42 pictures. The inner frame was then incorporated as e.g. a window, painting, poster, book page, aquarium or cinema screen, to mention just a few. Context therefore governed the size of the original motif. As regards the second assignment (test pictures 7-10), 30 subjects produced an average of 12 depictions of events (150 pictures) preceding and following each picture (pictures, in one instance). On the average, six different motifs were drawn by more than one subject. The most common motif was selected by nine persons.

The results showed far closer agreement between the subjects' perception of events "before - after" than of events "around". The latter produced fewer motifs (40% vs. 58%). In addition, the most common motif was represented in more pictures (30% vs. 18%). However, the number of motifs drawn by more than one subject was about the same for both assignments (20% vs. 18%).

The results show that the subjects have treated the visual information in a conscious and analytical manner. The results suggest that each subject placed available information in a wider, expanded, "personal" context. All the interpretations were realistic and about equally credible. We are apparently capable of sensing far more information than is explicitly displayed in a given picture. Adult perception tends to be holistic rather than detail-oriented. No one, except the picture creator, can state with absolute certainty what is *really* going on around a particular picture's events or what *really* happened before or after the situation depicted in a picture. All the subjects still expressed opinions

Perception, learning and memory

about circumfluous events on their drawings. They also tended to feel that their particular interpretations were the correct ones.

So consensus about the way a picture's explicit and implicit contents should be perceived is extremely limited. Opinions about implicit context are even more wide-ranging. Every picture can be said to possess an "individual interpretation dimension" which depends on available stimuli (the signs used to form the picture, the faithfulness of depiction, etc.) and the individual viewer's cognitive capacity. Since people are different, pictures will always be interpreted in different ways.

Pictorial capabilities
Backman, Berg, and Sigurdson (1988) researched pictorial capabilities of comprehensive school students. They wanted to know if there is any difference in the pictorial capabilities of intermediate level vs. senior level students in the Swedish compulsory, comprehensive school. (The 9-year Swedish compulsory, comprehensive school is roughly equivalent to American elementary school + junior high school, although Swedish students start school at the age of 7. The Swedish comprehensive school is divided into three levels, i.e. junior, intermediate and senior levels). "Pictorial capability" comprises the *production* and *reception* of visuals. Differences between the pupil categories can be expected with respect to 1. the production of visuals, 2. the analysis of visuals, 3. the perception of visuals and 4. the communication of visuals. Empirical studies with a random selection of sixty 5th, 6th, 7th and 8th year students respectively, i.e. a total of 240 subjects, participated.

For *picture production* the assignment was to produce a picture showing sky, mountains, forest, a lake, a house, a field, a meadow, a fence and two trees. The subjects were supplied with paper, a pencil, brushes and eight colors (80 min.). The use of tools, the number of colors, color mixing, perspective, and areas was evaluated.

For *picture analysis* the assignment was to submit answers to questions about the way a picture had been made (40 min.). The presence of comments on shapes, color, figures, composition and technique was evaluated.

For *picture perception* the assignment was to submit a written description of everything the test picture conveyed (40 min.). The presence of comments on emotions, imagination, associations and events was evaluated.

Picture communications was divided in two parts. For *production* the assignment was to produce a picture which supplies information about the significance of red and green as traffic signals (40 min.). Communications was evaluated as unequivocal, not quite unequivocal or incomprehensible. For reception the assignment was to write down the message conveyed by a series of instructive pictures (40 min.). Whether the student understood fully, partially or not at all was evaluated.

The study comprised a total of 1,200 visual and verbal statements submitted by 240 comprehensive school students. All the evaluations were performed by two of the authors, both teachers of method at the Department for the Training of Visual Arts Teachers at the University of Umeå.

The students displayed very poor pictorial capabilities. They were poor at producing pictures and in reading pictures. Only 5% of the senior level students were able to produce a picture which supplied information on the importance of red and green as traffic signals. Only 43% of the senior level students were able to supply a written description of the message conveyed by a series of instructive pictures.

The results showed that the two comprehensive school categories did not display any significant difference in pictorial capability (exception: intermediate level students used a brush more often than senior level students. However, this is probably not a particularly good measure of tool usage).

The teaching of visual arts does not live up to the expectations teachers should have on the basis of existing curricula. There is probably a very considerable need for further training of teachers of visual arts. The authors concluded that teachers of visual arts must adopt a new approach. The subject "visual arts" demands the same competent, cognitive processing as e.g. English, Swedish or mathematics.

Approaches to picture perception

There are many approaches to picture perception. Based on the theory of linear perspective, invented during the Renaissance, Gibson (1971) defined picture perception as *a stimulus-driven process* in which information is picked up from optical array. The opposite view is held by Gombrich (1969) and Gregory (1978). While seeing a picture *the viewer constructs a meaning* based on experience and expectations. From this receptionist position neither the readers or the message remains the same. Meaning exists only for a moment within each individual reader. Another approach to picture perception is based on semiotics and symbol theory (Goodman, 1976). Intentionalism suggests that meaning is embedded in the message by a producer, leaving the reader to discover and unfold it. From this perspective meaning exists independent from the reader. For an intentionalist a painting means what the artist says it does. For a receptionist the painting does not mean anything until the reader says it does (Muffoletto, 1987). Boeckman (1987) makes a clear distinction between drawings and paintings, which have "signs" and photographs which have "recorded perceptional stimuli". "Before photography was invented there were two modes to learn about reality. Perception processing stimuli of the surrounding reality on the one hand and communication processing signs on the other. Now we have something in between: Recorded perception stimuli which are not reality but not signs either". And for Arnheim (1974) picture perception is a matter of responding to basic forms such as gestalt laws. An important point of Arnheim's is that visual perception includes the same behaviours that we commonly consider only as matters of cognition or thinking. A "percept" is a building block of visual thinking and as such analogous to the cognitive function of a concept.

The perception process is often assumed to consist of two stages. A fast overview is followed by a conscious analysis. When we first look at an image we only see that which is necessary to perceive and identify objects and events in a reasonable and meaningful manner. This is Gibson's "principle of economy" (Gibson, 1966).

Simple line drawings accompanied by various assignments caused very different reactions in subjects. It is obvious that the

different assignments have caused perception and image interpretation on different cognitive levels. It may be suggested that image interpretation on low cognitive levels follows these steps:
1. The subject looks at the image. A few rapid eye fixations are made.
2. The information is handled as a "whole" in parallel, simultaneous, tentative, rough, holistic and fast processing.
3. A "wholeness interpretation" occurs, recognition and meaning of the image content is formed very quickly - "immediately".
4. This interpretation is expressed by the use of a very limited number of words.

It may also be suggested that image interpretation on high cognitive levels follows these steps:
1. The subject looks at the image. A few rapid eye fixations are made.
2. The information is handled as a "whole" in parallel, simultaneous, tentative, rough, holistic and fast processing.
3. A "wholeness interpretation" occurs, recognition and meaning of the image content is formed very quickly "immediately".
4. Certain details in the image attract more eye fixations.
5. The information is processed again, maybe several times, detail by detail. The process demands attention and is sequential.
6. Our verbal memory is activated in a search for suitable expressions. Various hypotheses about the image content are weighed against one another and tested. Segmented codes have to pass through several levels of recognition and interpretations before meaning occurs.
7. The interpretation of the image contents is expressed by the use of a large number of different words.

In both cases, I believe, both halves of the brain are involved in the interpretation of image contents. In the first case there might be a dominance of right brain activity. However, in the other case there might be a dominance of left brain activity. Interpretation of verbo-visual information such as a television-program is likely to take place simultaneously in both parts of the brain. *How we actually create meaning is an area where much research still is needed.*

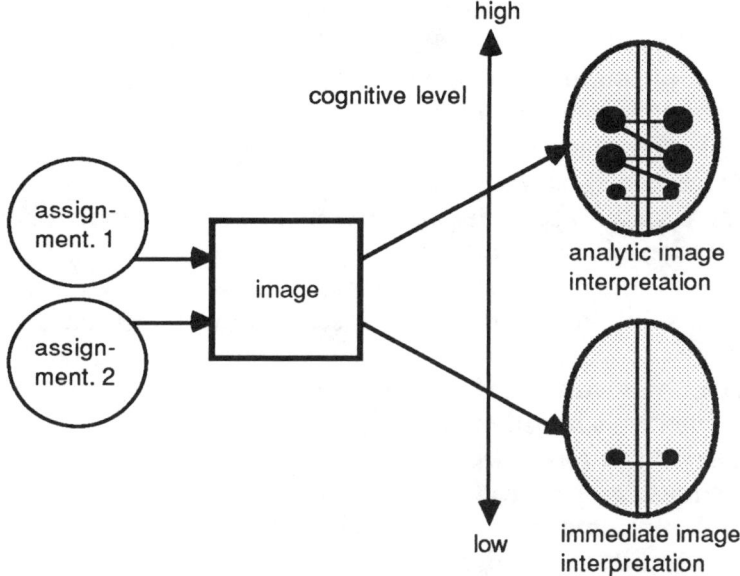

An image is interpreted in different ways depending on the assignment. An immediate image interpretation is handled on a low cognitive level. An analytic image interpretation needs high cognitive level activities.

It can be concluded that:
- Perceived image content is different from intended image contents.
- Different assignments may cause different interpretations of image contents.
- Some assignments cause interpretation of image contents on a low cognitive level.
- Some assignments cause interpretation of image contents on a high cognitive level.
- Even simple pictures may cause many different associations.
- A given set of basic elements can be combined to form completely different images.
- The design of a picture can be changed a great deal without any major impact on the perception of the image contents.
- Content is more important than execution.

- Picture readability is positively correlated with both aesthetic ratings and assessed usefulness in teaching.
- Legends should be written with great care. They heavily influence our interpretation of image content.
- Content is more important than format.
- To a large degree readers see what they are told to see in an image.
- There seem to be no major difference between gender in interpretation of image contents.
- Students display poor pictorial capabilities.
- Most subjects have their own ideas on how to finish a story.
- There are major differences between intended and perceived levels of quality in informative materials.
- Computer-based indexing systems should rely on full text image descriptions.
- We must learn to read image content.
- How we actually create meaning is an area where much research still is needed.

Message design

Seeing pictures, a movie or TV program clearly seem to be an active process. Some of the retina's 125 million sensory cells record the light impulses by chemical conversion of visual purple, signals are transmitted to the cortex and the cortex converts the signals into a sensation of vision. In the case of movies and TV program, dialogue, music and sound are additional effects which are transmitted by the auditory apparatus to the brain where they are incorporated into a unified perception of the total information. We must never commit the error of confusing still pictures, movies or TV programs with reality. They are only representations and always render a subjective, selective view of reality. Some general principles of information message design to be used in instruction may be given on the basis of different research results:
- Introduce novel or unexpected events at the start of instruction.
- Inform learners of expected outcomes.
- Recall relevant prerequisite information.
- Present only relevant information.
- Organize content and present "organizers".

Perception, learning and memory 93

- Progress from simple to complex.
- Provide prompts and cues.
- Vary information presented.
- Present examples and non-examples.
- Provide appropriate practice.
- Provide immediate feedback or knowledge of results.
- Review and repeat.

A cognitive model

An outline of a cognitive model to clarify differences between the concepts "see - look - read" and "hear - listen" is presented below. The model should be viewed as a theoretical device, based on empirical findings and extensive research on eye movements and fixations as summarized above (Eye movements), clearly showing that we are capable of perceiving picture contents in many different ways.

A single fixation of a picture is sufficient to enable us to recognize it subsequently among other pictures. If we e.g. go shopping in a department store, we are *virtually unaware* of the large number of advertising pictures/messages and background music to which we are exposed in the store. Everything merges into a kind of "noise". We probably only process most of the stimuli in this noise on a superficial level. We see and hear but do not look or listen. When we listen to the radio while engaged in some other simultaneous activity, such as cooking a meal, fixing a punctured tire or glancing through a newspaper, we are aware of words, music and images. Looking at a picture consumes more mental energy and demands a higher cognitive level than merely seeing a picture. Visual impressions are conducted from the sensory to the short-term memory, i.e. operative memory. We only become aware of the information which succeeds in passing through the brain's filtering system. Most of the information disappears after a while.

When we e.g. study material in books or on TV we process that material actively. We *read* texts, *listen* to music and *read* pictures. Perceived information is processed, sorted and stored in certain parts of the brain's long-term memory. Many fixations of a picture are required for people to recall it subsequently and e.g. be able to describe it.

Conscious analysis of linguistic messages, such as texts, music and pictures (e.g. research), probably demands an even greater consumption of mental energy and a higher cognitive level. The brain actually uses about one fifth of our daily consumption of energy, that is, more than a hectogram of glucose.

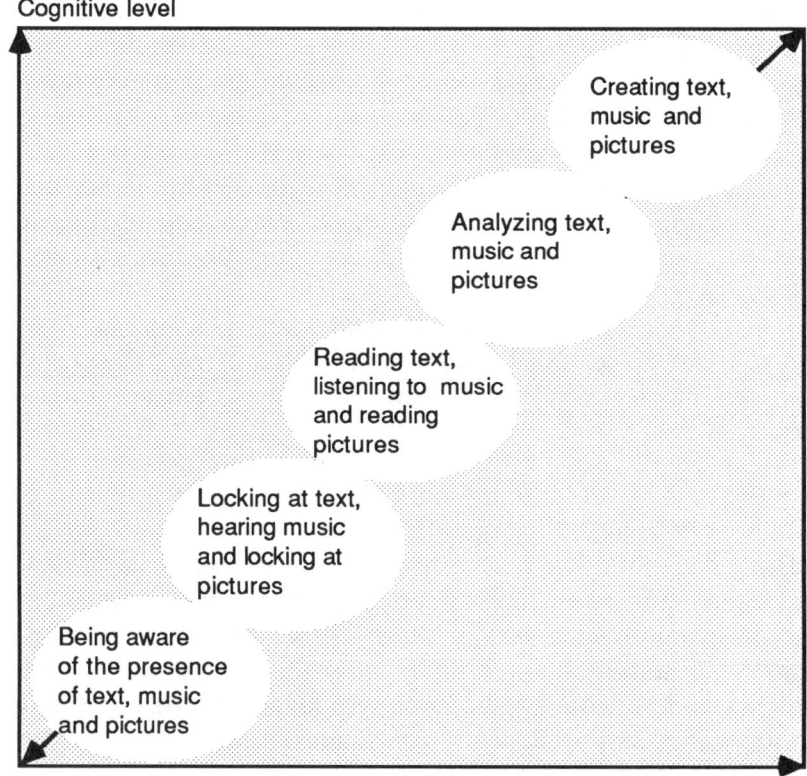

The relationship between cognitive level and mental energy consumption in different activities.

The most demanding processes are those leading to the creation of text, music and pictures. Creative people have often described the mental effort which is often associated with creativity.

The model assumes the existence of a dynamic relationship in which we consciously and unconsciously switch cognitive levels.

Our sensory organs respond to changes in our environment. We are normally capable of resolving changes with a gradient greater than about two percent. But we adapt to slow, gradual changes and often fail to notice them. So our senses are normally in the resting state but have a rapid response capability. In the corresponding manner, we are unable to remain on the highest cognitive levels for more than relatively brief periods of time, since this would otherwise be too enervating and lead to some form of mental "cramp". Like a pike lurking in the reeds or a cat poised outside a mouse hole, we know what our surroundings look like. When changes occur in those surroundings, we are capable of responding rapidly and powerfully by activating our bodies both in physical and mental terms. Sometimes, everything goes according to plan. The pike gets a minnow, the cat gets its mouse and we find the information we are looking for. At other times, efforts may fail. A predator may miss its prey, and we may spend a great deal of time and energy gathering information which turns out to be useless.

No clear distinctions can be made between the five cognitive levels discussed here. But there are probably major differences between individuals due to cultural, social and personal factors. So the model should not be interpreted too literally. However, it can be employed to elucidate the fact that there are major differences between the concepts "see - look - read" and "hear - listen". Active reception of linguistic intelligence comprising text, sound or pictures, individually or in concert, always requires exertion. Reading and listening are mentally and physically exhausting. Uninteresting or poorly designed material reduces our interest in the subject described by that material. So the sender of a message should strive *to design text, music and pictures in the most attractive, relevant manner possible* so receivers are encouraged to process the message on the highest possible cognitive level.

This should be the case irrespective of whether the "message" involves "information", "entertainment", "education" or "news". The principles apply irrespective of the medium involved, although different media transmit messages from senders to receivers in completely different ways.

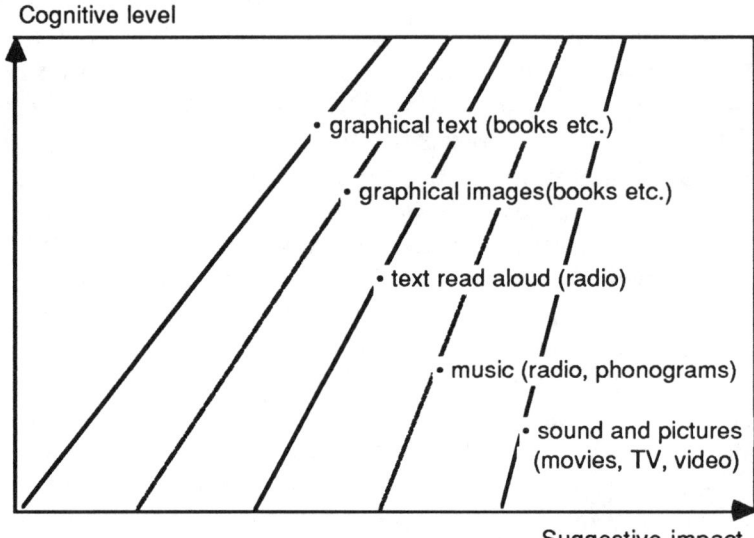

The relationship between cognitive level and suggestive impact for different kinds of representations. Suggestive impact increases as the cognitive level increases. Writing a text may have a greater suggestive impact than viewing a completed film or TV program. Creative involvement in the making of a movie or TV program may have a very considerable suggestive impact and evoke powerful emotions.

Compared to a book an interactive computer program, phonograms, films, TV and videograms have a highly manipulative effect on receivers. Message contents change continuously in a predetermined manner with respect to subject selection, time and space. The receiver's active efforts to seek information are therefore largely disabled. A reader can "digest" the textual and visual contents of a book at a self-selected pace. In a structured information context, i.e. lexivision, the reader is able to process information in about the same way as in a "natural" situation. This is probably the reason why lexivisual information seems to work so well in practice. For example, interactive videograms are now possible with the aid of a computer. Here, the advantages of using sound and moving pictures can be combined with a high degree of user involvement. Interactive videograms will encourage and demand activity on a high cognitive level and should therefore be effective in information transfer and learning.

Interactive videograms can be viewed as three-dimensional lexivisions.

The aforementioned discussion could conceivably explain why pictures have such an impact and a much greater ability to influence us than e.g. a text. Children are more easily frightened by *watching* an act of violence on TV than by *reading* about the same act in a book or in a newspaper. This is because things we see appear to be more "real" than things we merely read about and because a higher cognitive level is required for reading than for seeing. Many scientists, such as Tröger (1963) and Noble (1975), have shown that small children are incapable of actively processing the contents of and understanding contexts in a TV or video program. This is something most parents of small children have also experienced.

Just as we learn to read texts, we can also learn to "read" pictures. Tailoring pictorial language in all media is therefore essential so the degree of "reading" difficulty increases progressively in e.g. school textbooks. It is reasonable to assume the following regarding informative and educational pictures:
- A picture which is easy to read and understand conveys information better and more readily than a picture which is difficult to read and understand.
- A picture evoking a positive response conveys information better and more effectively than a picture evoking a negative response - when motivation is identical in both instances.
- A "poor" picture may work well when motivation is high, but a "good" picture would then work even better.
- An easily read picture can be assumed to have a greater functional, communicative impact than a picture which is difficult to read.

LEARNING AND MEMORY

We receive a lot of information about the outside world. We ultimately learn to interpret and "read" different coded messages such as those contained in e.g. text and visuals.

Learning

The ability to read and understand pictures is learned. This learning takes place more rapidly in a culture where pictures are used and seen frequently.

Learning must always be an active process. Just sitting passively and receiving information is not a particularly effective learning method. It must not be assumed that "disseminated" information is the same as "received" information. In language teaching, it has been found that a foreign word has to be repeated an average of 34 times before it has been learned. Learning should take place in a natural situation to the greatest possible extent.

An old teaching principle states that you should first tell your students what you plan to tell them. You then tell them what you wanted to tell them. Afterwards, you tell them what you have just told them. An old Chinese proverb states the following:

> *That which I hear, I forget.*
> *That which I see, I remember.*
> *That which I do, I understand.*

These old observations from reality have been confirmed by a number of different studies. We now know with great certainty that representations, such as text and pictures, sound and pictures or sound, text and pictures with redundant or relevant relation, provide the basis for much better learning than sound, text or pictures alone. We also know that representations with irrelevant or contradictory commentaries make for poorer learning than sound, text or pictures alone.

Bloom and colleagues (1956) proposed three domains of learning, the cognitive domain, the psychomotor domain and the affective domain. Gagne and Briggs (1974) identify five types of learning which they call Human Capabilities. These are, a) intellectual skills, b) cognitive strategies, c) information skills, d) motor skills, and e) attitudes.

The ability to recognize stimuli develops with age. Kids in all ages recognize visual stimuli better than auditory stimuli.

We all develop our individual behaviours while we are learning. The expression "learning style" refer to these individual preferences. These preferences concern our environment, like sound, light, temperature, moisture and design of the room, our emotions and our sociological, physiological and psychological situation. We receive and process information from our sensory systems in various ways. Preferences for different kinds of information or "modalities" do exist. Thus people may have visual, auditory, kinesthetic and/or tactual modality. Some people have a mixed modality.

In the US it has been found that 30 percent of elementary school children have visual modality, 25 percent have auditory modality, 15 percent have kinesthetic modality. The remaining 30 percent have a mixed modality (Duffy, 1983).

Children with *visual modality* rely very much on seeing things and on their internal visualization. They learn by seeing, they are "visual learners". Thus these children remember faces rather than names. They must take notes and write down verbal information if they need to remember it. Visual modality children are very quiet. They can not listen for a long period at a time. Visual learners have vivid imagination. They think in images and visualize in components and details rather than the whole. Visual learners are not particularly responsive to music.

Children with *auditory modality* rely very much on hearing and verbalization. They learn by hearing, they are "auditory learners".Thus these children remember names rather than faces. They learn from verbal directions and descriptions. They think in sounds. Auditory modality children talk a lot. They like to hear their own voices. Auditory learners miss significant details in pictures. However, they may appreciate a work of art as a whole. They favour music.

Children with *kinesthetic and/or tactual modality* rely very much on their movements and muscular involvement. They learn by doing and remember what was done rather than seen or heard. Imagery is not important, nor pictures. Kinesthetically oriented children prefer sculptures which they can touch. When communicating these children use a lot of bodily expressions. They respond to music by physical movements.

Children with mixed modality strength learn from visual, auditory as well as kinesthetic and tactile stimuli.

It is important to consider these various learning styles when we are producing instructional materials. Such materials should have a good balance between verbal and visual messages and maybe also suggestions for practical, hands-on-exercises.

A verbal response to visual stimuli or a visual response to verbal stimuli requires a transformation from one modality to another. Research concerning the effects of verbal as well as visual modalities shows that children pay more attention to visual than to verbal information. Zuckerman et. al. (1978) found that children tend to be more accurate in recognizing visual than auditory segments in television commercials. Hayes and Birnbaum (1980) showed pre-school children cartoons in which the audio track either matched or mismatched the visual information. In both cases kids had a higher retention of the visual than of the auditory information. Pezdek and Stevens (1984) found that when children had to choose which of two incompatible channels to process they preferred the video channel. The auditory information sustains attention and facilitates comprehension. Pezdek and Hartman (1983) found that video without sound reduced comprehension among pre-school children. Rolandelli et. al. (1985) concluded that children used the auditory component of television to direct attention to important visual information, as well as to process auditory, especially verbal, content.

Dwyer (1978, 1982-3) and his associates have conducted more than 200 studies on the effects of pictures on the learning of factual information. The studies are based on a 2,000 word text and various sets of illustrations of the human heart. A variety of formats such as booklets, television and slide-audiotape presentations have been used. Pictures have been found helpful in identifying the parts of the heart, e.g. when visual discrimination is needed. It has also been concluded that line drawings generally are most effective in formats where the learner's study time is fixed and limited. More realistic versions of art work however, may be more effective in formats where unlimited study time is allowed.

Locatis and Atkinson (1984) summarize the principles of cognitive learning in the following points:

Concept Learning
1 Determine whether to present a definition.
2 Present very clear, unambiguous examples of objects belonging to the concept class, and indicate the class name.
3 Present examples that clearly are not of the concept class but potentially may be confused as class members.
4 Provide practice/feedback in discriminating between positive and negative examples.
5 Provide practice/feedback in distinguishing between more ambiguous positive and negative examples, depending upon the degree of discrimination required.

Principle Learning
1 Ensure that students have learned prerequisite concepts.
2 Indicate the relationships among concepts.
3 Demonstrate, or have students demonstrate, the principle.
4 Provide practice and feedback in demonstrating the principle.

Problem Solving
1 Ensure that students have learned prerequisite concepts and principles.
2 Present the problem.
3 Provide direction and guidance.
4 Provide problem-solving practice/feedback.

Memory

Common to all the phases of the analysis performed on incoming information is the need to store the signals for varying lengths of time so that the information processing can be carried out. The processes which carry out this information storage are referred in psychological terms as "memories". There are many models seeking to explain the function of these memories (see Sinatra, 1986, and Levie, 1987, for reviews). One way of viewing memory functions is based on information processing in several steps.

The first of these steps is the sensory memory which carries out the storage of stimulus information on the peripheral level, i.e. far away from the brain. An example of sensory memory is the biochemical processes in the eye. The visual cells there possess some inertia and function therefore as a kind of memory. The sensory memory normally stores information for one half to one second (vision). Loftus, Shimamura, and Johnson (1985) showed that for one tenth of a second as much information can be extracted from this sensory memory icon as from the picture itself. The iconic memory (vision) and the econic memory (hearing) are closely related to the sensory memory. These memories precede the integration of signals from various sensory systems.

After being processed in the iconic memory and the econic memory, some information is passed on to the short-term (or operative) memory (STM) where it is only retained for a brief period of time, i.e. not more than one to two seconds. A number of complex operations are carried out here during solution of problems. But the short-term memory has severe capacity limitations. Any information to be retained in this memory must be repeated every few seconds otherwise it will be lost from the short-term memory.

Information which has entered the short-term memory can proceed through a filter (reception) which selects the information to be passed on. Once this filtration has taken place and certain information units have been assigned priority over others, these priority units are given access to a P system (register) with a limited memory capacity. This is the point at which a person becomes aware of the stored information. All other non-priority information disappears, normally forever if it is not re-transmitted to the filter when the filter is able to accept the traffic. The filter scrutinizes the information received from the outside world and identifies the special properties of this information. When the information involves e.g. aural signals, the filter notes whether the signal is strong or weak. When visual signals are involved, the signal is scrutinized for information on color, size, any movement etc.

The information which passes the P system can proceed in different ways. The information can be stored in a long-term memory (LTD). This is what normally happens with the knowledge we do not need for the moment. This long-term memory then affects the selection filter so the filter makes selections related

Perception, learning and memory

to previous experience. The long-term memory is what most people mean when they refer to the "memory". The long-term memory has carrying contents, episodic memories (i.e. recollections of events, feelings, experiences etc)., words, pictures, concepts etc. The short-term and long-term memories are actually theoretical models which cannot be related to any activity pattern or any particular anatomical structure in the human brain. The distinction made between the STM and LTM is probably too clear-cut.

Information can also be passed on to an "output system" which emits signals to the muscles which are to carry out a given act. The information can be switched back from the P system to the reception or to the short-term memory. The information can also get lost.

Comparisons are sometimes made between the human brain and a computer. However, the brain differs in many ways from a computer. As a rule, a computer must be able to process considerably more information than a human in any given situation, since the computer program is unable to distinguish between important and unimportant information. The machine is therefore incapable of ignoring any information the way the human brain constantly does. This is one of the reasons why a person's ability to process sensory information is far beyond the capability of even giant computers, even though the individual processing steps are carried out much faster in a computer than in the human brain, about one million times faster. The dual-code memory model (Paivio, 1971, 1978) proposes a verbal system specialized for processing and storing linguistic information and separate nonverbal system for spatial information and mental imagery. These systems can function independently but are also interconnected. Other memory models include a single-code approach. All information is coded as abstract propositions. Complex cognitive processing of information involves the use of both visual and auditory cues. According to cue information theory (Adams and Chambers, 1962) information that is shared between channels facilitates learning. Cues that occur simultaneously in auditory and visual channels are likely to be better recalled than those presented in one channel only. Drew and Grimes (1985) showed that close co-ordination between audio and video improved audio recall of television news and that redundancy aided story understanding.

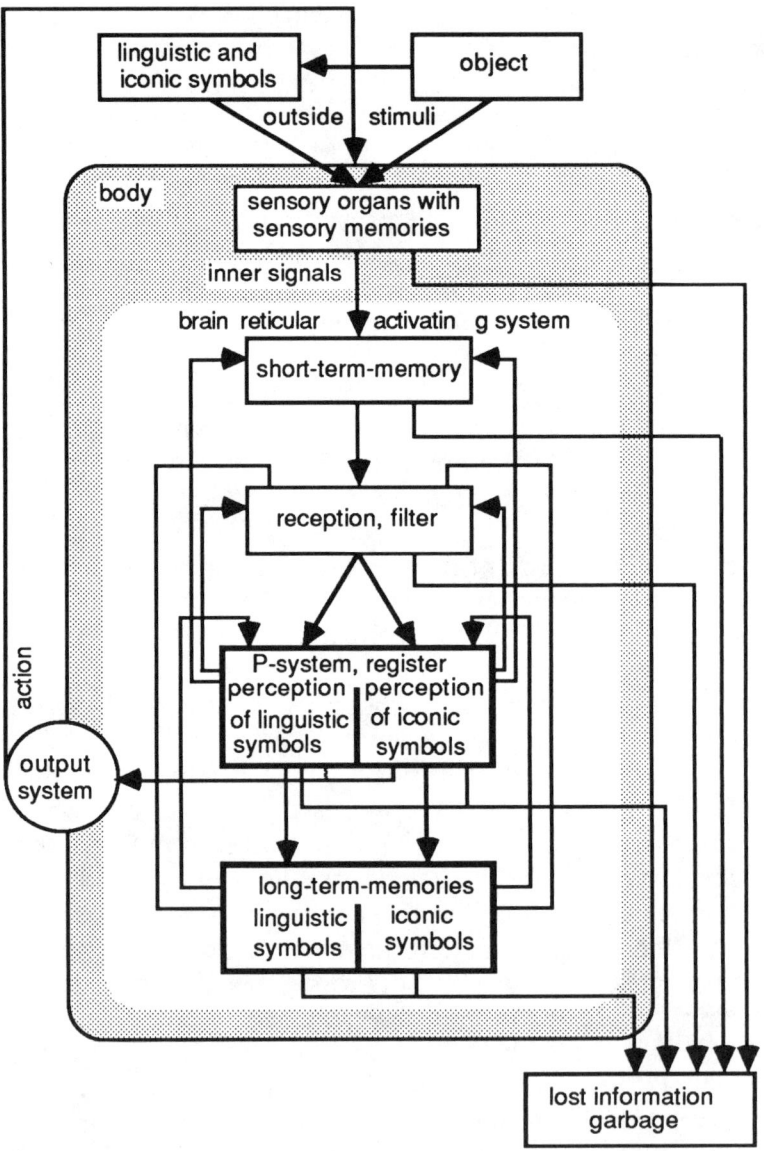

A suggested model for the perception of linguistic and iconic symbols.

Numerous scientists, such as Nickerson (1965), Shepard (1967) and Standing et al. (1970), have shown that subjects are capable of recognizing previously seen pictures with very considerable certainty. After showing subjects 10,000 slides over a five day period, Standing (1973) reported recognition accuracy of 83%. Haber (1970) described our ability to recognize pictures as virtually perfect. According to Potter & Levy (1969), a person only needs to look at a picture for a second or two to be capable of recognizing it subsequently. (Also see Picture perception: Assignments). Loftus (1972) found that the number of fixations governs our proficiency in recalling a picture. He found that pictures which subjects studied several times were recalled more readily than pictures which where studied less extensively. Brigthouse (1939), Haber & Erdelyi (1968), Haber (1970), and Nesbit (1981) studied just how much subjects really remembered about picture contents. They found that much more time was required for subjects to remember a picture than merely to recognize it. The fixations can be guided and determined by a picture legend or by a spoken commentary. Meaningful material is learned more easily and remembered longer than meaningless material. Thus, we are normally forced to make a continuous selection from the information which constantly bombards us. Paivio (1983) showed that our memory for pictures is superior to our memory for words. This is called the *"pictorial superiority effect"*. It is also known that memory for picture-word combination is superior to memory for words alone or pictures alone (Haber and Myers, 1982).

By the mid-1970's it was well established that children's immediate, factual recall of simple fiction was improved when picture content was completely redundant with prose content (Levin & Lesgold, 1978). More recent reviews (Levie & Lentz, 1982; Scallert, 1980; Levin, Anglin & Carney, 1987) substantiate the Levin and Lesgold conclusions.

Levin et. al. (op. cit.) discuss different functions of pictures used in prose. According to them four functions are "text-relevant". These are called representation, organization, interpretation and transformation functions. Illustrations are representational when they serve to reinforce the major narrative events in the text and "tell" the same story i.e. are redundant with the text.

Representational pictures add concreteness to the prose since memory for pictorial materials is better than memory for verbal materials.

Illustrations are organizational when they provide a framework for a text. They add coherence to the prose since memory for organized materials exceeds memory for unorganized materials.

Illustrations are interpretational when they clarify passages in the text that are difficult to understand. Interpretational pictures add comprehensibility to the prose since materials that are initially well understood are remembered better than materials that are more poorly understood.

Illustrations are transformational when prose content is recoded into concrete form and related in a well-organized context. These pictures provide readers with a systematic means of retrieving the critical information. Transformational illustrations are designed to impact directly on reader's memory.

After a meta-analysis of results from some 100 experiments on functions of pictures used in prose, published in 87 separate documents, Levin et. al (op. cit). concluded that all types of text-relevant pictures facilitate learning from reading prose. There was an increasing learning effect from representational pictures ("moderate"), organizational and interpretational pictures ("moderate to substantial") to transformational pictures ("substantial"). It was also concluded that when illustrations are not relevant to the prose content no prose-learning facilitation is to be expected, on the contrary there can be a negative effect.

Pressley and Miller (1987) reviewed experiments concerning children's listening comprehension and oral prose memory. They concluded the following ordering of conditions with respect to their potency for affecting children's learning of prose: sentences only < sentences + single incomplete pictures (i.e. partial pictures) < sentences + two incomplete pictures < sentences + complete pictures.

In conclusion results from several experiments show that *when content is the same in visual, audio and print channels learning is maximized.* Conveying information through both linguistic and iconic symbols makes it possible for the learners to alternate between functionally independent, though interconnected, and complementary cognitive processing systems.

Inner images

When we look at a visual or at an object this obviously results in a perception; we create an inner image. However, we do not require external stimuli to create inner images. It is enough to think about a specific object, a visual, a person or an event. Then we retrieve a "copy" of an inner image, stored in the long term memory, to the perceptive and cognitive level. It is known that inner images can result in physiological reactions that can be measured. Sportsmen are sometimes training mentally before an important athletic contest. In their minds they make adjustments to fine details in their performance. They imagine themselves on top of the winners' stand. Such a training session can be as demanding as a real training session.

When we think about a non-specific object or a non-specific person we probably retrieve "copies" of visual elements like dots, lines, areas, colors, shapes, patterns etc. to the cognitive level and then combine them to form inner images. These inner images are representations of reality as visuals are. However, when we think about something non-existent, e.g. when we are creative, we can combine copies of existing visual elements with images stored in the long-term-memories to form completely new images of our own. These images are not representations of reality, since the objects, or whatever content the images have, are non-existent. However, such images can be transformed and transferred to drawings, paintings, models etc. These visuals do not represent reality as we know it but the artist's inner images or "inner reality".

Many persons can "see" and experience complicated inner images, e.g. in dreams when external stimuli are shut out to a large extent. During sleep, the right half of the brain usually takes over the role as the dominant part of the brain. In our dreams we live in an image-world. According to Kosslyn (1975) more details of a mental image of an object are remembered when the object is imagined next to a smaller object. Thus the relative size of a part of an image may affect our ability to remember and recognize it.

Modern systems for computer-aided design make it possible to actually display a similar kind of "inner images" on a screen or on paper with the help of a plotter before the object itself actually exists. It is often possible to rotate the screen image of the object and study it from all possible angles. It is often also possible to "take the object apart".

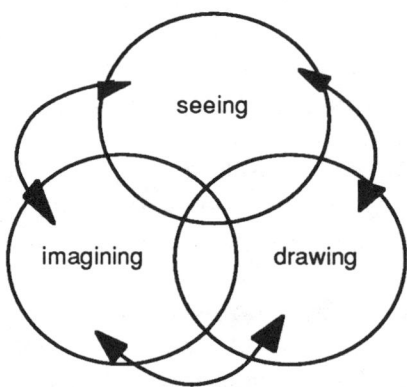

In "Thinking Visually" Robert H. McKim (p.8) illustrates the interactive nature of seeing, imagining and drawing with a figure of this kind. The three partly overlapping circles symbolize the idea that visual thinking is experienced to the fullest when seeing, imagining, and drawing merge into active interplay. The visual thinker utilizes seeing, imagining, and drawing in a fluid and dynamic way, moving from one kind of imagery to another.

Development

The relationship between color and shape as stimuli has been studied by many researchers. Otto and Askov (1968) found that the importance of these stimuli is related to the respective subject's level of development. For small children (three to six years), color stimuli have greater impact than shape stimuli. However, the reverse is true of older children; i.e., shape becomes more important than color. Modreski and Gross (1971) found that four-year-olds were better at pairing objects by shape than by color. Ward and Naus (1973) studied preschool children and found that they were also better at identifying objects by their shape than by their color. Macbeth (1974) found that children from three to eight emphatically tended to sort colored paper by shape rather than by color, so shape is often more important to children than color.

When a person attempts to copy a drawing made by someone else, he generally simplifies the subject so that it increasingly assumes simple, basic geometric shapes such as circles, rectangles, and triangles. When small children begin to make pictures of their own, the circle is generally their first definable area, followed by the square and then the triangle. The external contours of an image and its "total shape" are probably very important to the way we perceive image content. Segall, Cambell, and Herskovits (1966) pointed out that one of the most striking things about a photocopy is its rectangular shape and its white frame. These properties may very well have an effect on and interfere with our perception of the image subject itself.

My own study of the image creativity of children (Pettersson, 1979) showed, among other things, that the paper's edge, the corners in particular, attracted the children's attentions. This influence was apparent in one-third of the pictures made by children from two to seven. Yarbus (1967) and many other scientists have shown that we only fix our attention on certain elements of a picture's image, so it is possible that the corners of rectangular and square pictures are distracting to small children reading a picture. The corners may demand attention which should be conferred on image content. An ideal picture should probably be oval with blurred edges; i.e., the image should emerge from the background, about the way Gibson (1966) described our perception of "selected visual fields". Pictures in our books and newspapers have not always been rectangular and square and we can find interesting differences in different cultures (Pettersson, 1982). Today, we live in an age increasingly dominated by television. Children may ultimately expect all images to have the same format as a TV screen.

The ability of children to decipher the contents of a picture is governed by their mental development, previous experience and social circumstances. According to Piaget, chronological age is the most important factor in a child's mental development. He described four stages of that development:

1 The sensory-motor period (0 to 2 years)
2 The pre-operational period (2 to 6 years)
3 The period of concrete thought processes (7 to 12 years)
4 The period of formal or abstract though processes (from 13 years)

Noble (1975) analyzed the way in which children of different ages perceive the content of TV programs and found very wide differences between children in the different stages of development. Children from 2 to 6 tended to either strongly like or dislike what they saw. They had difficulty in distinguishing between internal and external experiences, i.e. between imagination and reality, and felt involved in and able to influence events in TV programs. They are unable to comprehend how different aspects of an event may be interrelated and therefore view TV programs as a succession of mutually unrelated happenings.

When children acquire the ability to carry out reversible thought processes in the third stage of their development, they begin to respond systematically to concrete stimuli in their surroundings. Their world of thought is no longer restricted to the present, and it becomes possible for them to foresee events and understand relationships. At the beginning of this stage of development, the children concentrate on special events in a TV program, but they gradually begin to understand the plot. Children from 11-12 are only capable of understanding the concrete, psychical behaviour of the TV performers, not the emotions supplying the motivation for a given action. From about the age of 13 children begin to be capable of dealing with logical thought processes on an abstract plane. Only at this stage do they acquire the ability to understand the indirect symbolism often found in movies and TV programs.

Illustrations in materials for use with children under thirteen should be strictly relevant to the text. Younger children can not ignore incidental illustrations. If pictures do not help they will probably hinder the understanding of the content.

Noble found that TV producers could accurately predict what children would like but not what children would understand.

Social circumstances, in addition to chronological age and intelligence, play an increasingly important role in the ability of children to understand the events in a TV program.

Various studies have shown that middle-class mothers talked and discussed things with their children to a greater extent than working class mothers. In Noble's view, therefore, we can expect to find similar differences as regards TV programs. The socialization process in middle-class children means that these children tended to receive more encouragement in understanding the programs.

Tröger (1963) felt that children first have to learn to comprehend individual pictures before they can comprehend the plot of a movie. A basic requirement here is that the children really are capable of distinguishing between an object and a picture of that object. Only after this is possible is a child mature enough to deal with various subjects on an abstract level. Tröger suggested that children do not achieve picture comprehension until they reach the age of about six. Comprehension of movies is therefore only possible after this age.

Tröger defined the following stages in movie comprehension:
1 The child attains picture comprehension, i.e. the ability to distinguish between an object and a picture of the object.
2 The child comprehends individual scenes in a movie. But these scenes are not perceived as being related to prior and subsequent scenes.
3 The child begins to comprehend the interrelationship of individual scenes.
4 The child begins to comprehend all the relationships in the film.

Tröger's view is in close agreement with Piaget's and Noble's with the exception of age level. Actually, children probably attain facility in picture comprehension at a much earlier than six, possible as early as three years.

In Tröger's view, children under seven perceive movie reality differently than adults. Even here Tröger described four stages of development which arise in chronological order but at different ages for different children, depending on their development in other respects:

1 The child lacks movie comprehension and views a movie realistically.
2 The child views a movie as a reproduction of reality, i.e. the events on the screen have really happened. The photographer just happened to be passing and made the movie.
3 The child perceives the movie as possible reality, i.e. they understand that the movie was made but that the events in the movie could actually happen in reality.
4 The child perceives the movie as selected and processed reality. Not every adults reach this stage.

In the United States, TV programs made for children are basically designed in the same way as programs for adults. In programs such as Sesame Street, for example, children see a series of rapid and varied scenes which are frequently unrelated to one another. The programs are chopped to pieces by commercials in which admonitions to buy seem to be hammered into their heads. Children's programs in Sweden are better tailored to children's prerequisites. The Soviet Union is even more advanced in this respect. The state-run Soviet TV company produces programs for five age groups: up to the age of 7, 8-10, 11-14, 15-18 and over 18 years of age. By now, the Eastern Bloc countries must have amassed considerable know-how about the way TV programs should be designed to suit different age groups. However, less is known about this subject in the West.

Results indicate that visual languages exists, at least for three-, five-, eight- and twelve-year-olds, and that these languages are apparently more efficient than verbal languages in memory tasks. A verbal response to visual stimuli or a visual response to verbal stimuli requires a transformation from one modality to another. The ability to transform from verbal to visual modality develops more rapidly than the transformation from visual to verbal modality. As previously noted we may have one kind of memory for pictorial material and another for linguistic material. Pictorial stimuli are stored as images and not as words. The stimuli cannot be recalled without extensive cognitive efforts to retrieve the stored image, transform it into words and then verbalize those words.

Reynolds-Myers (1985) suggests that we put the theories of Piaget, Bloom and Gagne together to be able to meet the principles of visual literacy.

Basic assumptions of Piaget's theory:
1 The ability to think and reason occurs in developmental stages through which individuals progress in an invariant order.
2 These stages are dependent upon several interacting factors; physical maturation, experience, social transmission, and equilibration.
3 Although the stages develop in a fixed order, individuals move from one stage to another at different ages.
4 An individual may function in one stage for some bodies of knowledge, while he function in a different stage for other bodies of knowledge.

Basic assumptions of Bloom and Gagne:
1 Desired learning outcomes can be described and classified into levels of learning.
2 A higher class of learning subsumes all lower levels of learning.
3 Instruction can be designed to allow the learner to develop the desired level of learning.

However, before we can do this we must refine the means of testing for learning. At the present time, most learning is measured or assessed through verbal means. Although neither Gagne nor Bloom describe cognitive learning outcomes as the ability to verbalize aloud or in writing, the majority of the instructors assume that testing or assessment implies paper, pencils and written words. Learning can be assessed in a number of ways.

Illusions

One and the same stimulus can easily be perceived in different ways on different occasions. A very famous example of this is the Necker cube. It is perceived in one of two ways. There are many examples of "transformation" pictures of this kind. Some artists have become specialists in making pictures which can be perceived in different ways. Victor Vasarely, M. C. Escher, Norman Ives and Malcom Grea are especially well-known.

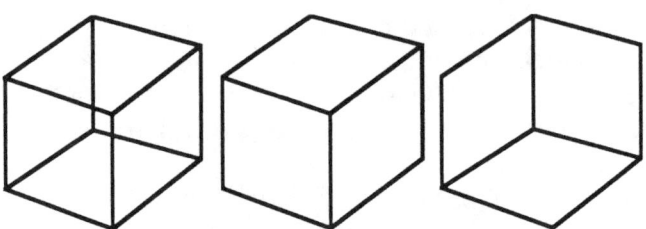

The Necker cube left and the two ways we can perceive it.

When the brain analyzes new data, it automatically adds or subtracts information in an effort to obtain a "sensible" interpretation of that data.

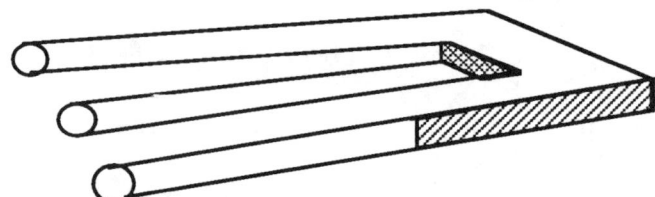

This figure is "impossible". The depth ambiguity means that the eye is unable to obtain all the information necessary to locate all the figure's parts. The brain becomes unable to determine how to interpret the image.

We often think we see things which are not really there. The black lines here are interpreted by many viewers as forming the word "word". An illiterate person would be unable to interpret the lines as forming a word.

We often have difficulty in interpreting simple relationships. For example, horizontal lines are often perceived as being shorter than equally long vertical lines.

Open and light forms are perceived as being larger than closed and darker forms of the same shape.

The left figure seems to have a longer horizontal line than the right figure. (Müller-Lyer's illusion).

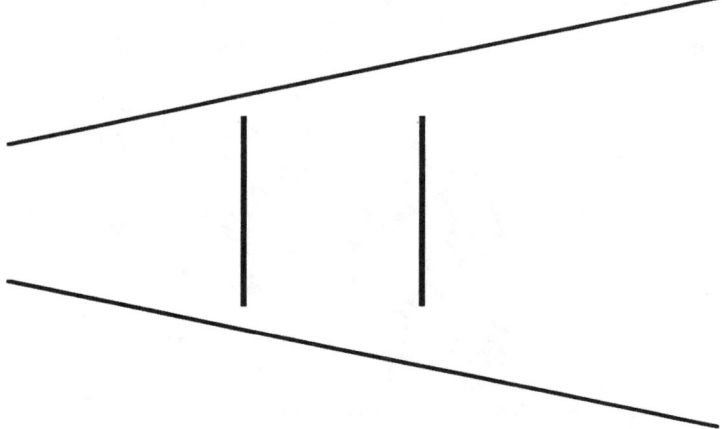

The left vertical line seems to be longer than the right vertical line. (Ponzo's illusion).

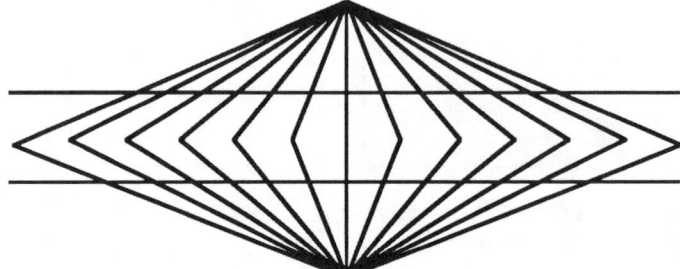

Intersected straight lines no longer appear to be straight but bent or serrated (Wundt's illusion).

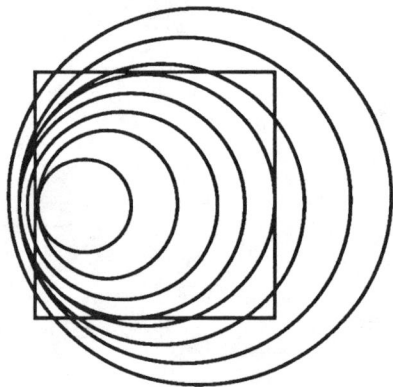

These intersected parallel lines no longer appear to be parallel.

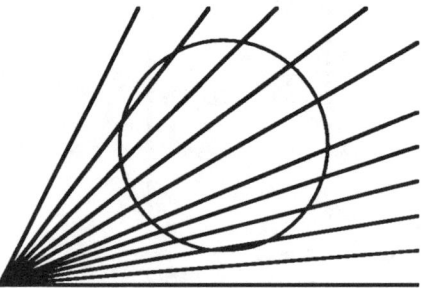

An intersected circle no longer appear to be a circle.

Perception, learning and memory

In regular patterns like these the areas in the intersections of the white and black lines look gray. The total black and, respectively white area must be considerably larger than the white and, respectively black area for this phenomenon to arise.

Changes in scale produce an illusion of elevations or depressions in a figure.

REFERENCES

Adams, J., & Chambers, R. (1962). Response to Simultaneous Stimulus of two sense modalities. *Journal of Experimental Psychology, 63,* 125-198.

Arnheim, R. (1974). *Art and visual perception: A psychology of the creative eye.* Berkerly, CA: University of California Press (rev.ed.).

Backman, J., Berg, T., & Sigurdson, T. (1988). *Grundskoleelevers produktion och reception av bilder.* Umeå: Umeå Universitet. Institutionen för bildlärarutbildning. Rapport nr 7.
Baron, L.J. (1980). Interaction Between Television and Child-Related Characteristics as Demonstrated by Eye Movement Research. *ECTJ, 28,* 4, 267-281.
Barthes, R. (1977). The rhetoric of the image. In *Image, music, text, essays.* Translated by S. Heath, London: Fontana.
Beitl, D. (1962). Das Bilderleben im frühen Kindesalter. *Jungenliteratur,* 8, 440-461.
Bergström, S.S. (1974). *Varseblivningspsykologi.* In B. Allander, S.S. Bergström, and C. Frey. *Se men också höra.* Stockholm.
Berlyn, D.E. (1966). Curiosity and exploration. *Science,* 153, 25-33.
Bloom, B.S., Englehart, M.D., Furst, E.J., Hill, W.H., & Krathwohl, D.R. (1956). *A taxonomy of educational objectives. Handbook I: The cognitive domain.* New York: Longmans, Green and Co.
Boeckman, K. (1987). *The Sign Structure of Realistic Images.* Paper presented at the Symposium on Verbo-Visual Literacy: Research and Theory. Stockholm, June 10-13.
Brody, J. (1982). *Affecting instructional textbooks through pictures.* In D.H. Jonassen. *The technology of text.* Englewood Cliffs N.J.: Educational Technology Publications, 301-316.
Brigthouse, G. (1939). A study of aesthetic apperception. *Psychological Monographs,* 51, 1-22.
Buswell, G. T. (1925). *How people look at pictures.* Chicago: University of Chicago Press.
Cronholm, M., Rydin, I., & Schyller, I. (1979). *Samspel mellan TV och barns lek, moral och bildmognad.* Stockholm: SR, Publik- och programforskning Nr. 1-79.
Dessoir, M. (1913). Uber das Beschrieben von Bildern. *Zeitschrift für ästhetik, 1913,* 8, 440-461.
Drew, D. G., & Grimes, T. (1985). *The effect of audio visual redundancy on audio and video recall in television news.* Paper presented at the annual meeting of the Association for Education in Journalism and Mass Communication (68th, Memphis, TN, August).
Duffy, B. (Ed.) (1983). *One of a kind. A practical guide to learning styles 7-12.* Oklahoma State Department of Education.
Dwyer, F. M. (1971). Color as an instructional variable. *AV Communication Review,* 19, 399-413.
Dwyer, F. M. (1978). *Strategies for Improving Visual Learning.* State College, PA: Learning Services.
Dwyer, F. M. (1982-83). The program of systematic evaluation - a brief review. *International Journal of Instructional Media,* 10, 23-39.
Edwards, D. C., & Coolkasian, A. (1974). Peripheral vision location and kinds of complex processing. *Journal of Experimental Psychology 102,* 244-249.

Ekwall, E. (1977). *Diagnosis and Remediation of the Disabled Reader.* Boston: Allyn and Bacon.

Elkind, D. (1975). We can teach reading better. *Today's Education. No. 64*, 34-38.

Faw, T. T., & Nunnaly, J. C. (1967). The effect on eye movements of complexity, novelty, and affective tone. *Perception and Psychophysics*, 2, 263-267.

Faw, T. T., & Nunnaly, J. C. (1968). The influence of stimulus complexity, novelty, and affective value on children's visual fixation. *Journal of Experimental Child Psychology*, 6, 141-153.

Fleming, M. (1969). Eye movement indicies of cognitive behaviour. *AV Communication Review 17*, 383-398.

Fleming, M., & Levie, W. H. (1978). *Instructional Message Design.* Englewood Cliffs. N.J.: Educational Technology Publications.

Gagne, R. W., & Briggs, L. J. (1974). *Principles of instructional design.* New York: Holt, Rinehart, and Winston.

Gazzaniga, M. (1967). The split brain in man. *Scientific American, 217,* 24-29.

Gazzaniga, M. S., & Le Doux, J. (1978). *The integrated Mind.* New York: Plenum Press.

Gibson, E. J. (1969). *Principles of Perceptual Learning and Development.* New York: Meredith Corp.

Gibson, J. J. (1950). *The perception of the visual world.* Boston: Houghton-Mifflin.

Gibson, J. J. (1966). *The senses considered as perceptual systems.* Boston: Houghton-Mifflin.

Gibson, J. J. (1971). *The information available in pictures. Leonardo,* 4, 27 - 35.

Gombrich, E. H. (1969). *Art and illusion: A study in the psychology of pictorial representation.* Princeton, N.J.: Princeton University Press.

Goodman, N. (1976). *Languages of Art: An approach to a theory of symbols (2nd ed.).* Indianapolis. IN: Hacket Publishing .

Gregory, R. L. (1978). *Eye and brain (3rd ed.).* New York: McGraw-Hill.

Gould, J. (1967). Pattern recognition and eye-movement parameters. *Perception and Psychophysics,* 2, 399-407.

Gould, J. (1973). Eye-movement during visual search and memory search. *Journal of Experimental Psychology,* 98, 184-195.

Guba, W., Wolf, W., deGroot, S., Knemeyer, M., Van Atta, R., & Light, L. (1964). Eye movements and T.V. viewing in children. *AV Communication Review,* 12, 381-401.

Haber, R. N. (1979). How we remember what we see. *Scientific American* 222, 104-115.

Haber, R. N., & Erdelyi, M. H. (1967). Emergence and recovery of initially unavailable perceptual material. *Journal of Verbal Learning and Verbal Behaviour.* 6, 618-628.

Haber, R. N., & Myers, B. L. (1982). Memory for pictograms, pictures, and words separately and all mixed. *Perception.* 11, 57-64

Haubold, M. (1933). *Bildbetrachtung durch Kinder und Jugendliche.* München.

Hayes, D.S., & Birnbaum, D.W. (1980). Preschoolers' retention of televised events: is a picture worth a thousand words? *Development Psychology.* 16, 5, 410-416

Hellspong, L., Melin, L., Pettersson, R., & Propper, G. (1987). *Intended and perceived content in informative materials.* Paper presented at the Symposium on Verbo-Visual Literacy: Research and Theory. Stockholm, June 10-13.

Hochberg, J., & Brooks, V. (1978). *Film cutting and visual momentum.* In J. Senders, D. Fisher and T. Monty, (Eds.). *Eye movements and the higher psychological functions.* New York: Erlbaum.

Hinkel, H. (1972). *Wie betrachten Kinder Bilder?* Steinbach - Giessen.

Hubel, D.H., & Wiesel, T.N. (1962). Receptive fields, binocular interaction and functional architecture in the cat's visual cortex. *Journal of Physiology,* 160,106-154.

Ibison, R.A. (1952). *Differential effects on the recall of textual materials associated with the inclusion of colored and uncolored illustrations.* Unpublished doctoral dissertation. Indiana University, Bloomington.

Judson, H. (1972). *The Techniques of Reading, (3rd ed.).* New York: Harcourt, Brace, and Jovanovich.

Kossllyn, S.M. (1975). Information representation in visual images. *Cognitive Psychology,* 7, 341-370

Krugman, H. (1965). The impact of television advertising: learning without involvement. *Public Opinion Quarterly,* 349-356.

Krugman, H. (1966). The measurement of advertising involvement. *Public Opinion Quarterly,* 583-596.

Krugman, H. (1967). Brain wave measures of media involvement. *Journal of Advertising Research,* 11.

Krugman, H. (1977). Memory without recall exposure without perception. *Journal of Advertising Research,* 17, 7-12

Lassen, N., Ingvar, D., & Skinhöj, E. (1978). Brain function and blood flow. *Scientific American,* 239, 62-72

Lawson, L. (1968). *Ophthalmological factors in learning disabilities.* In H. Myklebust, (Ed.). *Progress in Learning Disabilities, (Vol.1)* . New York: Grune and Stratton.

Leckhart, B. T. (1966). Looking time: The effects of stimulus complexity and familiarity. *Perception and Psychophysics,* 1, 142-144.

Levie, W. H. (1987). *Research on Pictures: A Guide to the Literature.* In D. M. Willows and H. A. Houghton. (Eds.). *The Psychology of illustrations. Vol I.* NY: Springer-Verlag, 1-50.

Levie, W. H., & Lentz, R. (1982). Effects of text illustrations: A review of research. *ECTJ,* 30, 195-232.

Levin, J.R., Anglin, G.J., & Carney, R.N. (1987). *On Empirically Validating Functions of Pictures in Prose.* In D. M. Willows, and H. A. Houghton (Eds.). *The Psychology of illustrations.* NY: Springer-Verlag, 51-85.
Levin, J.R., & Lesgold, A.M. (1978). On pictures in prose. *ECTJ,* 26, 233-243.
Limburg, V. E. (1987). *Visual "Intrusion": A two-way street in Visual Literacy.* Paper presented at the Symposium on Verbo-Visual Literacy: Research and Theory. Stockholm, June 10-13.
Lindsten, C. (1975). *Hembygdskunskap i årskurs 3, Att inhämta, bearbeta och redovisa kunskaper.* Lund: Liber Läromedel.
Lindsten, C. (1976). *Aktiviteter i hembygdskunskap: Elevpreferenser i årskurs 3. En faktoranalystisk studie. (Activities in Science and Social Studies: Pupils preferences in grade 3. A factorial study.)* Pedagogisk-psykologiska problem (Malmö, Sweden: School of Education), Nr. 310.
Lindsten, C. (1977). *Bilder i hembygdsboken: Elevpreferenser i årskurs 3. En faktoranalytisk studie. (Pictures in the Science and Social Studies book. Pupil preferences in grade 3. Factorial studies.)* Pedagogisk-psykologiska problem (Malmö, Sweden: School of Education), Nr. 312.
Locatis, C. N. and Atkinson, F. D. (1984). *Media and technology for education and training.* Charles E. Merrill Publishing Company.
Lodding, K. (1983). Iconic Interfacing. *Computer Graphics and Applications,* 3, 2, 11-20.
Loftus, G. R. (1972). Eye fixations and recognition memory for Pictures. *Cognitive Psychology,* 3, 521-551.
Loftus, G. R. (1979). On-line eye movement recorders: The good, the bad, and the ugly. *Behaviour Research Methods & Instrumentation,* 11, 188-191
Loftus, G. R., Shimamura, A., & Johnson, C. A. (1985). How much is an icon worth? *Journal of Experimental Psychology: Human Perception and Performance,* 11, 1-13.
MacBeth, D. R. (1974). *Classificational preference in young children: Form or color.* Chicago: National Association for Research in Science Teaching. (ERIC Document Reproduction Service No. Ed 092-362).
MacLean, W. (1930). A comparison of coloured and uncoloured pictures. *Educational Screen,* 9. 196-199
Mackworth, N. H., & Morandi, A. J. (1967). The gaze selects informative details within pictures. *Perception and Psychophysics,* 2, 547-552.
Matsushita, K. (1988). *A summary version of the Comprehensive Report on Hi-OVIS PROJECT Jul.'78-Mar.'86.* Tokyo: New Media Development.
McKim, R. H. (1980). *Thinking visually. A strategy manual for problem solving.* Belmont: Lifetime Learning Publications.
Moray, N. (1970). *Attention.* New York: Academic Press.
Muffoletto, R. (1987). *Critical Viewing - Critical Thinking: Reading The Visual Text.* Paper presented at the Symposium on Verbo-Visual Literacy: Research and Theory. Stockholm, June 10-13.

Nelson, W. W., & Loftus, G. R. (1980). The functional visual field during picture viewing. *Journal of Experimental Psychology: Human learning and Memory,* 6, 391-399

Nesbit, L. L. (1981). Relationship between eye movement, learning and picture complexity. *ECTJ,* 29, 2, 109-116.

Nickerson, R. S. (1965). Short-term memory for complex meaningful visual configurations: A demonstration of capacity. *Canadian Journal of Psychology,* 19, 155-160.

Noble, G. (1975). *Children in Front of the Small Screen.* Beverly Hills, California: Sage.

Noton, D., & Stark, L. (1971a). Scanpaths in eye movements during pattern perception. *Science,* 171, 308-311.

Noton, D., & Stark, L. (1971b). Eye movements and visual perception. *Scientific American,* 225, 34-43.

Nugent, G. C. (1982). Pictures, Audio and Print: Symbolic Representation and Effect on Learning. *ECTJ,* 30, 3, 163-174.

Otto, W., & Askov, E. (1968). The role of color in learning and instruction. *Journal of Special Education,* 2, 155–165.

Paivio, A. (1971). *Imagery and verbal processes.* New York: Holt, Rinehart & Winston

Paivio, A. (1978). *A dual coding approach to perception and cognition.* In H.L. Pick Jr. and E. Saltzman (Eds.). *Modes of perceiving and processing information.* Hillsdale, NJ.: Erlbaum, 39-51.

Paivio, A. (1979). *Imagery and Verbal Processes.* Hillsdale, NJ.: Erlbaum, 1980.

Paivio, A. (1983). *The empirical case for dual coding.* In J.C. Yuille. *Imagery, memory and cognition.* Hillsdale, NJ.: Erlbaum, 307-332.

Perfetti, C. (1977). *Language comprehension and fast decoding: Some psycholinguistic prerequisites for skilled reading comprehension.* In J. Guthrie, (Ed.). (1977). *Cognition, Curriculum, and Comprehension.* Newark, Delaware, International Reading Association.

Pettersson, R. (1979). *Bildkreativitet, en pilotstudie.* Stockholm.

Pettersson, R. (1981). Cultural differences in the perception of image and color in pictures. *ECTJ,* 30, 1, 43–53.

Pettersson, R. (1983a). Factors in visual language: Image framing. *Visual Literacy Newsletter,* 9 and 10.

Pettersson, R. (1983b). *Picture readability.* Rapport till VI:e Nordiska konferensen för Masskommunikationsforskning, Volda 1983.
and also (CLEA-report No. 10). Stockholm: Stockholm University, Department of Computer Science.

Pettersson, R. (1984). *Picture legibility, readability and reading value.* In A.D. Walker, R. A. Braden and L. H. Dunker *Enhancing human potential.* Readings from the 15th Annual Conference of the International Visual Literacy Association. Blacksburg, Virginia, 92-108.

Pettersson, R. (1985). *Intended and Perceived Image Content*. Presentation at the 17th Annual Conference of the International Visual Literacy Association. Claremont. CA. Nov. 1-2.
Pettersson, R. (1986a). Picture Archives. *EP Journal*. June. 2-3.
Pettersson, R. (1986b). *Image - Word - Image*. Presentation at the 18th Annual Conference of the International Visual Literacy Association. Madison, Wisconsin, Oct.30 - Nov. 2.
Pettersson, R. (1986c). See, look and read. *Journal of Visual Verbal Languaging*. Spring, 33-39.
Pettersson, R. (1986d). Properties of pixels. *EP Journal*. December, 2-4.
Pettersson, R. (1987). *Linguistic Combinations*. Paper presented at the Symposium on Verbo-Visual Literacy: Research and Theory. Stockholm, June 10-13.
Pezdek, K., & Hartmann, E. (1983). Children's television viewing: attention and comprehension of auditory versus visual information. *Child Development*, 51, 720-729.
Pezdek, K., & Stevens, E. (1984). Children's memory for auditory and visual information on television. *Developmental Psychology*, 20, 1, 212-218.
Piaget, J. (1968). *Barnets själsliga utveckling*. Stockholm:Liber.
Pirozzolo, F., & Rayner, K. (1979). Cerebral organization and reading disability. *Neuropsychologia*, 17, 485-491.
Potter, M.C., & Levy, E.I. (1969). Recognition memory for a rapid sequence of pictures. *Journal of Experimental Psychology*, 81, 10-15.
Prawitz, M. (1977). Varför förstår du inte vad jag säger, när jag hoppar, skuttar och målar? In G. Berefelt. *Barn och bild*. Stockholm: AWE/Gebers.
Pressley, M., & Miller, G.E. (1987). Effects of Illustrations on Children's Listening Comprehension and Oral Prose Memory. 87-114. In D. M. Willows and H.A. Houghton, (Eds.). *The Psychology of illustrations. Vol I*. NY: Springer-Verlag, 87-114-
Reynolds Myers, P. (1985). *Visual literacy, higher order reasoning, and high technology*. In N. H. Thayer and S. Clayton-Randolph, (Eds.). *Visual Literacy, cruising into the future*. Readings from the 16th annual conference of the International Visual Literacy Association. Bloomington, Western Sun Printing Co, Inc., 39-50.
Rolandelli, D. R., Wright, J. C., & Huston, A. C. (1985). *Children's auditory and visual processing of narrated and non-narrated television programming*. Paper presented at the Annual Meeting of the International Communication Association (35th, Honolulu HI, May).
Rudisill, M. (1952). Children's preference of color versus other qualities in illustrations. *Elementary School Journal*, 52, 444-451
Salomon, G. (1979). *Interaction of media cognition and learning*. San Francisco: Jossey Bass
Schallert, D. L. (1980). *The role of illustrations in reading comprehension*. In R. J. Spiro, B. C. Bruce and W. F. Brewer, (Eds.). *Theoretical issues in reading comprehension: Perspectives from cognitive psychology, lin-*

guistics, artificial intelligence, and education. Hillsdale, NJ:Erlbaum, 503-524.
Segall, M. H., Cambell, D. T., & Herskovits, M. J. (1966). *The influence of culture on visual perseption, an advanced study in psychology and anthropology.* Indianapolis: Bobbs-Merrill.
Shepard, R. N. (1967). Recognition memory for words, sentences and pictures. *Journal of Verbal learning and Verbal Behaviour,* 6, 156-163.
Sinatra, R. (1986). *Visual Literacy Connections to Thinking, Reading and Writing.* Springfield. Illinois: Charles C Thomas.
Smerdon, G. (1976). Children's preferences in illustration. *Children's literature in Education,* 20, 17-31.
Snodgrass, J. G., & Vanderwart, M. (1980). A standardized set of 260 pictures: normes for name agreement, image agreement, familiarity and visual complexity. *Journal of Experimental Psychology: Human Learning and Memory,* 6/2, 174 -215.
Spangenberg, R. (1976). Which is better for learning? Color or black and white? *Audio Visual Instruction,* 21 (3), 80.
Sperry, R. W. (1973). *Lateral specialization of cerebral function in the surgically separated hemispheres.* In F.J. McGuigan and R.A. Schoonorer, (Ed.). *The Psychophysiology of thinking.* Academic Press.
Sperry, R. W. (1981). Changing priorities. *Ann. Rev. Neuroscience,* 4, 1-15.
Sperry, R. W. (1982). Some effects of disconnecting the hemisphere. *Science,* 217, 1223-1226.
Standing, L. (1973). Learning 10,000 pictures. *Quarterly Journal of Experimental Psychology,* 25, 207-222
Standing, L., Conezio, J., & Haber, R.N. (1970). Perception and memory for pictures: Single-trial learning of 2500 visual stimuli. *Psychonomic Science, 19* , 99, 73-74.
Tidhar, C.E. (1987). *Verbo/visual and print interactions in television presentations - effects on comprehension among hearing and hearing-impaired children.* Paper presented at the Symposium on Verbo-Visual Literacy: Research and Theory. Stockholm, June 10-13.
Tröger, W. (1963). *Der Film und die Antwort der Erziehung.* München: Basel Reinhardt.
Ward, W. C., & Naus, M. J. (1973). *The encoding of pictorial information in children and adults.* Princeton, New Jersey: Educational Testing Service. (ERIC Document Reproduction Service No. ED 085-073).
Webb, W.W., Matheny, A., & Larson, G. (1963). Eye movements and a paradigm of approach and avoidance behaviour. *Perceptual and Motor Skills,* 16, 341-347.
Wilson, D. A., Reeves, A., and Gazzaniga, M. S. (1982). "Central" commisurotomy for intractable generalized epilepsy: Series two. *Neurology,* 32, 687-697.
Vogel, D. R., Dickson, G. W. & Lehman, J. A. (1986). Driving the Audience Action Response. *Computer Graphics World,* August.

Wolf, W. (1970). *A study of eye movement in television viewing. Final report.* Columbus: Ohio State University, (ERIC Reproduction Service No. ED 046 254).

Yarbus, A. (1967). *Eye movements and vision.* New York: Plenum Press.

Zuckerman, M., Zeigler, M. & Stevenson, H. V. (1978). Children's viewing of television and recognition of commercials. *Child Development,* 49, 96-104.

Zusne, L. & Michels, K. (1964). Nonrepresentional shapes and eye movements. *Perceptual and Motor Skills ,*18, 11-20.

Chapter 3

LITERACY

There are many different kinds of languages. In this chapter special attention is paid to characteristics of visual language. Its functions, levels of meaning, properties and structure are discussed.

Combinations of different kinds of languages are used in mass-communication. Yet little is known about the effects of various linguistic combinations. Some linguistic designations are suggested. Different verbo-visual representations are presented.

It is concluded that different linguistic combinations must be studied in detail before optimum combinations can be found for various purposes, such as education, information and entertainment.

LANGUAGE

According to Skinner (1957) language is a *behaviour which is learned by habit*. Children imitate adults until they learn the language spoken by them. Eriksson (1968) cites Chomsky (1959) who argued that language is not "a set of habits". Instead, the development of language is a continuous and creative process working in concert with the surrounding. The brain develops *verbal proficiency* making it possible for Man to formulate and understand an infinite number of sentences. This view has been supported by the findings of a number of scientists after Chomsky (e.g. Slobin, 1973, and Littlewood, 1984).

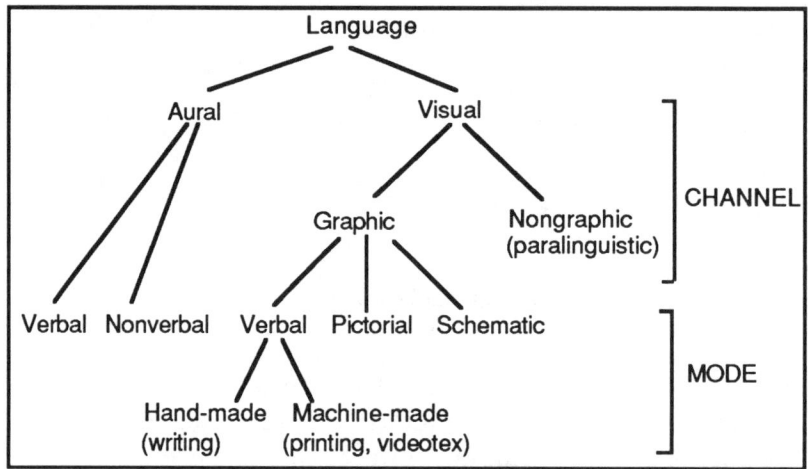

Twyman's (1982) language model devised to accommodate the approaches to language of linguistic scientists and graphic designers. Reproduced by permission of the author.

According to semiotics all cultural processes may be seen as communication processes (Eco, 1971). Thus, there are different languages, such as spoken, written, and visual languages. Lotman (1973) suggested that any system used as a means of communications between people can be regarded as a language. Cochran (1987) concludes that humans cannot transfer ideas whole and intact from one person to another. Human communication depends upon an interactive series of successive approximations presented in metaphors. She finds "languaging" useful in directing attention to the actions of people as they share their own ideas, listen to others, or learn from technologically produced sights and sounds. There are many approaches to language and language classification systems. Twyman (1982) pointed out that while linguistic scientists distinguish between spoken and written language graphic designers distinguish between verbal and pictorial language. From a design point of view written, printed or displayed texts or *"verbal graphic language"* are important components of visible language. Examples of poor design which hinder the comprehension of text contents are far too commonplace.

However, if the linguistic representation (e.g. the medium and its content) is placed at the forefront, another approach is natural. In this model, linguistic differentiation is based on the form of the messages: words, sounds, images and other forms. Thus, *verbal language* has spoken (aural), written (visual) and tactile categories, *audial language* comprises sound effects, music and paralinguistic sounds (all aural), *visual language* has symbols, pictures and paralinguistic visual expressions (all visual) and *other language* is based on smell, taste, touch etc. This latter approach is used in this book.

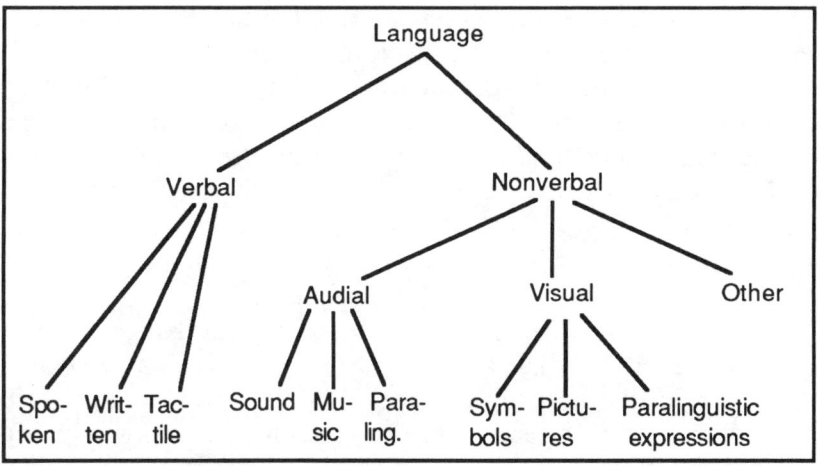

Language model based on the form of representation. The model can be broken down into additional sub-categories.

Languages differ in their ability to express concepts with precision and flexibility. Physics, chemistry and mathematics, for example, employ *non-ambiguous* symbol and equation languages. In verbal and technical descriptions, the language of specialists must be as unambiguous as possible. Languages such as these can only be understood by people with the appropriate specialized knowledge. Normal prose is often open to multiple interpretations, i.e. it is *ambiguous*. Fiction and poetry in particular offer abundant opportunities for individual interpretations. Pictures are normally ambiguous too.

In the animal world various body signals supply most of the communications between individuals. Animals send messages by displaying parts of their bodies in various ways. Message receivers "respond" with equivalent displays or movements. Bees have developed an advanced "language." After returning to the hive, a bee can perform a dance informing other bees about e.g. the location of a source of food.

Body language, paralinguistic and extralinguistic signals are also important in Man. Some scientists suggest that body language accounts for up to half, or more, of all our communications with others. Many movements and gestures can be interpreted without ambiguity in a given cultural community but not outside that community. In some societies, for example, the raising of an eyebrow, consciously *or* unconsciously, designates surprise. Or shrugging the shoulders designates indifference. But confusion and misunderstandings can occur before visitors to foreign cultures learn to understand the body language prevailing there.

Our body language is partly instinctive, partly learned and imitative (e.g. Fast, 1971). An interesting fact is that bilingual persons change their body language, gestures and eyelid movements when they switch (spoken) languages.

Brun (1974) gives many examples of sign languages. We can see examples of "formal" signs almost every day. Deaf people are often very skilled in using their highly developed and structured visual verbal sign language. Other less sophisticated kinds of sign languages are used by e.g. umpires in sporting events, traffic policemen, people directing aeroplanes on the ground etc. Further examples are the sign languages used in making radio and television programs or movies.

Thousands of alternatives are available to a sender wishing to transmit a rendition of some reality to receivers. Senders always utilize a "filter" and quality checks before selecting one of the many available text and picture options. The choice is based on the sender's *subjective opinions*. She/he selects the option believed to be the most efficient for each purpose and each transmission situation. The selected pictures/ texts are then edited in one of many ways for the purpose of enhancing reception impact.

Literacy 131

Thus, a selected, edited version of reality is transmitted to receivers. In mass communications, message reception can be affected in countless ways. For example, television reception may range from very bad to very good. Different viewers also perceive the same text and/or image in different ways, since there are always great inter-individual differences in perception (Pettersson, 1986b).

The context in which a message is seen can convey a "pre-understanding" of the message's contents. Pre-understanding is vitally important to our perception of any message. The language we choose to use in any given situation is in itself a device conveying preunderstanding to the reader/listener/ viewer. Message response is sometimes easy to predict. This predictability is often heavily exploited in movies, television and theatre.

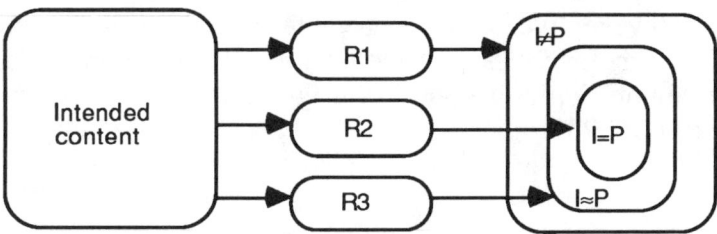

A large number of different representations, texts and/or pictures are always possible. The representations convey discrepant (R1), identical (R2) or acceptable (R3) perceptions (P) of the intended content.

There is no unambiguous verbal or visual language. In a closed, homogeneous cultural group, "ordinary" pictures and texts probably give rise to similar interpretations and perceptions of a specific reality, single object, event, message or content. However, we do not know the magnitude of the individual "tolerance ranges" in which different texts and pictures generate *reasonably identical perceptions*. One representation may produce accurate perception of content by one person but a completely different perception by another person. Perception of a given text/image by a random receiver in exactly the manner intended by the sender is extremely unlikely. However, senders do not often require identical perception of transmitted messages by all receivers. A large number of approximate interpretations may suffice. A well-written explanatory and elucidating caption can enhance understanding of the content. One study (Melin, 1986a) of student perception of texts and pictures in lexivision, (i.e. openings in a book where documentary and analytic pictures and descriptive texts interact) showed that pictures were better at expressing contrast and specification and that texts were better at expressing logical relationships such as cause and effect. Some lexivision presentations utilize the respective advantages of text and image.

VERBAL LANGUAGES

Usually we understand what we are saying. We know what we mean. However, we can never be sure that other people perceive our verbal messages as we have intended. On the contrary people perceive and depict a given message in widely differing ways (Pettersson, 1986b).

Spoken languages
Many animal species are capable of communicating with the aid of sounds. The messages they convey often express simple concepts, such as hunger or repletion. These acoustic messages are usually sent to individual(s) of the same species. However, the noisy cries emitted by a jackdaw or crow to "warn" the flock are actually a form of "mass communication" rather than personal messages.

One of the simplest forms of communication between humans, the crying of an infant are to some degree specific for that specific individual. Parents often quickly learn how to understand the meaning of different kinds of acoustically similar crying. They can also distinguish their own child's crying from the crying of other infants. After some time the child acquires linguistic facility enabling it to express a wide range of needs and emotions.

More than 2,000 languages and countless dialects have long been said to exist. However, Gunnemark & Kenrick (1985) claim that there are probably 5,200 living languages, certainly no less than 4,500 and possibly as many as 6,000. Tens of thousands of years ago, our ancestors were able to communicate with one another by means of some linguistic expressions. Over the millenia, language ultimately evolved into Man's most important means of expression.

Man is the only terrestrial species to acquire a language in the true sense of the word. However, the ability to form concepts is not unique to the human brain. Primates and several lower animals are capable of entertaining general, picture-based concepts. Concepts probably form in their brains in a similar way as in Man's brain. Several scientists in the U.S. have succeeded in teaching chimpanzees to communicate by means of visual sign language. Chimpanzees can deal with more than 100 words and display linguistic creativity, i.e. they are independently able to form new, logical word combinations. To a certain extent, their language has a grammatical structure. Previous attempts to teach apes to learn a language probably failed because they involved efforts to teach apes to speak, despite their anatomical inability to produce human language sounds.

Even very primitive societies often have advanced languages providing scope for great expressiveness. These languages sometimes contain many subtle terms for concrete concepts.

A pioneer in the field of semiotics, Ferdinand Saussure, divided the phonologic components of language into their smallest, non-meaningful parts, i.e. phonemes. Phonemes are basic units of sound. When combined, they form units with meaning. A language's smallest meaningful grammatical unit is referred to as a morpheme. Morphemes are combined to form syntagms (Fredriksson, 1979), i.e. words, phrases, sentences and complete texts. Spoken and written languages are formed from a limited number of phonemes (usually 20-40). These phonemes can be inter-combined in a limited number of ways. We can make a distinction between individual language, i.e. speech, and super-individual language, i.e. the language itself. When we speak and write, the phonemes, morphemes and syntagms we use must follow one another in a particular sequence if our messages are to be understood. Language is consequently hierarchic and linear.

The term "spoken language" is almost always taken to mean direct, informal verbal language. A sender and a receiver share a highly interactive communications situation. This situation offers immediate feedback and opportunities for explanations and corrections. However, the situation is highly transient and impossible to rehear/resee. On the other hand, the spoken word in technical media lacks any interactive component to facilitate communications. However, TV does have limited, sender-controlled or simulated interaction. These media all lack immediate feed-back but are non-transient, at least in principle, and their messages can be played back. Speech conveyed by technical devices depends on the quality of the reproduction technology employed and even on factors such as cost. Speech reproduction devices often clip higher frequencies, thereby impairing reception conditions for the listener and conveying speech less adequately than direct conversation.

This all means that the reception conditions of the spoken word conveyed by technical media are beginning to approach the reception conditions of the printed word. The sender must plan her/his message carefully. She/he must practice cognitive clarity and avoid ambiguity - both acoustically and optically. As is the case for the printed word, the language used by broadcast media for recurrent messages, such as weather forecasts, can be rationalized and formalized. Since computers can be taught to "speak", we run the risk of being stricken by the impoverished language of computer-synthesized speech.

Dahlstedt (1979) predicted that the verbal language used in media would not only develop on its own terms but even exert an impact on the spoken language as a whole. The media probably do have a leveling effect on the spoken language and thereby contribute to the disappearance of dialects. As a result of its wide-ranging coverage, the language of broadcast media tends to become a national standard to a greater extent than direct conversation. As is the case for the written language, the language of broadcast media is tailored to be understood of a wide range of listeners/viewers with widely varying backgrounds. This development is bound to retard language development, since the use by message senders of old and familiar phraseology maximizes the likelihood of message comprehension by receivers.

Written language

Man's ability to communicate was greatly enhanced when knowledge and information began to be stored with the aid of simple pictures and, subsequently, symbolic characters a few thousand years ago. *Pictographic languages* ultimately evolved in different cultures. They initially depicted objects and events as realistically as possible. These early pictograms were drawn with a stick in sand or clay or on the wall of a cave with a piece of charred wood or bone. Ultimately, people began depicting abstract concepts, largely religious or magic in nature, using pictograms to represent concrete objects. Pictograms of concrete objects were often combined to designate some abstract concept or thought. The pictograms became increasingly stylized and evolved into simple symbols or characters. Each character was equivalent to one or more concepts and came to represent a word. The Chinese language is an example of a living pictographic (ideographic) language in which each character represents one or more words. Other pictographic languages have developed in other ways. *Alphabetic* languages and alphabets evolved when characters designating words began to be used to represent the initial sounds of words.

The utilization of written languages, composed of individual letters, provided the bases for mass storage of knowledge and information and for communications between people at a great distance from one another in terms of both time and space. Most alphabetic written languages evolved from the Phoenician language which appeared around 1200 B.C. The wide-ranging sea voyages undertaken by the Phoenicians spread their language to many places. It reached the Greeks in 800-900 B.C. They added vowels to the Phoenician alphabet, which only consisted of consonants, and began writing from left to right instead of right to left. Many languages have alphabets based on the Greek alphabet, including the Latin of the Romans. Latin, in turn, has given rise to the alphabets employed in most modern written languages in Western countries.They use only a few dozen characters to represent thousands of words and concepts.

English is often said to contain no less than 750,000 words. Many languages are closely related. However, Japanese is an example of an interesting and extremely complicated language which is probably unrelated to any other tongue. Words borrowed from Chinese and European languages (English in particular) have been adapted to the Japanese phonetic system, but many of them remain recognizable. In Japanese many inflections share the same explicit significance but differ in implicit meaning, depending on the prevailing social and other circumstances.

Japanese script originated in China and is highly complex.It is said to comprise about 48,000 different characters, *kanji*, designating different words. Each kanji character can be written in three different fonts and has two or often more meanings, sometimes as many as 15-20. Combining different kanji characters can create a large number of new words and concepts. In elementary school, children learn the 996 most important kanji characters. About 1,850 kanji characters are used in the basic set employed in daily newspapers. A few thousand more are used on special occasions. Few Japanese are able to read and write more than 10,000 kanji characters. The older generation frequently complains that "the schools just aren't teaching children to read well anymore." This might be true, but Japanese children must spend a lot of time and effort on learning to read and write, since their language is so difficult. In addition to kanji, Japanese has *kana*, a 48-character syllabic language developed in Japan. These characters are used in two versions, *katakana* and *hiragana*. Kana writing is used for various inflective elements and for the phonetic writing of e.g. borrowed words.

There are very exact rules on how to write different characters. Calligraphic beauty is judged on the basis of the amount of physical and emotional effort perceived in it. As previously noted, kanji characters had their origin in Chinese characters. The latter evolved at least 3,400 years ago. The art of writing reached Japan during the 6th century A.D. It evolved into a domestic calligraphic language during the Heian period (794-1192). *Shodo* is Japanese calligraphy executed with brush and ink. Interest in Japanese calligraphy has spread to many other countries, including Sweden. For example, an exhibition of calligraphy and ink paintings by the Japanese artist Ken Sato was held at the House of Culture in Stockholm in the summer and fall of 1985. Ken-san described some of his feelings in the exhibition catalogue: "Japan's cultural

Literacy 137

heritage, with its aesthetic emphasis on everyday life, has had a great impact on my artistic studies and work. Shuichi Kata put it this way: "There must be harmony between human thought and Nature and a transfer of everyday life to art. *Not* art for the sake of art, *but* life for the sake of art." Ken-san concluded his presentation with the following comment: "My calligraphy-inspired paintings with their spontaneous brush strokes are a kind of personal handwriting containing poetic allusions. Ink paintings have a long tradition and demand freedom, rhythm and immediacy."

A printed message
Written or printed verbal messages basically consist of a number of characters such as those used here, i.e. a mixture of letters, spaces, punctuation marks and sometimes even numerals. Most letters are lower case, but upper case letters occur from time to time.

aaaaaaaaaaaaaaaaaaaaaaaaaaaaaaaAAbbbbbbbbbccccccdddddddddd ddddddeeeeeeeeeeeeeeeeeeeeeeeeeeeeeeeeeeeeeeeeeeeeeeeeeeeeeeeeeff ffffffffffffffggggggggggggggggggghhhhhhhhhhhhhhhhhhhhhhhhhhh hhiiiiiiiiiiiiiiiiiiiiiiiiiiiiiiiikkkllllllllllllllllllllmmmmmmmmmmmnnnnnnN nnnnnnnnnnnnnnooooooooooooooooooooooooooooooooooooo ppppppppppqrrrrrrrrrrrrrrrrrrrrrrrrrssssssssssssssssssssttttttttttttttttttttt ttttTTTTttttttttttttttttttuuuuuuvvwwwwwwxxxxyyy-,,,,,,......

The 428 characters above can be combined in many different ways. Here is one ...

ta eb ni si oN fo fo fo oros tao tuo, adn rae are. acn orf tis lge eth hTe thp topo ckba byoed. bgtod esey infef fomr frm frae,om frnaom eh htad heiad eaflt, lsreft le-hft lirine pdoart rehst ene seoen sch thateil tha iel thsatan tahin, wieng an,ogle. btlt apck heotuse otgther. rgihht right tmrin ihagflht heioa uhse htitwe inws. wAings dgea tasil eexpt muar mbtin fortked aebotve halves, hg her little strAong upfper. boaymote toncm botltom execept lihdig oliqe iaonl dinal oards, exwtea wnding peog erigorst edshaed

... not very successful example. It looks like a genuine text, but no combination of characters represents any intelligible concept.

There are much better ways of combining the characters in the original example. These characters can easily be used to form both short and lonf words. Here is an example with more than one hundred real words of successively increasing length.

a a a a A A an as at be in is is No of of of or so to to and are are can for its leg the the the the the the the the the The The The The top top back body body eyes fine form form from from from from head head left left left line part rest seen seen such tail tail tail than thin wing angle black house other right right flight house white wings wings detail except martin martin forked above halves higher little strong upper bottom bottom except gliding oblique diagonal diagonal towards extending posterior wedgeshaped- ,,,,,,,.......

These words can, in turn, be combined to form meaningful sentences.

A house martin in flight A house martin seen at an oblique angle from above are gliding so its body form a diagonal from top left to bottom right The wings form a strong diagonal from bottom left to top right The tail is a little higher than the head The wedge-shaped wings the upper halves of the head back and the forked tail are black The rest of the body is white except for a thin line extending from the tail towards the posterior part of the left wing No other fine detail such as eyes or leg can be seen -,,,,,,.......

The addition of punctuation marks at appropriate points make the text much more cohesive.

A house martin in flight
A house martin, seen at an oblique angle from above, are gliding so its body form a diagonal from top left to bottom right. The wings form a strong diagonal from bottom left to top right. The tail is a little higher than the head. The wedge-shaped wings, the upper halves of the head, back and the forked tail are black. The rest of the body is white, except for a thin line extending from the tail towards the posterior part of the left wing. No other fine detail, such as eyes or leg, can be seen.

Many other words could be formed and the new words arrayed in sentences and texts with completely different meanings. It is easy to conclude that a text retains its content even when type size is changed. Here are several examples of the same text in different sizes (character size is designated in typographical points -p).

<small>A house martin in flight (9 p)</small>
A house martin in flight (10 p)
A house martin in flight (12 p)
A house martin in flight (14 p)
A house martin in flight (18 p)

Individual characters can be designed in many different ways. Here are a few examples of the same text rendered with different fonts.

A house martin in flight (Times 12 p)
A house martin in flight (Helvetica 12 p)
A house martin in flight (Geneva 12 p)
A house martin in flight (New York 12 p)
A house martin in flight (Chicago 12 p)

Each type font is usually available in different versions. Here are some examples of the same text with different versions of the same font.

A house martin in flight (12 p, normal)
A house martin in flight (12 p, italic)
A house martin in flight (12 p, bold)
A house martin in flight (12 p, bold, italic)
A house martin in flight (12 p, outline)

So type size, fonts and font versions can be combined in very many ways. However, these options should normally be used sparingly and only a few different versions utilized in a text. Verbal characters also retain their meaning even if rotated in different directions or if turned upside down as in this example.

Visuals for information

A house martin in flight (upside down)

A mirror-reversed text (written from right to left, below) can also be read.

A house martin in flight (mirror-reversed)

So the contents of a verbal message are *relatively independent of its form*. However, its readability is strongly influenced by its design or topology. The basic rule is quite simple, that the most common type sizes are easier to read than uncommon sizes. The combinations employed most frequently in newspapers and books have the greatest readability. Characters may obviously neither be too small, nor too large. In the first case we can not read them. In the other case we can only have a few words on each line. The optimum line length seems to be about 40 characters and spaces. Aspects such as margin width, the number of paragraphs, number of columns, the number of lines per page and the line width are also important to our ability to read text. (Also see Context: Text).

Characteristics of verbal languages
- Verbal languages have digital coding using combinations of letters (and/or numerals) to represent content (Elkind, 1975).
- There is no direct correspondence between groups of letters, words, and reality. Each meaning is defined and must be learned (Elkind, 1975).
- The properties of letters are limited. A letter has a given position in an alphabet, it has a name, it is represented by one or more sounds and is used in a context (Elkind, 1975). The way letters are written is of minor importance (Pettersson, 1983a).
- Verbal languages have varying levels of meaning (Eco, 1971)
    - phonemes (without meaning)
    - morphemes (with meaning)
    - syntagms, sub-meanings
    - complete meanings

Literacy 141

- Semantic codes, grammar and syntax must be defined (exactly) (Chomsky, 1959).
- The perception of linear representations requires slow, sequential, processing for comprehension of content (Perfetti, 1977, Sinatra, 1986).
- Memory retrieval is a serial integration process and entails sequential processing by auditory-motor per-ception systems (Sinatra, 1986).
- Perception of a text is relative. Different people perceive and depict a given text in widely differing ways (Pettersson, 1986b).
- Dissatisfaction with the execution of a message may cause dissatisfaction with the content of the message.
- Perception of verbal content is apparently easier when a text is read than heard. Thus it is easier to assimilate and profit from a rich language by reading than by listening (Pettersson, 1986b).
- A written text can convey information, contain analyses and describe feelings and facts (Melin, 1986a).
- Verbal depiction of the content and execution of even simple pictures requires relatively long descriptions (Pettersson, 1986b).
- The more abstract a word is the harder it is to relate it to any specific activity (Melin, 1986a).
- People usually have no difficulty in reading the jargon used in professional or technical languages but understanding the concepts the words represent may be difficult for a non-specialist (Melin, 1986b).

VISUAL LANGUAGES

It has probably always been natural for man to express himself by means of visual messages. Since the beginning of mankind we have been using body languages and different kinds of signs for communication.

Prehistoric Man made murals and rock inscriptions with mythological meaning. In everyday life, people probably made drawings on the ground to show the location of game etc. Simplified images ultimately evolved into characters, letters and numerals.

Pictures helped Man communicate long before we had written languages for our messages. Our children make pictures, they draw and paint long before they learn to read and write.

For 20,000 years we have had murals. For about 2,500 years we have had rock inscriptions. For about 700 years we have had framed paintings and put them on our walls as pieces of art. For more than 500 years we have had printed illustrations in books. We have had photos for 150 years, films for 80 years, electronic pictures for more than 40 years and computer images for more than ten years. Electronic "live-pictures" last only for one twentyfifth of a second, but they can be stored for example on videotape or videodisc.

Nowadays, pictures are to be found almost everywhere. They differ in character. It is not possible for every one to stand out on every occasion. People "drown" in a flood of general "pictorial noise", a kind of mental pollution of the environment. Visuals can be classified according to several different criteria such as sender, receiver, content, execution, format and context and even according to criteria such as function, use and the means of production etc. Thus, there are many possibilities for classification. However, one and the same visual can and will be classified in different ways at the same time depending on the criteria applied in each case. Often the boundaries between different groups partially overlap each other.

Functions

From a theoretical point of view, a visual can possess many different functions and effects or combinations of functions and effects. Thus, a distinction can be made between *symbols and pictures*.

In western civilizations a symbol is usually something which "represents" something (Lee, 1959). We "apply" words to things or names to persons. These "signs" stand for the things to which they have been applied. However Agrawal et. al. (1987) point out that in the context of the ancient Indian civilization the symbol is not a representation. A symbol is a concretisation of reality having intrinsic power of its own. It is a part within the whole belief system, and a link between the past, the present and the future.

Signposts, traffic signs and labels are examples of symbols. They are unambiguous by convention. *We agree and decide on their meaning.*

All pictures are *representations* of reality and depict the physical structure of the objects they represent. As is the case for other kinds of representations, pictures are always open to different interpretations by different people at different times. Some pictures are open to many interpretations, others to only a few. Cochran (1987) distinguishes between actual events/objects, iconic re-presentations and arbitrary representations. Examples of iconic re-presentations are film and TV-images, still photographic pictures and realistic art work. Symbols, signs, computer graphics and words are all examples of arbitrary representations. Here no cues from actuality are left.

"Pictures" may be classified as *realistic;, suggestive;* and *schematic.* "Realistic" pictures can provide reasonably objective documentation of a situation, product or course of events. Photos and movies, X-ray films, satellite photographs, thermographic pictures, ultrasonograms and certain documentary drawings are examples of "realistic" pictures. "Suggestive" pictures also cover a wide field. A picture in this category can serve to *express* the picture creator's particular circumstances and convey messages about this person's internal or external reality. Examples of "schematic" pictures are various kinds of maps, charts, graphs, engineering drawings, EEG and ECG recordings etc.

Pictures can attract *attention* to and create interest in a given material or in a given subject.

Pictures may be *cognitive* and convey knowledge and information to the reader or viewer. They can facilitate learning from a text by enhancing comprehension and memory. Pictures can be used e.g. for instructing, exemplifying, identifying or providing variation, authority or information as a supplement to text and sound. Pictures are often used for content that is important, hard to understand and new.

It should be remembered that pictures can have a negative effect. The inability of children younger than thirteen to ignore incidental images means that effects are unlikely to be neutral: if the pictures do not help, they will probably hinder. *Illustrations should be strictly relevant to the text.*

Pictures can be *affective* and provide readers with entertainment and reinforce an experience. They can trigger associations and influence emotions and attitudes, especially in movies and TV. In advertising and television pictures often carry subliminal messages. Ads for liquor for example sometimes use sexual symbols.

Pictures can be *compensatory,* making it easier for poor readers to comprehend, learn and recall things they read in a text.

In various ways, pictures often have important *social functions* in the home, at school, in organizations and in society. *Picture creation* is more important than the visual results in certain instances. Some pictures may not have any or only a limited function once created. Modern cameras which automatically set the exposure, focus the lens and advance the film have made it possible for anyone to take pictures. More than 90% of all Swedish families own at least one camera. Two thirds of the population make a movie or take still photographs at some time during any year. Millions of amateur photographs are the result. The advent of lightweight, portable VCR equipment has opened up new horizons for non-professional creators of moving pictures.

Pictures may also have a generally *decorative effect* and be used to improve our environment.

Results from several experiments show that learning is facilitated and maximized when visual, audio and print media contain the same information. In normal situations, the addition of visual embellishments has not been found to enhance the learning of information which is only conveyed in printed form. The presence of text-redundant visuals will neither help nor hinder the learning of information given in the part of the text without illustrations. Some picture editors admit that some of the pictures they use in textbooks are only there to to "stimulate" the reader, to have "a life of their own" or merely to provide a "breathing space" within the text. This seems doubtful. Many illustration (often without legends) in contemporary textbooks appear to serve no useful purpose whatever. It is even possible that certain types of illustrations, incorporated to "stimulate" the reader's imagination and interest, could instead have a heavily governing effect which stifles the imagination and diverts interest from the information and knowledge the author wishes to convey.

In the selection of visuals for reference books and textbooks, picture editors often ask themselves questions such as the following:
- Does the picture depict the right thing?
- Is the presentation of the subject satisfactory?
- Is the picture technically acceptable?
- Is the picture aesthetically satisfactory?
- Is the picture "flexible", i.e. will it work with different formats?
- Will the picture fit into a given area?
- Will the picture fit in with the other pictures on the same page?

In practice, many picture editors find that *procurement time*, *availability* and *image clarity* are the most important considerations in making actual choices among visuals. A number of authors have described different methods for the editing of visuals so as to change their importance and impact. Some important changes which can be made to a visual prior to publication should be mentioned. For example, a picture editor may elect to crop or expand the original picture. Parts of the picture can be deleted, added, altered, moved or changed in shape. The picture can also be enlarged or reduced. A color can be changed, removed or added. The picture's expressiveness can be altered by the choice of repro method etc.

Visuals cost money, often quite a lot of money. But in many situations a "good" picture need not cost more than a "bad" picture! Spending a lot of time on the visualization process and on sketches (usually a less expensive process than the cost of originals, "masters" and printing runs) may therefore be worthwhile. When material is going to be used in another culture, extreme care must be used in preparing the illustrations.

Levels of meaning

Everyone appreciates the need to learn the meaning of words and that words and texts are things you have to learn. However, we also have to learn to "read" and understand the meaning of visual information and the components of visual language. The learned ability to interpret visual messages accurately and also to create such messages is *visual literacy*. Thus interpretation and creation in visual literacy can be said to parallel reading and writing in print literacy. Visual languages differ just as spoken and written languages differ. The codes used in visual language differ in different cultures as well as in many sub-cultures. Even within a western mass-media country like the U.S., visual codes differ in different parts of the country, in different socio-economic groups etc. Visual languages have their own "grammars", syntaxes etc., just like spoken and written languages. To a limited extent, some of the factors involved in the grammar and syntax of visual languages are known. However, most of this linguistic work still remains to be done. One obvious problem is the lack of simple and general systems for classifying visual messages.

Reynolds-Myers (1985) postulated the following "Principles of visual literacy theory":

- Visual languaging abilities develop prior to, and serve as the foundation for, verbal language development.
- Development of visual languaging abilities is dependent upon learner interaction with objects, images, and body language.
- The level of visual language development is dependent upon the richness and diversity of the objects, images, and body language with which the learner interacts and upon the degree of interaction.
- The level of visual language development is facilitated by direct learner involvement in the process and equipment used to create objects, visual images, and body language.

Literacy

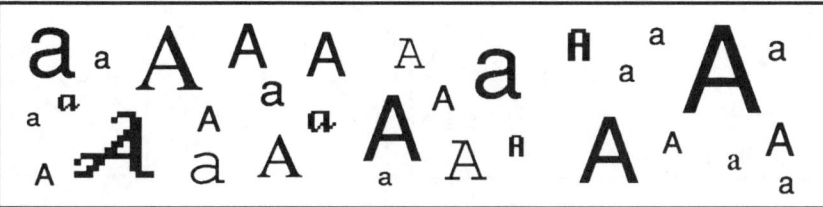

In a printed text a=a. The execution of the letters usually does not affect their meaning and content.

In contrast to spoken and written languages pictures have no general, distinguishing elements which are not bearers of information. Visual languages have analog coding. Visuals are iconic. They normally resemble the thing they represent. The simplest components in a picture, i.e. its *basic elements,* are dots, lines and areas which can be varied in a great many ways. A dot may vary in size, shape, color, value, grain, position and context. A line may be varied with respect to its starting point, length, direction, curvature, shape, thickness, evenness, points of changes, printing, color, value, grain, brightness, orientation, terminus and context. An area can be varied with respect to size, "emptiness", shape, color, value, grain, texture, shaded, non-shaded, gray scale, color combinations, brightness and context. Three dimensional pictures also possess *volume* in different forms. Basic graphical elements are sometimes meaningful, sometimes not. The number of ways in which the smallest image components can be inter-combined is unlimited, and the importance of certain combinations varies from one picture creator to another.

So basic picture components are not equivalent to the phonemes in spoken and written languages. If there were some kind of "visual phonemes", it would be possible for people to learn to draw and paint in about the same way they learn to read a text. In a picture, the basic image components - dots, lines and areas - form *shapes* which form *visual syntagms* or sub-meanings. These components interact to form complete meanings in stills, picture series or moving pictures.

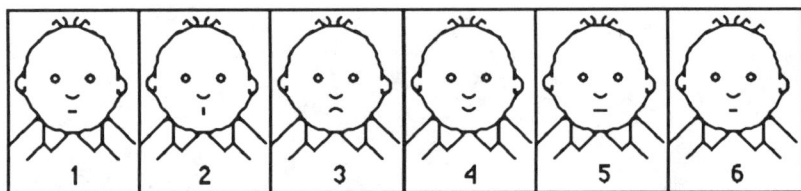

However in a pictorial presentation, a dot or a line may have widely varying meanings. Here, execution influences content. To illustrate this, six copies were made of a simple drawing. Figure 1 was left unchanged. The mouth was changed in figures 2 - 5 by the addition of small lines which completely altered our perception of the illustrations. In Figure 6 a small line was added to the hair, but this addition has no effect on our perception of the illustration.

In visual language, a small dot is usually a meaningless or non-significant image element, such as one of many halftone dots, but it could also be a syntagm, such as an eye in a cartoon-face Or it may even have a complete meaning, such as a ball in midair. It all depends on the situation depicted. So like written and spoken languages, visual language has numerous but varying levels of meaning. The following levels can be listed in an ascending order of complexity:
1 Basic elements, dots, lines, areas and volumes (non-significant)
2 Shapes (non-significant)
3 Syntagms, sub-meanings
4 Complete meanings
   a) Stills
   b) Picture series, such as comic strips
   c) Lexivisions
   d) Moving picture depictions, such as TV programs.

Dots, lines and areas can be put together in many ways resulting in different contents. Changes of the basic elements will result in different images sometimes of great and sometimes of minor importance.

Literacy 149

Non-significant basic elements (dots, lines and areas) are arrayed into shapes which form syntagms or sub-meanings (here an eye).

The syntagm eye can be a part of the complete meaning face, which in turn can be a syntagm in other complete meanings. This specific face may be a part of pictures of jacks as well as kings in all suits. Here the complete meaning is specified by the symbols for suits and numeric values.

Here is another example with eight black areas.

These areas can be combined in many different ways. Here is one example ...

... not particularly successful. No combination of characters corresponds to any intelligible concept. The picture gets no concrete image content. There are better ways of combining the characters in the original set. In the following example the elements are combined to form a bird, a house martin in flight.

Simple image elements, such as those used to depict this house-martin, can be rotated, turned upside down and re-combined to form a series of completely different but still intelligible representations of real concepts. On the next page are two such examples.

Literacy 151

Contrary to the situation with verbal messages the contents of a visual message are highly dependent on its shape. Size variations for example are only possible within certain limits. The image can be made rather small ..

... or rather large, but will then not convey the same message.

152 *Visuals for information*

There is an optimum size for every pictorial subject. This size can only be established by trial and error. In this instance, the small version is probably too small and the large version needlessly large.

If two different sized pictures of objects such as house-martins are placed next to one another, one is perceived to be near the viewer and one farther away. Or the birds are perceived as being of different sizes. Maybe one bird is adult and the other still a baby bird. Or maybe the two birds belong to different species.

Visual signs do not retain their meaning in the same way as verbal signs when rotated and turned in different directions. Turn the page in different directions and see in what way the impact of the pictures change. Also the actual placement on the page, the layout, is important.

This is an "upside-down" mirror image. Here the house-martin is ascending to the right and not descending to the right as in most of the previous pictures. This picture supplies the viewer with the same basic information about the bird's appearance but completely different information about the bird's actions.

In this "side-ways" mirror image the house-martin is apparently descending to the left. Again the image contains the same basic information as the original image about the bird's appearance but completely different information about the bird's actions.

However, Cossette (1982) claims that it is possible to build an iconic "alphabet". He identified six families of basic graphic sign elements, which he called *graphemes*, e.g. "visual phonemes". Each of these graphemic elements is part of one of six continuum families: tallness, value, grain, color, orientation and form. The same variables were discussed by Bertin as early as 1967. Each grapheme signifies nothing in itself. A spot is nothing but a spot. Together with other graphemes the spot may be contextually enriched to a unit of iconic significance, an *iconeme*. In a photograph of a man one iconeme can be an arm, a leg, the head and so on. By analysis of an image it is possible to identify the iconemes which are important to the information content and identify the *key syntagm*, the "meaning nucleus" of the visual. By editing, eliminating or adding certain iconemes the effectiveness of an image can be altered.

In my view, the Cossette graphemes represent *qualities* more than visual phonemes. Graphemes would instead be dots, lines and areas, since they all can vary more or less with respect to tallness, value, grain, color, orientation and form. Anyhow they are all *variables in the visual language*.

Structure

The structure of visual language is formed by different image variables which jointly influence our interpretation of images. Image variables can be subdivided into four main categories: *content, graphic execution, context* and *format*.

Variables related to image *content* are the degree of realism, the amount of detail, objects, time, place, space, events such as "action", humour, drama, violence etc., time displacement, parallel action, metaphoric descriptions (symbolic actions), the relevance and credibility of the contents, comparisons and statistics, motion, sounds such as speech, music, sound effects, and emotions. Some of these variables apply to moving pictures in films or TV. Some apply to stills in printed media like books, newspapers etc. Others apply to both stills and moving pictures. The contents of pictures can evoke highly positive or negative responses in viewers, especially in children. Visual language can affect our attitudes and emotions more easily than speech and text.

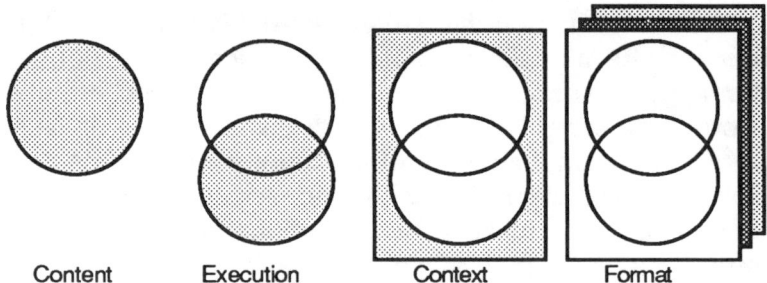

Variables in visual language can be related to content, execution, context and format.

Variables related to an image's *"graphic execution"* or art style may consist of image factors and image components. They are composed of non-significant image elements, such as dots, lines and areas in different combinations.

Examples of image factors and image components are image type, i.e. whether images are drawings, paintings, photos, computer-generated visuals etc., brightness, light, shape (external shape, external contour), size (image, subject, depth), color (color, hue, gray scale), contrast, emphasis, composition (organization, centers of interest, balance), perspective (depth, depth-of-field, image angle, image height), technical quality, symbols, signs and code signals in the image, pace, speed change (slow, fast), editing, zooms in and out, panning, visual complexity and visual effects.

A picture has both an *internal* and an *external context*. I regard factors inside the medium as "internal context." In books internal context is the interplay between text and illustrations, the interplay between illustrations and layout. Movies and TV programs have sound with speech, music and sound effects plus visual and audio metaphors. Some computer programs contain advanced animation with interaction between text, images and even sound. I regard the entire communications situation, i.e. senders and their intentions for the picture and receivers and their circumstances (e.g. time available), as external context.

The choice of *"format"* is of major importance to our perception of image contents. Our perception of a picture (such as a photograph) changes when we view it as a paper print, transparency projected on a white screen, as a computer image etc. If you watch a film on TV, cable TV or VCR at home alone, your perception of the film is very different from your response when you watch the same film on a wide screen with hi-fi sound in a cinema full of people. In analogical technical systems, letters and numerals are represented by defined "type" (a, b, c...). Pictures consist of lines and halftone dots. In digital systems, image elements are mathematically defined either as intersections of co-ordinates and vectors providing direction or as "pixels", i.e. small rectangular image components.

As an example of the interplay between different variables, let us consider an ordinary deck of cards. It consists in fact of fifty-two (or fifty-four) different visuals. Regardless of the suit, cards with small values, such as one to six are usually "very easy to read." It only takes one or a few glances for a card player to know which one of the fifty-two cards he has been dealt. Cards with values from seven to thirteen contain more information and can be classified as "easy to read." However, pictures of jacks, queens and kings are sometimes harder to read and distinguish from one another, depending on their design and execution complexity. Cards of the same numeric value, e.g. four, differ in their execution with respect to the symbols for the four suits. Thus, they differ in content. Different decks of cards can differ in design and execution. Thus e.g. the king of spades looks different in different decks but the king always represent the same content. A card seen together with other cards is seen in different contexts. Thus, the value of one card (or of any other visual) is different for the player (or for the user) in different contexts.

Ratings of variables
In a study of picture readability (Pettersson, 1983.1), 15 experienced "visual design experts" in Sweden were asked to rate the importance of each of 21 individual visual language factors to the

total readability of a picture. They indicated their ratings on a questionnaire with a semantic scale from "very slight importance" to "very great importance". The results suggest that it is very difficult to rank the variables. Only a few of the variables were regarded as being of very slight or very great importance. A number of respondents noted that in their view the variables varied in importance depending on the context. Thus a variable may be very important in one context but of only slight importance in another.

The same task was later given to 25 students in the USA. Also the results from this rating suggest that it is difficult to rank the variables and that the variables vary in importance. In these model experiments the number of subjects was limited. In an attempt to get more information, copies of a somewhat extended and partly different questionnaire were sent to members of IVLA, International Visual Literacy Association, who distributed them among their students. In this case a semantic differential scale which combined verbal statements with numeric values (0-100) was used. This scale has been successfully used in several studies (e.g. Pettersson et.al., 1984). The use of numeric values makes it possible to calculate mean values.

The idea was to collect information from several different cultures and compare the results. Questionnaires were sent back from Canada, Holland, Japan, United Kingdom, United States, Sweden and Switzerland. An analysis of more than one hundred answers shows enormous variations between individual subjects. For most of the 24 variables there is a difference of 70-80 points with mean values ranging from 58 to 76, corresponding to "great importance". Standard deviations were also very high (15-22).

In this study it is not possible to find any certain differences between the opinions of subjects in different countries. Basically the study support earlier findings and shows that people have very different ideas about the importance of various aspects of visual language to the readability of a picture. However, on average all variables are "important". Several subjects also noted that variables varied in importance depending on the content and the context. A few subjects noted that it was very hard to isolate and rate the importance of individual variables since they all interact in forming the visual message. Future research in this field will probably have to use sets of actual test pictures for people to react on. These test pictures will probably be judged differently by individual subjects. However, there might also be cultural differences.

Properties

Spoken and written languages, like text and music, are linear. They must be read (listened to) in a particular sequence to be comprehended. However, visual language is two-, three- or four-dimensional and can be "read" by letting the eye scan a picture or sculpture in many different ways. Time is an important dimension, not only in film and TV, but also in still pictures. Our "decoding" of an image, and our subsequent perception of it, may vary considerably with respect to which of the visual cues we see first. Studies of eye movements have shown that we often scan pictures in search of simple shapes providing structural simplicity. Missing information is filled in by the brain so a logical and "complete" visual impression is created. Influenced by our reading habits, people in western countries often scan pictures from left to right.

In comparison to a written text, a visual contains an infinite amount of information (Pettersson, 1985). By selecting and utilizing different parts of a picture's information on different occasions, we can experience completely new and different perceptions when we re-see a picture in new contexts. Like other languages, pictures consist of coded messages which are comprehensible in a given social context and in a given age. For example, we often find it difficult to interpret the messages in pictures from unfamiliar cultures and ages. "Modern art" puzzles its public who have not yet learned to decipher the new codes. The reader (viewer) always has greater freedom in interpreting a visual message than a verbal message. Pictures almost always convey multiple messages. Extraneous messages may compete with the messages the sender regards as significant and important. So pictures always incorporate some ambiguity and numerous "correct" interpretations, although not always a picture creator's intended or anticipated interpretation. The way in which a picture is interpreted depends to a great extent on the reader's code in relation to the sender's code. Studies of intended vs. perceived image content give clear evidence that there are major differences between intended and perceived image content.

There are many ways to depict even the simplest object. Many pictures are appropriate to and representative of a given designation, such as "Easter", "Christmas", and "flowers", "children", "horses", "dogs", "cats", "cards" etc. The depiction of e.g. "Jesus Christ" and "Buddha" is commonplace in the classical art of the respective religions. The number of pictures capable of depicting a concept declines as the degree of descriptive detail increases. Many pictures may be regarded as "visual synonyms." A message may always be expressed in different pictures. A picture will always be interpreted in different ways. Thus it may be concluded that pictures used in instructional materials always should have captions to guide understanding of the content.

As far as ambiguous pictures are concerned, there is often a major difference between their *denotation*, i.e. their literal meaning, and their various *connotations*, i.e. their associative meanings, and their *private associations* .

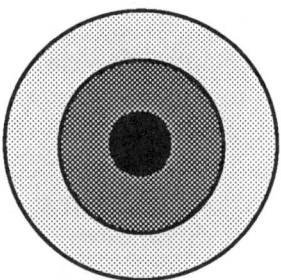

Each complete meaning can be interpreted in different ways by various persons. We can define fields of denotation (centre), connotations (middle) and private associations (outer area).

By e.g. exaggerating perspective, deforming shapes, making symbolic use of colors etc., a picture creator can easily create works which evoke extra associations in viewers. This is in fact the very idea behind an artistic picture. However, the *informative picture* should not be open to different interpretations. The pic-

Literacy

ture's message should then be the message intended by the person/agency commissioning the picture.

The total amount of information presented varies very considerably in different media. A typed A4-sized page can hold up to 2,500 characters, whereas a TV image consists of 250,000 pixels whose color content and gray scale can be changed 25 times a second. By editing a text we can reduce the number of words required to convey a "content." The amount of information in synthesized (computer-generated) speech can sometimes be reduced by up to 99% without obliteration of message comprehension. A number of graphic elements in pictures can also be reduced without any major impact on content. We can *delete, add* or *relocate* information. Graphic elements which constitute boundaries between different image elements are more important to our perception of the image than other graphic elements. In principle, it should be possible to delete a rather large number of *non-significant* elements in e.g. a photograph. As long as some of the *significant* picture elements are retained, we can still get some idea of the image content. So *image design can be changed a great deal without any major change in the perception of image content.*

Image design can be changed a great deal without any major change in the perception of image content. In this example one hundred pixels were successively changed.

Since the brain fills in missing information and, in certain instances, attempts to make the best possible interpretation of a given stimulus, certain significant graphic elements can also be deleted from images. Missing lines in cartoons can sometimes be as important as the lines actually used. Employing about the right amount of graphic elements and finding the right visual balance are characteristics of skilled and experienced artists, photographers and graphic designers. Inadequate information results in an inadequate picture. Excessive information results in visual overload making a picture hard to interpret. There is an optimum trade-off for each content and application.

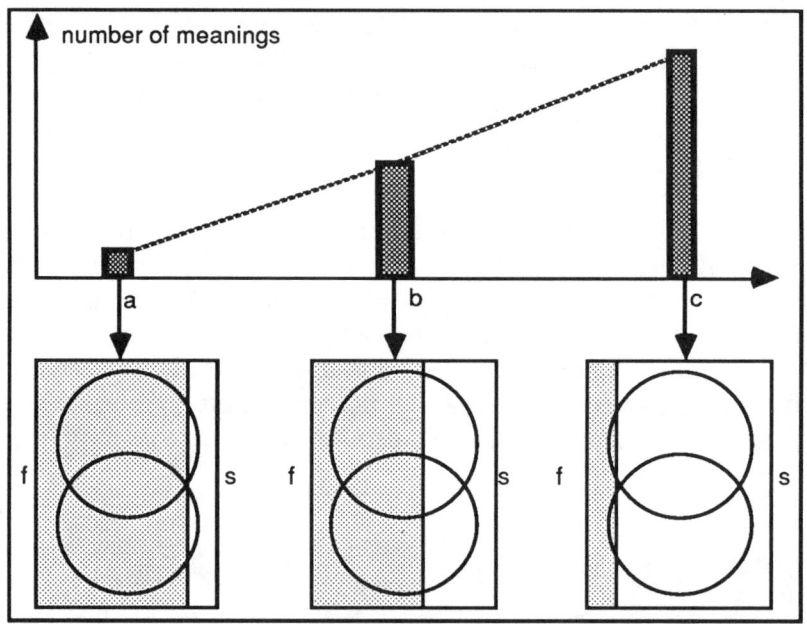

A symbol (a) usually has only a denotation and very few connotations and private associations. It is unambiguous. All other visuals have one or more connotations and private associations. They are more or less ambiguous. In realistic pictures (b), used in instructional message design, functional properties are more important than suggestive properties. In a suggestive picture (c), like a painting, the reverse is true. (f = functional properties and s = suggestive properties).

The graphic execution of a visual can be measured by objective as well as by subjective methods. The content can only be measured by subjective means. Each content has an execution, and each execution has a content. The variables in visual language have both functional and suggestive properties. *Functional properties* are related to cognitive factual information in contents, execution and context. *Suggestive properties* are related to emo-

Literacy 161

tions, conceptions, aesthetic perception, tension, fright etc. The choice of format also comprises a large measure of emotional content.

Functional properties predominate in symbols. They are also more important than suggestive properties in "informative", "information-dissemination" or "educational" pictures, since their task is to convey certain knowledge, information etc. in the simplest and most effective manner possible.

The objective of an "information-dissemination" picture is also to convey certain emotions and arouse the viewer's interest and involvement (e.g. regarding conditions in other countries or in past times).

Suggestive properties are more important than functional properties in "artistic" pictures. Art is not primarily a question of objects. It is actually a visual language for dissemination of ideas and experiences which are difficult to put across in words. Irrespective of the sender's intentions, different receivers may respond in an emotional manner to a picture with mainly functional properties. In the corresponding manner, some viewers may respond unemotionally and functionally to pictures with predominantly suggestive properties.

Examples of visual synonyms, three queens from different decks of cards. The variation between the different decks may be greater than the differences between cards of different values in the same deck, with the exception of the symbols. In several cases it is only the symbols that are differentiating between individual cards. In some cases the symbols of the suit may be integrated in the design of the figure.

Picture readability

All sighted people are capable of "looking at" a picture. But people can also learn to "read" pictures the same way they learn to read words. The language of pictures used in all media should be tailored to reader perceptions. For example, the degree of reading difficulty should gradually increase in textbooks intended for different school grades. It is reasonable to assume the following as regards pictures designed to convey information and knowledge:

- A picture that is easy to read and comprehend conveys information more readily than a picture that is hard to read and comprehend.
- A picture that evokes a positive response conveys information more effectively than a picture that evokes a negative response when motivation is identical in both instances.
- Even a "poor" picture will work when viewer motivation is high but a "good" picture would then work even better.

An easily read picture can be assumed to have greater communicative impact than a hard-to-read picture. What makes a picture easy to read?

In view of our understanding of the importance of the way a picture is executed with respect to different variables in the visual language, the author has devised a proposal for a measure of a picture's readability, i.e. a picture readability index (Pettersson, 1984). (BLIX, an acronym for this term in Swedish). BLIX values may range from 0, i.e. a virtually incomprehensible picture, to 5, i.e. a very comprehensible picture, and was initially calculated on the basis of the rating of up to 19 variables, that researchers had found being important for instructional message design. When the research started in 1979, 17 variables were directly connected to the content and execution of the visual and 2 to the context. The 17 variables were: 1 external shape, 2 external contour, 3 size, 4 color versus black and white, 5 color intensity, 6 contrast, 7 gray scale and darkness-lightness, 8 degree of realism, 9 number of details, 10 number of centres of interest. 11 location of centre of interest, 12 presence of symbols and reading aids, 13 perspective, 14 illusions, 15 subject common or uncommon, 16 size of main subject and 17 technical quality. The

Literacy

remaining 2 variables were: 18 legend, and 19 relationship between legend and picture.

The BLIX-test was constructed in such a way that all kinds of pictures could be indexed. Relations between different pictures or layout was not taken into account here. Experiments with ranking and rating of test-pictures showed that pictures with high BLIX-values were ranked and rated better than those with lower values by children as well as by adults.

2. En blåmes sitter på en gren. Blåmesen är en liten fågel, som är blå på hjässan, vingarna och stjärten. Kinder och panna är vita, undersidan är gul.

6. Den som vid utfallsanalys inte har implicit tillgång till explicit futural klärvoajans beträffande kombinations-komponentens betydelse kan med fördel använda sig av formeln $k = r_a(q_a - q_b)$.

Two of the six versions of the picture "a blue titmouse perched on a branch". The intended BLIX ratings are 5 (left) and 2 (right). Here the visuals are very much reduced and not in color.

Experiments with the actual making of pictures showed that despite detailed instructions on the execution of the visuals there was still plenty of scope for individual creativity. It was also shown that informative pictures drawn so that their BLIX-ratings were high (more than 4.5) a, were to a large extent rated as a aesthetically pleasing, b, rated as "suitable" or "very suitable" for teaching, and c, did not take more time to make than pictures with lower BLIX-ratings.

As expected, analysis of the importance of different variables showed that adults had a better grasp of picture variables than children.

Adults are therefore, naturally, better equipped than children to understand visual language. These analyses gave as a result a

164 *Visuals for information*

revised BLIX-rating-scheme that may be used as a practical tool in instructional message design.

Instructions on the execution had to be followed if reliable and satisfactory results were to be obtained.

Two of the visuals produced in the experiment with actual making of pictures. These visuals got BLIX ratings 4.8 (left) and 2.5 (right). Here the visuals are reduced and not in color.

Revised BLIX-rating-scheme
Questions   *Yes/No*
1 a) Color picture: The picture is executed in a true-to-life color.
   b) Black & white picture: The contrast and gray scale in the picture are clear.
2 The picture has a shape other than a square or a rectangle or covers an entire page.
3 The picture has a legend which is brief, easy to understand and deals with the picture.
4 The picture is unambiguous and not too "artistic", and ambiguous.
5 The picture has a dominant centre of interest at or near its optical centre (middle of the picture) and few details which can be regarded as distracting.
Total number of yes answers.   _____

The total number of "yes" answers provides a direct value for picture readability in which 0 = "a virtually incomprehensible picture", 1 = "very hard to read", 2 = "hard to read", 3 = "neither hard nor easy to read", 4 = "easy to read" and 5 = "very easy to read".

BLIX must not be an end in itself. There is always a risk associated with index values since they can be interpreted as absolute values. BLIX actually represents the average difficulty or ease with which a picture can be read. It also yields some very valuable information and detailed knowledge on the importance of individual picture variables. The ability of the receiver to study the contents of a word-picture message is likely to increase considerably if the word-picture is designed with this in mind. Knowledge of picture readability, i.e. our total ability to interpret and understand a visual message in terms of our *perception of the content, execution and context of the visual, enables us to make a visual description* .

A visual description is a description in words and outlines of a visual which does not yet exist. The accuracy with which the intentions of the instructor are carried out can subsequently be checked, at least in part, by means of picture analysis, i.e. an evaluative description of a visual, and partly by means of various practical tests. The results of these tests lead to a revised visual description which leads to another still more effective instructional material etc. in a spiraling process of feedback interaction.

Picture Quality

A question such as "what is good or poor picture quality?" may seem trivial. But there is no widely accepted definition for "picture quality" nor any unambiguous or sufficiently comprehensive measure of this parameter.

Any visual produced to convey information or knowledge must obviously contain the information to be conveyed. Such a visual's content, execution, context and format elicit a response, a perception, and possibly subsequent learning and memory. The information producer should produce representations in such a way that perception, on the average, is optimized.

The sender of a message must define the objectives for each picture used. What emotions and information should the image convey? Who is the receiver? And in which medium will the visual be distributed? Correspondingly, the receiver (viewer) should attempt to identify the sender's intentions. Which emotions and information are conveyed by the picture? Who is the sender? What are the picture's apparent objectives?

Which pictures are "good" and which pictures are "bad"? In this context, "good picture quality" can be defined as the degree of coincidence between the sender's and receiver's subjective perception of the picture and the reality (external or internal) represented by the picture.

According to this definition, the concept "picture quality" is related to the entire communications process, encompassing both sender and receiver, representation and reality.

A "good" visual has a high level of picture quality. It is well worth reading and is executed so as to be legible and readable and be displayed in an optimum context in an appropriate format. The visual should convey information without ambiguity. It should be stylish and attractive and is often, but not necessarily, also aesthetically pleasing.

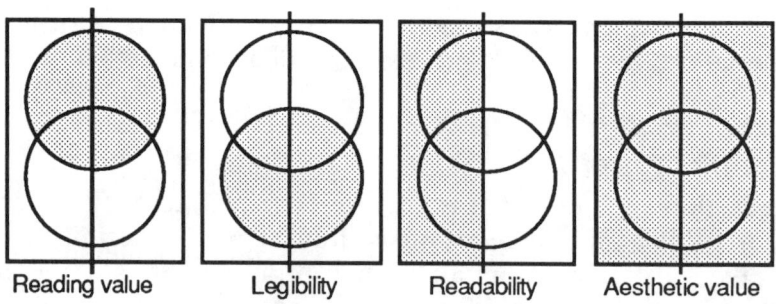

Reading value   Legibility   Readability   Aesthetic value

A visual is well worth reading and has a high reading value when the content is interesting to the reader from a functional and/or from a semantic point of view. The legibility is mainly depending on the execution of the visual. The readability is mainly depending on the functional properties of the visual. The aesthetic value of a visual is a combination of all the different variables.

A "poor" visual has a low level of picture quality. It displays poor legibility and poor reading value. It conveys information poorly, is seldom aesthetically pleasing and often ambiguous.

Reading value is governed by picture variables related to picture contents

Legibility is governed by the functional properties of picture execution.

Readability is governed by the functional properties of picture variables. A picture's aesthetic value is the aggregate effect of all picture variables.

Measuring picture properties

There are several ways of "measuring" picture properties. These "tools" can be used before the original is finished, before the technical production and after the actual publication of the images.

Before the original

A picture description can be drawn up on the basis of our knowledge of man's ability to interpret and understand a visual in terms of perception, contents, execution, context and format. A "picture description" is a depiction in words and sketches of a visual that does not yet exist.

Before technical production

OBS and reading value ratings

Larssen and Skagert (1982) employed two "preview tests" in order to assess reader response to as yet unpublished advertisements. A simple interview test provides a good forecast of future OBS (observation) and reading value ratings. The two central questions were (p.28): "1) If you encountered this ad in a newspaper, would you stop to look at it? 2) If you encountered this ad in a newspaper, do you think you would read any of the text in it?" When numerous subjects respond affirmatively, an ad can be expected to receive high OBS and reading value ratings. The opposite is also the case, i.e. if numerous subjects respond negatively.

Utility/Originality rectangle

The second preview test entailed assessment of ads according to the concepts "utility" and "originality". First, the extent to which the reader derived any benefit from reading or taking a closer look at an ad was rated. The rating scale ranged from "no utility" to "great utility". The degree of execution originality was then assessed. Ads with positive originality and great utility (field 1 in the "utility/originality" rectangle) were usually subsequently rated as "good ads" by readers. Publication of an ad with negative originality and little or no utility (field 4) is virtually pointless.

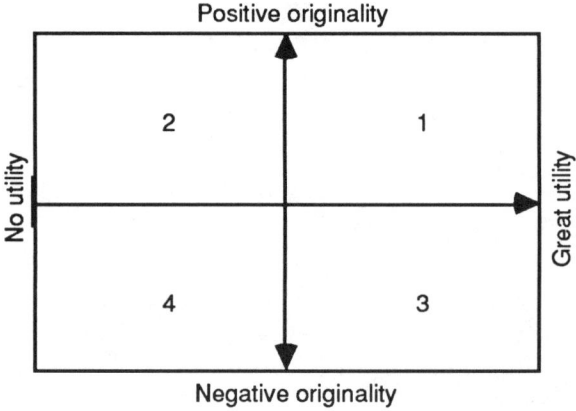

The "utility/originality" rectangle.

Redundancy/Information
Berefelt (1976) suggested that experience grows in steps in the power field lying between events previously observed and not observed, between the familiar and unfamiliar and between banality and originality. The greater the amount of information supplied (the less the redundancy), the greater the amount of energy needed by the information recipient in order to register and comprehend the new data. Berefelt used a horizontal line with maximum redundancy and maximum (new) information as the line's theoretical end points to describe registration and processing of stimuli. Maximum redundancy elicits complete familiarity with the material, e.g. a picture. Maximum information elicits a total inability to comprehend the signals. Our perception of different pictures probably falls between these two extremes. Berefelt assigned seven proportionally spaced perception positions from an

infinite number of possible positions on the line. These perceptions, from a high degree of redundancy to a high degree of information, were referred to as "boring" (unpleasant), "neutral", "harmonious" (pretty?), "fascinating" (nice), "interesting" (exciting), "neutral" and "irritating" (unpleasant).

A picture creator who is very familiar with her/his target group can easily ensure that redundancy/-information in a picture is on a level relevant to the picture's aim. The redundancy factor provides the picture creator with an opportunity to relate viewer perceptions to picture contents.

Redundancy/information/communicative impact
A refinement of Berefelt's ideas could result in a model that also includes consideration of the communicative impact of pictures. Our perception of a picture probably affects the picture's communicative impact. Pictures found to be boring or irritating are likely to have poor communicative impact. However, a picture perceived to be "wonderfully fascinating" is bound to be very good in communicative respects. The fact that the communicative impact of a given picture may differ for different people must obviously be kept in mind. Different people also respond to the redundancy factor in different ways depending on e.g. previous experience, social factors and cultural circumstances. So for these reasons, plus the fact that identification of the degree of both redundancy/information and communicative impact may be difficult, the model may be unsuitable for use in practical work.

Interest/Perception
In a world in which it is becoming increasingly difficult to avoid unsolicited information and, at the same time, increasingly difficult to find information we really wish to find, our interest in material may be decisive to the way in which we perceive that material. Interesting material arouses our emotions to a greater extent than material we regard as boring. The degree of interest can be described with a rating between "no interest at all" and "maximum interest". So the interest factor is one way to define the viewer's relationship to picture contents. When interest is zero, our emotional response is negative or, possibly, indifferent.

170   *Visuals for information*

Emotional response increases as the interest factor increases and becomes increasingly positive. However, a given picture may evoke different emotional responses in different people, even when they share a common degree of interest in the picture. Different people also perceive the interest factor in different ways. As is the case with the Redundancy/ Information/ Communicative impact model, the Interest/Perception model may be hard to use in practical work.

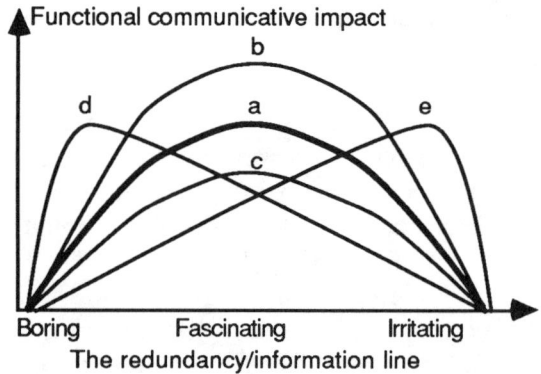

The redundancy/information/communicative impact model (a). The communicative impact of a given picture may differ with different people (b and c in this example). Different people also respond to the redundancy factor in different ways (d and e in this example).

The Legibility/Reading value rectangle
A picture can also be rated according to legibility and reading value. First, the extent to which the picture is readable for the intended reader is rated. Does the picture have considerable reading value and interest or does it have poor reading value and little interest? The picture's legibility is then rated. Is the picture distinct and easily read or is it indistinct and difficult to read with a view to its execution? An informative picture with positive reading value and legibility (field 1 in the "legibility/reading value" rectangle) is probably "very good". A picture is "good" if it is readable but difficult to read. The picture is "bad" if it has limited reading value and is easy to read but "very bad" when it has poor reading value and is also difficult to read. Initial experiments

Literacy

suggest that a preview test of this kind could prove to be very useful.

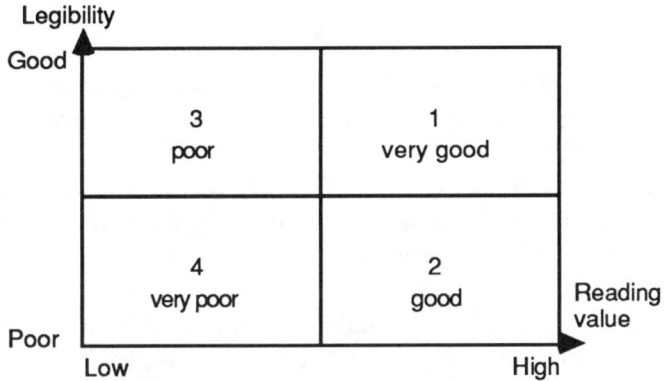

The "Legibility/reading value" rectangle.

Picture readability index
A picture's readability can be assessed by calculating the BLIX-value.BLIX was designed for informative pictures. It takes functional picture properties into consideration and is a measure of the ease or difficulty with which a picture can be read. A picture that is incomprehensible is incapable of conveying any factual information or knowledge. Its functional, communicative impact will then be very slight. The greater the readability of a picture, the greater its functional, communicative impact. Different people obviously respond in different ways to different pictures.

In the corresponding manner, a suggestive communicative impact can be discussed as a function of BLIX. The correlation here is the antithesis of the previous correlation since the suggestive, communicative impact is high when the BLIX rating is low and low when the BLIX rating is high.

After publication
A picture analysis, i.e. a descriptive rating of a picture, and various practical tests can be carried out to determine whether or not an information disseminator's intentions are accurately realized.

The results of these tests can be used for revision of the picture description which, in turn, could result in even more effective informative material etc.

Picture analysis

A picture analysis can comprise a description and, possibly, a rating of picture language, contents, execution, context, format, medium, distribution method, sender, receiver, objectives etc. Different sets of questions can be used in picture analysis depending on the objective of the analysis. The following questions may be useful in a brief, general analysis.

- *Visual language.* Is the visual language clear and distinct? Is the visual language adopted to the culture and to the audience? Is the picture's "meaning nucleus" obvious? Does the picture contain a lot of insignificant information?
- *Content.* What is (are) the subject/s in the visual? Is (Are) the subject/s easy to understand? What are the relationships of the different subjects? Is one part of the picture dominating over the others and why? Is the picture a typical or a non-typical example of the subject? What is the degree of realism and details? What is the degree of credibility? How are motion, time, sound and emotions expressed?
- *Execution.* What type of visual is it? Is the subject large and clear? What is the shape, size, color and contrast? How is the composition in terms of organization, centres of interest and balance? What are the depth, picture angle and picture height? What is the technical quality like? Does the picture have symbols and explanatory words?
- *Context.* What is the context? Is there a legend, texts, other pictures or sound in connection with the picture? How is the layout done?
- *Picture readability.* What is the picture readability index?
- *Medium.* In which medium is the picture used? Is the picture used in mass-media, in group media or in personal media?
- *Distribution.* How is the distribution organized?
- *Sender.* Who is (are) the sender/s? Who is (are) the producer/s? Are the views of the sender important to the use of the picture?

- *Receiver.* Who is (are) the receiver/s? Do the receivers form a homogeneous group? Is the group small or large?
- *Aims.* Why has the picture been produced? Has the picture been produced for advertising? Are "hidden" intentions imbedded in the image?
- *Impact.* Is the picture likely to have an effect on learning, human feelings, attitudes or opinions? What impact is it likely to have?

The various preview tests can also be transformed into true readability tests. The results of these tests can also lead to revised picture descriptions...

Peterson (1984) is working on an analysis of comic strips and has proposed the following model (p. 104) based on a semantic approach.
- An analysis of the storyline. Which hidden values do the figures represent? How are conflicts presented in the story? How are conflicts resolved? Are any myths created?
- An analysis of picture structure and meanings on both denotative and connotative levels. When characters conveying meaning are interpreted, both internal and external context are taken into consideration.
- An analysis of the importance of balloon texts.
- A study of the location of emphasis in the communications process.

This should lead to identification of the comic strip's function, e.g. to be poetic or challenging. How is imagination employed? In an emancipative, compensatory or power-confirmative manner? Which attractive properties do the pictures have? Fascinating, aesthetic shapes? Do they play on any particular emotions, needs or dreams? Which dialectic relationships prevail between the strip's design and e.g. receiver context?

Values and attitudes
Semantic differential scales in which the sender and/or receivers report how positively or negatively they respond to a given picture in overall terms or with respect to individual picture variables

can also be employed in measuring how "good" or "bad" a picture is.

Semantic differential scales can comprise e.g. general attitude toward a picture (Bad - Good), aesthetic value (Ugly - Pretty), reading value (Uninteresting - Interesting), technical quality (Poor - Good), legibility (Hard to read - Easy to read), educational value (Slight - Great) and credibility (False - True). The combination of verbal *and* numerical scale steps makes possible statistical calculations of e.g. mean values, standard deviations and confidence intervals. This makes the method very suitable for large groups of subjects.

Classifications of visuals

A visual always has a sender and a receiver, as can be seen in the communications models. A visual also has a content seen in the image. The visual is executed e.g. as a drawing. It is structured or executed e.g. according to size, shape etc. The visual has a physical form, a format, e.g. as a 35-mm slide. The visual is used in a context, e.g. as an illustration in a textbook.

Visuals can be classified according to various criteria such as sender, receiver, content, execution, format and context and even according to criteria such as function, use and the means of production etc. Thus, there are many possibilities for classification. However, one and the same visual can and will be classified in different ways at the same time depending on the criteria applied. Often the borders between different groups partially overlap each other. The following is an attempt to exemplify one model of classification.

The Picture circle

Many visuals are made to affect us in one way or another. Pictures which affect us in an unambiguous way can be referred to as *symbols*. Signposts, traffic signs, labels etc. belong to this category. They are unambiguous by convention. We agree and decide on their meaning. All other pictures are representations of reality and depict the physical structure of the objects they represent. As is the case for other kinds of representations, pictures are always open to different interpretations by different people at different times. Some pictures are open to many interpretations, others to only a few.

Ambiguous pictures, which often express moods and emotions, are usually referred to as *suggestive pictures*. Even here the creators of the pictures are out to influence the viewer in some way. Paintings often belong to this category. It is often difficult and sometimes impossible to make clear distinctions between different kinds of pictures. Advertising pictures, propaganda pictures, pictures for information or instruction or educational pictures can be both ambiguous and unambiguous.

The role of a picture for instruction may be to convey a given piece of information in the simplest and most effective manner possible. But the picture may also have the task of conveying moods or to arouse the viewer's interest and involvement by disseminating certain information. An example of the latter might be information on conditions in other countries.

Objective documentation of a product, situation or course of events by means of X-rays, ECG, EEG, satellite photographs, thermographic pictures, ultrasonograms, photographs, drawings and charts is often necessary. These pictures are frequently *realistic* and simulate reality in ways unique to each documentation process. Apparently objective documentation can occasionally be extremely subjective and suggestive when the choice of images, the cropping, layout and caption contents are overtly selective. The expression "the camera never lies" can often be very wrong indeed!

As far as ambiguous pictures are concerned, there is often a major difference between their denotation, i.e. their literal meaning, and their various connotations, i.e. their associative meanings. By e.g. exaggerating perspective, deforming shapes, making symbolic use of colors etc., a picture creator can easily create works which evoke extra associations in viewers. This is in fact the very idea behind an artistic picture. However, the informative picture should not be open to different interpretations. The picture's message should then be the message intended by the person/agency commissioning the picture.

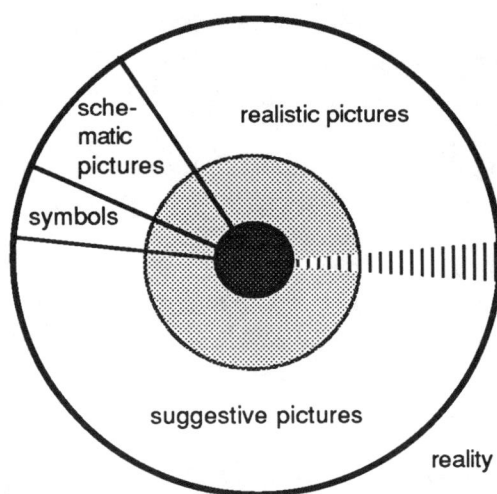

This is the picture circle. We have symbols, schematic pictures, realistic pictures and suggestive pictures. The borderline between realistic and suggestive pictures is indistinct. Scribble (the dark spot) is followed by handicrafted visuals (grey) and technically crafted visuals.

A hand-crafted visual such as a painting, drawing, diorama or sculpture takes a long time to make, is highly personal, exists only in individual, unique copies and only reaches a narrow public. Pictures made by children, for example, often display considerable spontaneity and reveal a great deal about the personality, degree of development and maturity of the children. In all hand-crafted pictures the relationship of information presented to reality is totally controlled by the artist. Photographic pictures are records of an event or object which actually existed.

Technically crafted visuals can be made in a relatively brief space of time and easily reach a wide public. A TV camera can take live pictures viewed simultaneously by millions of people in different countries. In this way, we can "attend" various happenings, such as sporting events, no matter where they occur. The ease with which news pictures can be produced and distributed may influence the selection of pictures. Sensational events, such as a disaster, may be assigned a relatively large amount of space in the mass-media because pictures such as these attract widespread interest. Here, the mass-media people bear an enormous responsibility in their editing and selection of pictures.

Hand-crafted pictures are now easy to reproduce in newspapers, books, television etc., but the technical reproduction processes do rob them of some of their original character. The halftone dots of the printing process or the special characteristics of electronic images are incapable of doing justice to e.g. a painting made with vivid colors and applied paint. This is even more true for sculptures, dioramas and other 3-dimensional pictures. In the future, holograms, stereo and laser techniques may hopefully solve some of these problems and re-create the third dimension. Current methods for making 3-dimensional pictures still require considerable development.

The manner in which we perceive a picture and the efficiency with which the image communicates the image creator's intentions depend not only on the technical reproduction method chosen but even on the manner and presentation to a large degree. We often need help and guidance in order to interpret a picture's message. Different captions or sound effects enable us to respond to one and the same picture in widely differing ways. This is especially true of moving pictures. The relative size of the picture, cropping, lighting and the location on the cover of a book or newspaper page are also important to the way in which the picture is perceived by people with differing values, feelings, attitudes, experience, background knowledge and philosophy. Pictures often serve as amplifiers, i.e. the viewer often readily accepts information verifying his own opinion on a given issue.

Pictures are always related in some way to reality. But they must never be confused with reality and are incapable of replacing reality. The "picture circle" is an attempt to provide a simple graphic description of the relationship between different types of pictures. The spot in the centre, the "bull's eye", represent scribble which is the same all over the world and our first attempt to make pictures.

Increasingly advanced picture techniques have evolved from scribbling. This development can be represented with a series of concentric circles. Scribble is followed by handicrafted visuals. Drawings with a pencil, charcoal, crayons and pens; paintings in water colors, acrylics, oils etc. simple flipover moving pictures, castings, models and sculptures of clay, plaster-of-Paris, wood, metal etc. are all examples. The borderline between handicrafted and technically crafted visuals is indistinct. Some picture techniques represent both hand-crafted and technically crafted methods. "Hand-made" prints, linocuts, etchings, lithographs, serigraphs etc. are examples. All handicrafted pictures can now be reproduced in any quantity desired with the aid of processes such as letter-press, offset, intaglio printing etc.. Examples of other technically crafted pictures are different types of machine-made prints, photos and films, electronic pictures, thermographs, radiographs, ultrasonograms, ECG and EEG records etc. The outermost circle is occupied by various 3-dimensional pictures such as holograms. In the future, they should be capable of making the closest conceivable approach to the reality surrounding the circle.

Every ring in the circle encompasses *symbols,* such as signs, signposts etc., *suggestive pictures* with mythological representations, artistic pictures, advertising, propaganda pictures, news pictures etc., *realistic pictures* for objective documentation, and *schematic pictures* such as blueprints and maps etc. The borderline between realistic and suggestive pictures is indistinct. Some visuals may be considered as suggestive pictures in one context but as realistic pictures in another context.

Symbols
Taking up only a very small amount of space, symbols can convey a message containing a large amount of varying information, equivalent to one or more sentences of text. Image perception is very rapid, virtually "instantaneous". Reading and comprehending the equivalent message in words takes much more time. So symbols permit *rapid reading.* This is important in numerous situations, e.g. in traffic, industry and aviation.

Symbols are often composed of simple graphical elements, i.e. lines, circles, ovals, squares, rectangles, triangles or combinations thereof. Distinctively shaped letters are often utilized.

Symbols often employ bright colors, such a pure yellow, red, blue or green, white and black or combinations of same.

Shape and color components are often used for designating a link or relationship between groups of messages. In traffic, for example, a triangle is used for warning signs, a circle for restriction signs and a rectangle for informative signs.

A good symbol is designed so it can be used in many different situations. For example, the McDonald's M is designed to work in every conceivable size from a few millimetres high in a brochure to more than six feet high in outdoor signs.

Symbols can be used for *creating an overview* and providing a holistic perspective. This property is utilized in maps and informative signs as well as in e.g. catalogues and project reports.

Symbols can be used for *supplying instructions and information* about appropriate behaviour in different situations. Numerous examples can be found in catalogues and timetables. Various traffic signs also belong to this category.

Symbols can be used for *illustrating* the spatial and geographic *position* of different objects or services. One example is the floor plan of an exhibition hall with symbols designating the location of telephones, lavatories, information booths and refreshment sites. Other examples are maps with numerous cartographic symbols for objects and conditions.

Symbols can be used for illustrating size relationships and supply numerical/statistical information. Some diagrams and many symbols in maps are examples.

Symbols can be used to represent an organization, service or product. Trademarks and logos are utilized in marketing, advertising, public relations etc. As a rule, promotion of the representation begins with text (e.g. a company or product name), followed by text + a symbol. Ultimately the symbol alone suffices. Examples: McDonald's yellow M and Shell's scallop shell.

Symbols are employed in different media. They are static and immutable in graphical media. They may be more changeable in computer media. When you select e.g. a brush in the menu for a Macintosh drawing program, the brush icon switches from positive to reverse video. This "acknowledgement" shows the user that the command has been understood. This makes communications more "reliable".

Every situation/context demands consistent utilization of symbols, an explanation of the symbols used and learning the meaning of those symbols. Well-designed signals can be used and work in different cultures in different parts of the world.

Computer pictures

Computers are currently capable of displaying many kinds of pictures on their monitors. Rapid technological innovations constantly increase the range of images displayable by computer. Computer-displayable pictures are always converted to digital form at some stage, i.e. a series of zeros and ones. The computer can process picture information as *vector* or *pixel* images. A vector image is based on mathematical functions and composed of lines and closed polygons. A pixel image is composed of a large number of individual picture elements, i.e. pixels whose gray scale and color scale are variable. The following classification, based on picture function and intended use, is proposed to facilitate discussions of various issues in the field of "computer pictures". Computer pictures may be classified in four groups: 1. Computer processed pictures, 2. Pictures analysed by computer, 3. Computer generated pictures and 4. Computer distributed pictures.

1 Computer processed pictures
Computer systems are being used to an increasing degree for editing, correcting, processing, retouching and supplementing the contents of pictures for e.g. books, magazines or other printed matter or for slides or overhead transparencies. The basic picture, such as a drawing or photograph, must be digitized with the aid of a scanner or special video camera. The computer can then feed the digitized images to some peripheral such as a laser printer, dot matrix printer, plotter, film or printing plate.

Satlight was used for the first time during the 1984 Los Angeles Olympics. Pictures were scanned, compressed by a computer, processed and sent by satellite to a receiving station in London. Pictures were stored on magnetic tape and distributed to various newspapers.

2 Pictures analysed by computer
Pictures analysed by computer may be divided into the following two groups: 1. Measurement pictures and 2. Photographic pictures.

2.1 Measurement pictures

Measurement pictures are representations of various measurements in e.g. medicine. Ultrasonograms and CAT scans are examples of pictures employed for identifying differences in the density of body tissues. The brain's activity can be visualised and measured with a positron camera. Measurement of thermal radiation is another example.

2.2 Photographic pictures

Photographic pictures are of several origins. Satellites with multispectral scanners continuously record and transmit digital TV images of the Earth. These images are analyzed and used for many different purposes in meteorology, geology, agriculture and forestry. The interpretation of satellite pictures is a widespread activity. Photographic pictures are also used for a wide range of military applications.

3 Computer generated pictures

The "concept computer-generated pictures", i.e. computer graphics, is employed in many different ways. However, image generation by computer is the common denominator. Computer generated pictures may be divided into the following four groups: 1. Computer art, 2. Information graphics, 3. Design pictures and 4. Entertainment graphics.

3.1 Computer art

Computer art is a young art form comprising visual presentations whose aesthetic aspect predominates. Computer art consists of images created on an interactive basis and of images and patterns generated at random. Computer art often contains animated sequences and is displayed at e.g. exhibitions, art galleries etc. Computer art can also be displayed on paper. Image information is often stored pixel by pixel, and not as mathematical functions.

3.2 Information graphics

Information graphics may be divided into several subgroups (See Lexi-visual representations: Infography). Business and news graphics.are often generated by computer. Sales, stock or production statistics are often illustrated with graphics. If the values of individual variables are stored separately, the user is often able to illustrate the information in different ways. Histograms, bar charts, pie charts or curves are examples of the options available. The graphics are usually reproduced on film (as a slide or overhead transparency) or paper. Grahics are being used to an increasing degree for presenting information in research and development.

3.3 Design pictures
Design pictures comprise the subgroups drawings, maps and patterns.

Drawings, two-dimensional representations of mathematical descriptions of objects, can be generated by various CAD (computer-aided design) systems. The systems are often able to "twist and turn" a depicted object to show it from different angles before the object ever leaves the drawing board stage. Car parts, ships, aircraft, machinery, buildings etc. are examples of objects being designed with the aid of CAD. CAD systems are often used in conjunction with CAM (computer-aided manufacturing) systems.

Maps are successfully produced in CAD systems, combined with vector systems. The systems make it easy to change both the scales and contents of maps.

Patterns, e.g. for textiles are also produced in CAD systems. But these CAD systems can also be used for producing patterns for e.g. wallpaper, wrapping paper and book covers.

3.4 Entertainment graphics
Entertainment graphics such as electronic games and animations are also produced in computer systems. Many kinds of interactive *electronic games* are on the market. Players manipulate space ships, robots, heroes and bandits in fantasy worlds. The electronic games often feature dramatic colors, symbols, changes in perspective and sound effects. Developments move at a furious pace. Only a few years ago, graphics were very primitive, but their sophistication and resolution have been vastly improved. Animation is becoming increasingly commonplace. Computers are being used to create advanced animation effects in *movies, TV*

and video. Some examples of computer-animated 3-dimensional films in color were shown at the 1985 Tskuba Expo in Japan.

4 Computer distributed pictures
Computer distributed pictures may be divided into the following two groups: 1. image data bases and 2. Fax.

4.1 Image data bases
Various forms of videotex belong to this category. They all entail transmission of information via the ordinary telephone network. Several online systems have very high transmission capacities.These systems usually store their information on magnetic media.

Optical storage media have a much greater text and picture storage capacity (hundreds of thousands of documents on each storage unit) than magnetic media. Each of the stored documents can be quickly retrieved and displayed on a screen or printed as hard copy if desired. *Filing* is a main application for optical storage media.

4.2 Fax
Fax is a collective designation for electronic copying and transmission of text and/or pictures to a receiver in which a facsimile of the transmitted information is reproduced .

Picture archives
Pictures are now being created more rapidly than at any time in history. Millions of pictures are produced every day. Sweden alone (with a population of 8.3 million) accounts for more than 200 million amateur photographs each year. And each of the country's 2,000 professional photographers produces a half million photographs before retiring. Many pictures are put to active use in various ways. But a large proportion end up in collections. Some collections evolve into archives. There are four main types of archives:
- Personal, private collections
- Commercial photo agencies

- (Personal) research archives in different fields
- Collections in museums and other public institutions

Many photo collections are small enough to be accessed without any special index. The owner knows which pictures she/he has and where they are stored. This ease of access is no longer possible in large photo archives holding hundreds of thousand or even millions of photographs. So a large number of different indexing systems have been devised. Pictures may then be indexed according to category, motif or subject. Era, geographic area and persons may be other classification concepts. Accession and negative indices and information on the dates photographs were taken, copyright etc. may also be provided. Commercial photo agencies usually permit direct, manual and visual perusal of originals or copies in each category. The feeling here is that the indexing or cataloguing of individual photographs takes too long, costs too much and conveys no decisive advantages. Institutional photo archives, as used in research and education, are usually unable to manage without some kind of cataloguing. Many indexing systems are based on hierarchic classification of picture subjects according to some pre-determined code or on systematic catalogues in which every index word has a corresponding alphabetical or alpha-numerical designation.

The Inconclass system, developed in Holland, has a systematic catalogue on theological subjects. The system is often used for classifying artistic pictures. Each picture can be assigned a classification comprising a few index words/codes. The method is based on a description of the picture's main subject. Picture details and minor subjects cannot be indexed .

Many museums use Outline, i.e. OCM (= Outline of Cultural Materials), for classifying pictures. Outline was designed to be a general classification and code system for social and cultural subjects and operates with computerized routines. However, finding codes (headings) which describe true picture contents is as hard with Outline as Iconclass. So classification is influenced by the perceptions of the individuals doing the coding. This makes it difficult for a visitor to find pictures complying with her/his requirements. Similar results have been obtained with many systems in other countries. The Iconograhic Archives in

Uppsala, in Sweden, employ a system with a much finer "mesh". Here, pictures with subjects in the field of ethnology/cultural history (e.g. ethnographic or folk-loristic scenes) are recorded. The date a photograph was taken, its country of origin and the source are recorded for each picture. After an analysis of the picture contents, the main subject and minor subjects are then recorded according to a systematic code catalogue subdivided into subjects. The entry of search conditions combined in different ways results in fast computer extraction of information on whether the desired picture subject is on file.

Results obtained in the U.S. suggest that classification and searches based on various code systems seldom work satisfactorily at large picture collections or photo achieves. Greater success has been obtained at archives in which search words are listed alphabetically for each subject. Modern computers are capable of processing plain language search words as easily as more succinct codes. Utilization of plain language words obviates the need for users to rely on archive specialists or learn special code systems when searching for a subject.

APIS (Agency & Photographer Information System), developed in the Federal German Republic, is a computerized system for managing picture archives and all the administration related to the lending of pictures and selling of rights. A serial number, heading number, a key word describing pictures contents, the photographer's name and the copyright holder are recorded for each picture. This information is printed on a label which also bears an optically legible bar code. The label is attached to the back of prints or to mounts of transparencies. All captions are stored in a database for full text searches. Desired photographic subjects can therefore be accessed very quickly. Photographs can be filed in numeric order or by subject (heading). The latter system makes it possible to conduct manual, traditional searches. The bar-code is read with a light pen for rapid entry of information on all pictures borrowed and returned. The system also supplies invoicing, bookkeeping, statistics, detailed reports to the photographer and other copyright holders etc. plus other administrative information.

Spectrum, the Dutch publisher of reference books, has developed an advanced system of databases for both text and picture administration (Thesaurus). The company has indexed 45,000 illustrations, each accompanied by information on up to seven parameters. These pictures have been published at 90,000 locations in different reference books, in various sizes, with different cropping etc. The computer system contains all relevant information on the illustrators/ photographers, copyright, costs, disbursements, archive locations of originals and films etc. The system offers several different ways of searching for pictures by means of search words.

Picture databases
The ability to store photographs in a database for simultaneous display of pictures and texts would be an attractive option to most people with a picture archive and facilities for database searches of indices or texts. A picture stored in digital form requires a vast amount of storage space compared to text. So some systems employ analog storage of pictures. An optical video disc is capable of storing up to 100,000 PAL-TV-quality images, i.e. 250,000 pixels per picture. Pictures are individually numbered and can be sought and displayed within seconds. Spectrum has stored its 45,000 pictures on a single analog, optical videodisc. The disc is used as a kind of "catalogue" in marketing the picture archives. A customer can obtain all the facts about a sought photograph on computer screen at the same time as the photograph is displayed on a TV monitor. A similar system has been developed by Image Bank, in collaboration with Brignoli Inc. in New York. Video discs holding picture archives provide people in different parts of the world with access to pictures previously unavailable to them. Art treasures from the world's leading museums can be displayed to the public, scientists and educators using this medium.
    Within the work of a computer based access system to image content the Dutch encyclopedia publishing company, Spectrum, experimented with models for image classification. An image classification system makes sense only if different classifiers apply the same objective criteria to the image and subsequently different picture researchers are able to locate the same illustration. In a first experiment in 1979 twelve editors had to classify 25

pictures by using catch words. Results showed a correlation as low as 0.2. In a following experiment a questionare regarding categories combined with requests for description was used. In this case the correlation was 0.67. In the final system, 1983, all indexing is made in the computer with a calculated correlation of 0.80, which seems to be very good.

The "International Veterinary Pathology Slide Bank" has been transferred to a video disc at the University of Georgia in the U.S. However, indexing the pictures has proved to be extremely difficult (Trice, 1986). Veterinary experts have been unable to agree on the most essential feature of each slide. So assigning multiple headings and index words for each picture is necessary. Full text searches are then made in a database. The Dutch publisher VNU New Media announced in 1986 their videodisc MEDDIX data with a collection of 30,000 medical slides for diagnosis and training. This system uses a highly advanced computerized thesaurus with cross-references between key-words. Images are also accessed by the use of a free-text database. In 1986 "The National Iconographic Research Center" in France also announced an interactive videodisc with 100,000 medical images with their captions. Even in systems in which text and pictures are stored on the same medium and displayed on the same screen, searches for picture contents can only be made, in practice, by means of verbal descriptions of main or minor subjects.

A large number of indexing systems has been devised to guide access to individual images (Pettersson, 1986a). However, real life experience, as mentioned above, shows that it is often very hard to find the intended image. It is known from several experiments that images are perceived in many different ways by various subjects (Pettersson, 1985, 1986 b). Even simple line drawings evoke many associations. Vogel et. al. (1986) showed that image-enhancement intended to improve interpretation of image content sometimes got in the way of the message. They concluded that image-enhancement graphics should be used selectively and carefully. When in doubt, they recommended, plain text should be used. Limburg (1987) pointed out that receivers have even more ambiguity or semantic diversity with visual images than with most expressions of written language with its manifold meanings. Lodding (1983) reported on the problems with misinterpretations of icons used in computer systems. However, he concluded that people find naturalness in dealing with images either as an aid to or, in some circumstances, as the sole means of communicating.

A picture in a database can be sought with the aid of verbal and visual indices. Each picture has a picture number as a heading and a verbal description. The pictures can be listed systematically in numerical order in a numerical index. Or they can be listed in alphabetical order (according to their headings) in an alphabetical index. Picture descriptions are stored in a free-text (or full-text) database, making it possible for users to access a picture via a number of different descriptive terms.

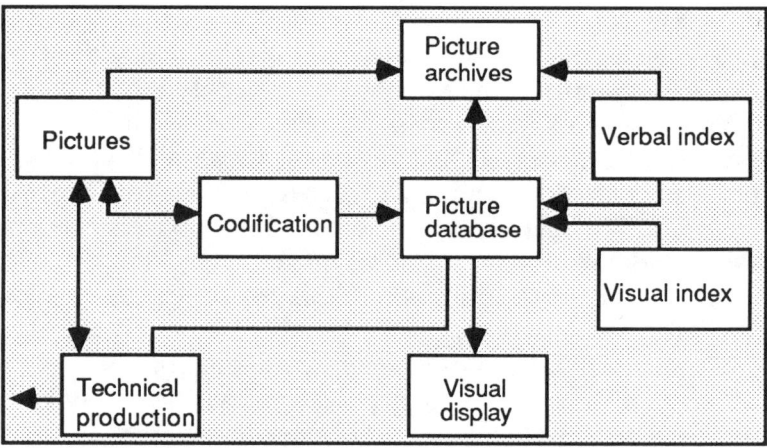

In picture archives pictures are stored as objects, that is as originals or as copies. This is a *primary storage*. For storage in picture databases a transformation of the image content to analogous or digital signals is needed. This is a *secondary storage*. Individual images can be found with the use of a verbal and/or verbal-numerical index. For technical production and e.g. mass communication pictures are taken from picture archives and image signals are collected from picture databases.

A verbal description of a picture should be rather comprehensive. It may sometimes apply to an entire picture series. A database search based on certain descriptive terms could produce several different pictures with the same description. All such pictures would then be displayed in separate "windows" on the terminal screen. Entry of a command causes full-screen display of

Literacy 189

any of the windowed pictures. For children it might be easy to point with a finger at the window on the screen. Pictures can be stored in files stored in other files etc. in a kind of a tree structure. When a file containing pictures is opened, the file contents are displayed in "windows" which can be as small as 1.5 x 1.5 cm. Thus, verbal searches are used on higher levels and visual, iconic searches on lower levels in the storage structure. Users who knows in which file a desired picture is resident can go straight to that file. Index searches are employed when the whereabouts of a given picture is unknown.

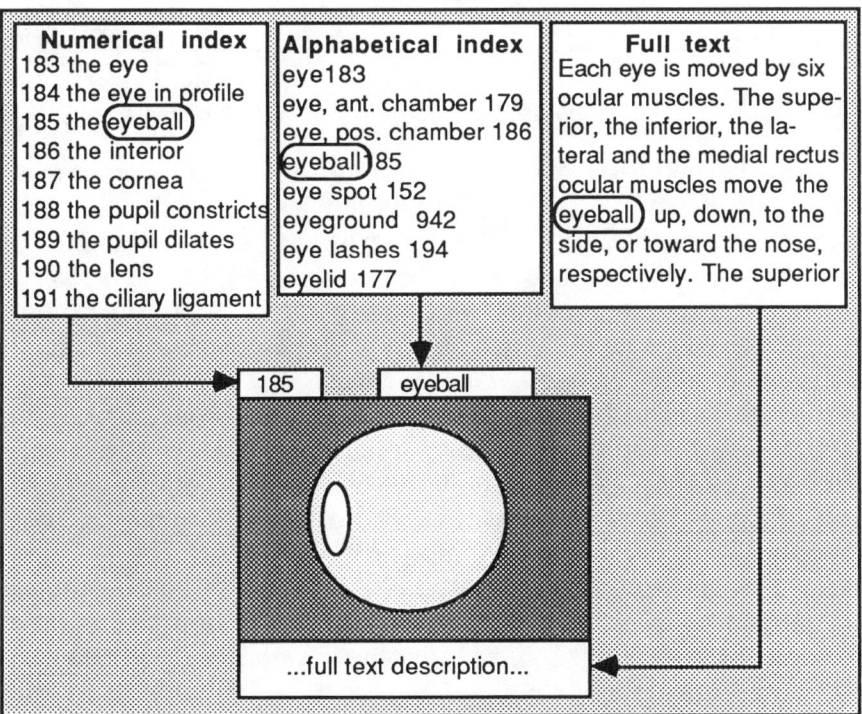

A verbal search for a picture. Examples are taken from a numerical index, an alphabetical index and a free-text database.

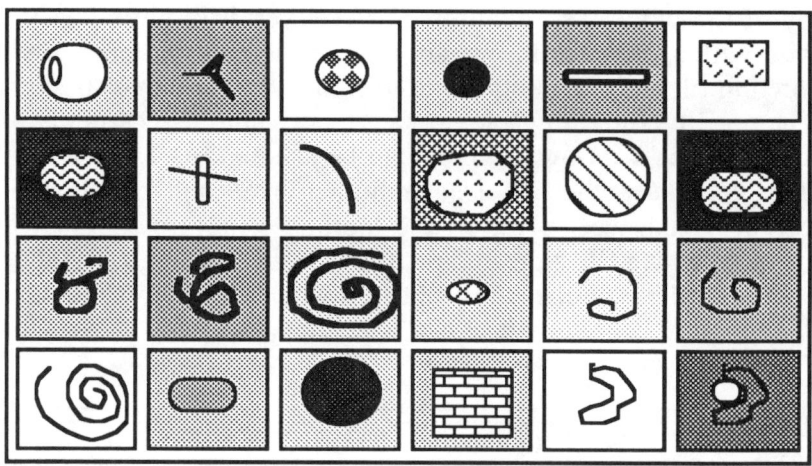

A visual search for a picture. Examples of "windows" shown on the screen.

Batley (1988) experimented with retrieval of pictorial information from a database on a videodisc. The videodisc was created specifically for the experiment. It contained 950 photographs selected from a collection of 40,000 photographs by a Victorian photographer. The photographs were arranged into broad subject groupings such as: Cathedrals, Castles, and Rivers. A program in the authoring language Microtext provides access to the database. The program allows users to scan through images in the database using a joystick ("serendipitous browsing"; step through groups of related photographs ("specific browsing"); or type in key-word descriptors ("key-word search"). Summary files keep a record of each user's interaction with the database. Users may request text information about the photograph currently displayed on the screen and store a record of photographs they retrieve. The findings indicate that the search strategies adopted by users are dependent upon two factors; the nature of the information need, and the individual user characteristics. Batley offers three proposals for the design of visual information systems:

1 Emphasis should be on providing a range of search options for the user - to accommodate both narrowly defined and exploratory searching and to accommododate individual user preferences.

2 Care must be taken in the design of the user interface - the emphasis should be on ease of use - so that the system is accessible to both naive and expert users.
3 Some attempt should be made to individualize searching - by allowing users the option of selecting their own range of scanning speeds, choosing between menu selection and typing commands, choosing which input devices to use, designing a screen layout, etc.

Research is being conducted on the possibility of using a computer to search picture files for image structures or patterns. So far, these system have very limited capabilities and are only being employed in e.g. industrial robots programmed for taking certain components from a conveyer belt and creating assemblies with other components. Developments are most advanced in the military sector, e.g. in target-seeking missiles capable of reading terrain and comparing readings to a pre-programmed map and a predetermined route to the target.

But there is yet another major, unsolved problem, since one and the same structure may occur in different pictures. Empirical studies (Pettersson 1987) have shown that subjects given a number of image elements combine them to form many different picture contents.

Picture dimensions

The development of different compact discs will open up fascinating, new opportunities to producers of e.g. teaching aids. They will make it possible to create "the total teaching aid" encompassing text, sound, pictures, numerical information *and* opportunities for various kinds of information processing in a single medium. A "total teaching aid" is a multimedia database offering the user complete freedom in moving back and forth between verbal, numerical, visual and audio information. This will enable children (and adults) with all kinds of modalities, i.e. verbal, visual, kinesthetic or mixed modalities, to actively seek and find information which is actively transformed into experience and knowledge. (Cf. Duffy 1983 for a discussion on modality). In supplying answers to assignments or writing reports, students will have easy access to the necessary background information. They will also be able to retrieve suitable examples, i.e. "quotes" from the individual databases, and incorporate them into their own presentations. Numerical information in tables, for example, can be processed and presented as bar charts, curves or pie charts providing a better overview. (Cf. Pettersson 1984 for an overview). A teaching aid could also contain different kinds of computer-based educational games and the like.

Kindborg and Kollerbaur (1987) point out that the use of graphical interfaces has made computers easier to use for people who are not computer experts. Visualization of system status and of on-going processes has enhanced the user's understanding of how various computer-based tools work and can be used. The Dynabook system (Goldberg et. al., 1977) and the desktop metaphor of the Xerox Star system (Smith et. al., 1982) and their successors are well known examples of graphical interfaces. One reason for their success is that the visual presentation techniques employed communicate the model of the system to the user in a clear way. In addition, interaction with a graphical interface is often considered to be stimulating and fun. In fact it is easy for a child to learn to use graphical interface computers like the Apple Macintosh.

Every published photograph has been involved in a selection process, not just once but repeatedly. First of all, the picture creator (photographer or artist) makes an extremely narrow selection from all the pictures which could be created on any given occasion. The picture editor then makes a selection from numerous alternatives in a collection or archive. As far as drawn illustrations are concerned, a number of alternative sketches often serve as the basis for discussions on the appearance of the final originals. So a picture only depicts a selected slice of reality, one person, one object or one event, for example, always surrounded by undepicted things and circumstances occurring before and after each selected picture. Most graphic products can only display a rather limited number of pictures depicting a situation. However, an optical/electronic system is capable of storing an extremely large number of pictures which need not be cropped as severely as "print published" pictures. So the user has a greater opportu-

Literacy 193

nity to utilize picture information as a "resource", "information bank", and retrieve information that is relevant and of interest on any given occasion.

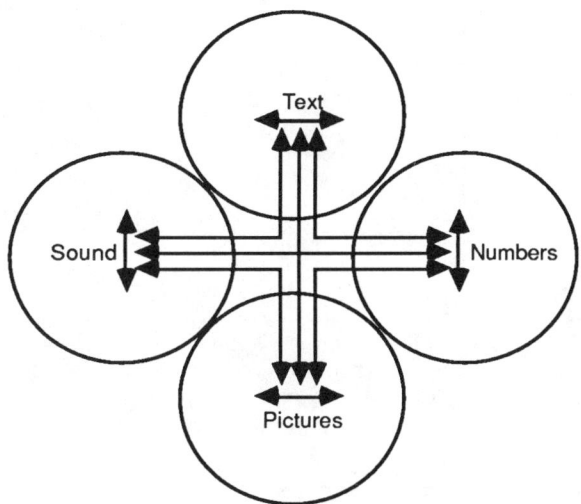

Search options in databases with verbal, numeric, visual and audio information. There are always four ways to proceed. The user can remain in the same database or switch to any of the others at ease.

A stored image is much larger than the image displayed on the screen. Only the central part is displayed. The entire picture can be viewed by scrolling the screen image up or down or to the side. Horizontal and vertical rulers with cursors outline the position of each displayed image window.

Here, electronic media are completely superior to all traditional media. For economic reasons, a book cannot contain multiple versions of a picture with different croppings. The sender's perception of what is important is the deciding factor in the choice of the picture selected for publication. With use of the "total teaching aid" the user of the system, the learner, can decide what is important to her or to him.

194 *Visuals for information*

The central (lighter) part of the image is displayed when the system starts. The image shown on the terminal screen is outlined by the inner frame and cursors. Here and in the following (printed) examples only a small picture is used (four times the size of the screen). Much larger pictures can be stored.

Scrolling the image up or down or to the side provides access to the entire image. Here, the viewing window has been shifted so the segment at the top left is the one displayed on the screen.

How can you get an overview? The stored image can be shrunk to a fraction of its normal size so the entire image fits on the terminal screen.

Literacy   *195*

The picture has been shrunk (in this example to one-fourth) so it all fits on the terminal screen.

How can picture details be viewed? You can zoom in on any detail displayed on the screen by enlarging that part of the image, thereby changing the scale. The result is like viewing part of the picture through a magnifying glass. If sufficient computer and storage capacity is available, stepless enlargement or fixed, multiple degrees of magnification could be allowed. Image magnification or shrinkage does not change image contents but it can have a major impact on image perception.

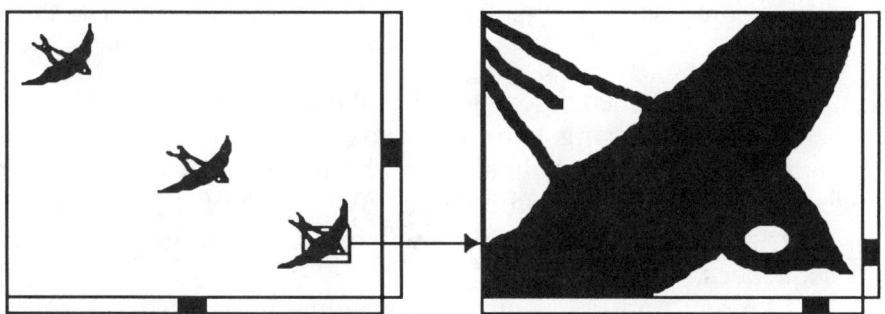

Enlargement of a detail in the framed section of the image can fill the entire screen. You can gradually zoom in on any section of the displayed image.

Possibilities for enlargement is already available in several systems. In the future this will probably be standard and with better and better performances.

How can an image be processed? Modern, computer-based systems for processing graphical images offer wide-ranging opportunities for simple editing and *manipulation* of image contents. In addition to changing scale, as previously mentioned, the user can change projection, crop or expand, reduce, delete, modify, move, turn, supplement, isolate or combine various image elements. (See Picture editing: Changes of image content). Pictures can be stored as object oriented descriptions, in bit-mapped form or as a combination of same.

Computerized image processing offers incredible opportunities. However, copyright laws and ethical rules make free use of these opportunities impossible. Manipulation or counterfeiting of image contents are condemned. In commercial situations the contents of a picture may not be changed without the expressed consent of the picture's copyright holder.

Entire picture sequences can be stored. This supplies information on "before" (picture to the left,) "now" (picture in the centre) and "after" (picture to the right).

What happened before and after the displayed picture? Picture sequences depicting various events can be stored instead of individual pictures. Animation, with the option of freezing each component image, could be used. By the use of advanced computerized image compression it will also be possible to show live sequences.

Among traditional media this technique is used with great success in comic strips. Comics are usually examples of presentations where text and pictures are highly integrated. Producers of teaching aids and producers of encyclopedias may learn a lot from the creation of comic strips.

Are additional levels possible?The displayed picture is a basic picture. It can be stored with several different overlays containing supplementary information in the form of various symbols, such as terms in different languages. This gives us an opportunity to adapt and structure information by rising above the picture plane.

Literacy

In certain instances, the user can also descend below the picture plane.

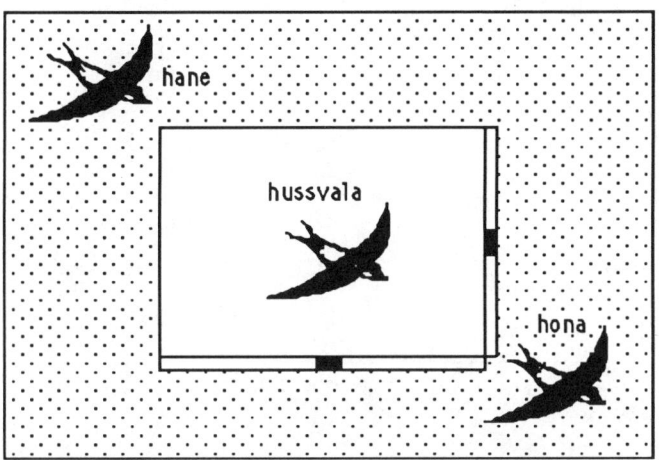

Example of a basic picture with an overlay (the words "hane", "hussvala" and "hona" are Swedish for "male", "house martin", and "female").

Experiences from the use of overhead transparencies may by used to guide production of several overlays.

How can you understand a picture? Pointing at different image elements opens one or more windows to other databases with information on picture contents. This information may comprise explanatory text or additional pictures. Pointing at a word in the text opens new windows containing even more detailed information etc. Sound can be used in some contexts. In an "electronic dictionary", for example, spoken words are displayed on the screen. Thus learning is enhanced. Music and sound effects can also be used.

How are text and pictures combined? Use of the windowing technique and electronic "clippings" makes it easy to combine images and text or parts of texts in the creation of new documents.

Examples of windowing. Only the window frames are shown. Here the text is only indicated.

Ferm, Kindborg & Kollerbaur (1987) point out that the computer as an aid for learning is far from having reached its potential. Its applications in education have mainly been restricted to the drill-and-practice of programmed instruction. Kollerbaur (1983) developed an approach where the computer is an aid or tool for learning. This approach is based on cognitive theories for learning, focusing on the learner and the learning problem rather than on the technology. It was concluded that:
- the learner should be active and creative
- the interactive system should be used to solve problems in the educational situation and improve learning
- programs should provide access to the special qualities of the computer as a means for handling, communicating and presenting information
- the system should only be used when existing methods and other aids are insufficient
- users (teachers and students) should be able to influence the systems, which consequently have to be flexible
- the systems should be easy to learn and use

So far computer systems have not been able to fulfil these requirements. Most of the options discussed earlier exist already today in various systems. Developments are very rapid. New

Literacy

products and new systems are released all the time. We can be sure that *"databases of the future"* will offer completely new options of very considerable theoretical interest.

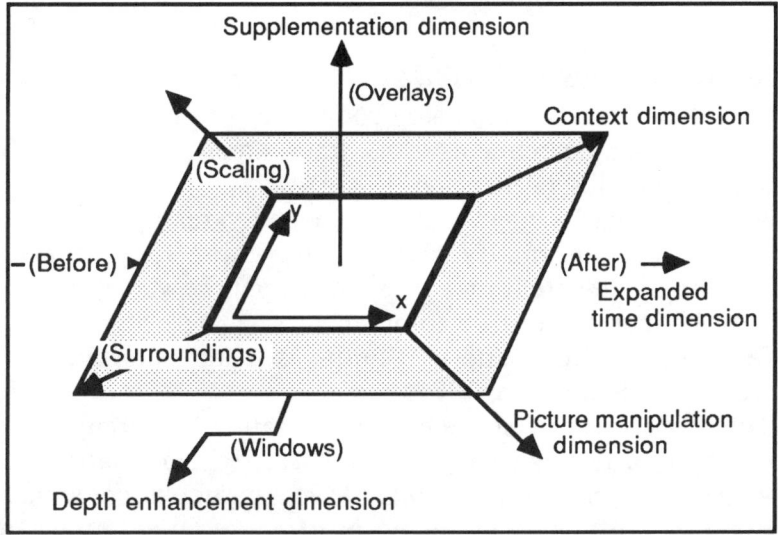

Databases of the future will offer completely new options of very considerable theoretical interest. Pictures get new dimensions.

A picture printed in a book is twodimensional. It has width and height (x and y axes). A time dimension develops when we study a picture. One comprehensive study of eye movements (Cf. Pettersson 1986c for an overview) showed that we read pictures in many different ways. We also select different picture information in different situations (Pettersson 1987a). The "total teaching aid" and the "total encyclopedia" employ some of the best qualities of the existing media. Furthermore new qualities are added. As our previous examples showed, *new dimensions* can be added to pictures stored in a database. We can attain an *expanded time dimension* by "before-now-after" picture storage. Or we can expand to a *movement dimension* by the use of animation. A *context dimension* is attained by not cropping too severely and retaining elements around the main subject. A *picture manipulation dimension* occurs when we enlarge, shrink, change projection, crop or expand, delete, change, move, turn, supplement, isolate or combine different image elements in new ways. Departure from the picture plane and utilization of overlays provide us with a *supplementation dimension*. We can attain a *depth-enhancement dimension* by employing windows opening on other databases.

Characteristics of visual languages

- Visual languages have analog coding employing combinations of basic graphic elements (dots, lines, areas and volumes) for depicting reality (Pettersson, 1983a).
- Visual languages attempt equivalence with reality. Visuals are iconic. They normally resemble the thing they represent. Meaning is apparent on a basic level, but the visual language must be learned for true comprehension. There are major differences between the concepts "seeing", looking" and "reading" (Pettersson, 1986a).
- The properties of visual elements are rather wide-ranging. For example, a dot can vary with respect to size, shape, color, value, grain, position and it its use in a particular context. The execution of basic elements is often of vital importance (Pettersson, 1983a).
- Visual languages have varying levels of meaning (Pettersson, 1983a).
- Guide-lines and conventions differ. Several variables and a structure can be described for visual language (Pettersson, 1983a).
- Visual languaging abilities develop prior to, and serve as the foundation for, verbal language development (Reynolds-Myers, 1985).
- Development of visual languaging abilities is dependent upon learner interaction with objects, images, and body language (Reynolds-Myers, 1985).
- The level of visual language development is dependent upon the richness and diversity of the objects, images, and body language with which the learner interacts and upon the degree of interaction (Reynolds-Myers, 1985).
- The level of visual language development is facilitated by direct learner involvement in the process and equipment used to cre-

Literacy 201

ate objects, visual images, and body language (Reynolds-Myers, 1985).
- Picture perception is relative. Different people perceive and describe one and the same picture in different ways (Pettersson, 1985 & 1986b).
- Perception of two- or three-dimensional representations entails fast, parallel, simultaneus, and holistic processing (Gazzaniga, 1967, Sperry, 1973 & 1982).
- It may take only 2-3 seconds to recognize the content in an image (Paivio, 1979, Postman, 1979, Pettersson, 983b), but 20-30 seconds to read a verbal description of the same image (Lawson, 1968, Ekwall, 1977) and 60-90 seconds to read it aloud (Sinatra,1986). In verbal and visual languages prior experience and context are very important to the perception of contents.
- Retrieval from memory involves parallel processing of memories (Paivio, 1979, Sinatra, 1986).
- Memory for pictures is superior to memory for words (Paivio, 1983). This is called the "pictorial superiority effect."
- Memory for a picture-word combination is superior to memory for words alone or pictures alone (Haber and Myers, 1982).
- An intended subject/content can be depicted with many different pictures (Pettersson, 1986b).
- Pictures with different executions may still have the same basic content (Pettersson, 1986b).
- Abstract content is expressed by concrete execution (Pettersson, 1985).
- Concrete content has no abstract execution (Pettersson, 1986b).
- Certain basic image elements are more important to the perception of the image content than others (Pettersson, 1986b).
- Pictures with abstract contents can be perceived in more ways than pictures with concrete executions (Pettersson, 1986b).
- Databases of the future will offer completely new options of very considerable theoretical interest. Pictures get new dimensions.

LINGUISTIC COMBINATIONS

Different combinations of linguistic expressions are usually employed in mass-communications. For example, a text-book or newspaper generally utilizes both the printed word *and* pictures. A TV program employs words *and* images *and* sounds such as music. Interesting effects can be produced by the combination of various linguistic expressions, thereby heightening interest and attractiveness. We get more interested in the material and pay attention to it. The results of several experiments show that learning is maximized when the contents of visual, audio and print channels are on the same level (cf. Levie and Lentz, 1982, for a review). Conveying information through both verbal and visual languages makes it possible for learners to alternate between functionally independent, though interconnected, and complementary cognitive processing systems. The cited categories yield 62 ways of combining spoken and written language, sound effects and music, symbols and pictures when producing representations of reality We have no designations for most of these combinations, and the designations we do have are often misleading. *AV* or *audio-visual* are common designations illustrating the problem. You never know exactly what is meant by the term "AV." It may refer e.g. to the use of slides *or* to slides with audio cassettes. The slides may contain images with pictorial content *or* images with verbal content *or* both. Braden and Beauchamp (1986) make a distinction between "reader slides" and "picture slides".

More distinct, specific designations are necessary to any serious discussion of linguistic expressions and different kinds of representations. There is no practical need for designations covering all the combinations possible. However, we should at least be able to distinguish between the categories "spoken language" and "written language" in the "verbal languages" category. Sound effects and music could be placed under the heading "audial language". Symbols and pictures could be referred to as "visual languages". This would leave a smaller, more easily managed number of combinations.

Literacy 203

In *verbal languages* spoken language or "audial verbal" (or "aural verbal") can be designated *oral.* Written language or "visual verbal" or "graphic-verbal" may be designated as *lexigraphic.* Combinations of these may be referred to as *oral-lexigraphic.* Examples of such representations are texts recited in a theatre, radio program or on audio-tape.

In *audial languages* both sound effects and music are *audial* (or aural). Examples may be found in radio programs and audio tapes.

In *visual languages* both symbols and pictures are *visual.* Symbols are used e.g. for traffic signs. Pictures can be found almost everywhere, usually in combination with verbal and/or audial languages. Paintings, drawings and other objects of art often stand alone. (Paralinguistic visual expressions are not discussed here).

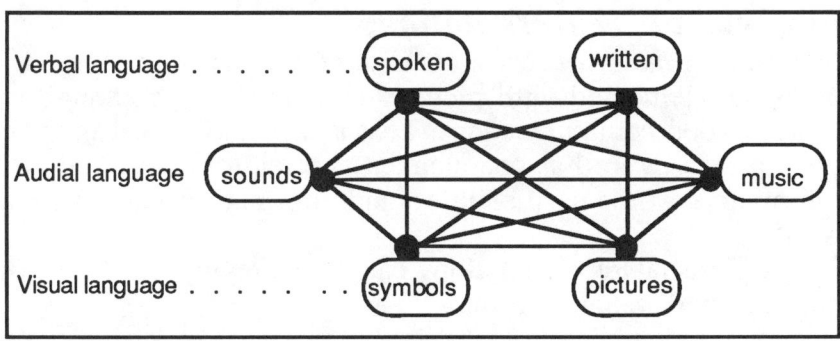

Many combinations of linguistic expressions are possible.

Combinations of *verbal language + audial language* can be designated *audio-verbal*. This designation can be used in describing representations on radio, audio tapes, records and compact discs.

Verbal language + visual language can be designated *verbo-visual* and sub-divided into *oral-visual* (e.g. a filmstrip with a spoken commentary) and *lexi-visual* (frequently found in books, magazines and other printed matter).

Audial language + visual language can be designated *audio-visual*. Many artistic slide-tape shows and multi-image presentations employing images, music and sound effects belong to this category.

Verbal language + audial language + visual language may be designated **verbo-audio-visual**. Motion pictures, television and video programs belong to this category. Audio-visual or verbo-visual films, TV shows and video programs are also possible and sometimes necessary.

However, this theoretical model may not be practical to use in everyday life. Based on how the *verbal information* is presented to the recievers we can distinguish between two forms of verbo-visual information. We *read* text in lexi-visual representations and we *listen to* speech in audio-visual representations (the term audio-visual is used here in the traditional sense as a designation for sounds and visuals).

Lexi-visual representations

Information materials often consists of text. This text is sometimes supplemented with pictures. But this is not enough to achieve good communications. Text and pictures must both be easy to read as well as complement and reinforce one another. Informative words need pictures, and informative pictures need words.

Lexi-visual representations can be manually produced or manufactured graphical media.

Interplay of text and graphic design
It is not enough for text to be well-edited, easy to understand and interesting. Text must also have a *typography* facilitating its legibility. Headings, sub-headings, main text, legends, boxes, summaries etc. must be clearly distinguished from one another. This must be accomplished in a purposeful, structured way. For example, the intermixing of an excessive number of fonts, point sizes and typefaces in the same document should be avoided. As a rule, a little space left between different text categories can contribute to the creation of a harmonious, functional product.

Literacy 205

Reference material, such as telephone catalogs, dictionaries etc. are examples of highly structured information. Here, a carefully thought-out, functional layout can facilitate the reader's ability to find the desired information quickly, easily, effectively and reliably.

A few examples of text pages.

Interplay of text and pictures
A picture without a caption has no or almost no informational value. A picture is too ambiguous on its own. A picture caption must describe the picture and guide the reader to the interpretation the informer wished to convey to the reader. (See Context: Interplay of words and visuals, Legends).

Interplay of text, picture and graphic design
Both words and pictures may possess an emotive force which is not easily foreseen. A number of different value judgements could slip into a text when the purpose of the text was merely to supply information. The reader's emotions could be aroused by seemingly insignificant details in a visual or nuances in the wording of a text. So sufficient effort must be invested in the editing of both texts and pictures. Interest can be centered on the central message in pictures through careful picture selection and editing, primarily by means of cropping. Sometimes different visuals benefit from being presented in a group. This may be the case for a photograph and an explanatory drawing, or several photographs or drawings forming a mini-series or related picture sequence.

When texts and visuals are collected for informative pages and spreads, "message transmission" must be a central consideration. This kind of information layout" differs from a "decoration layout" in which purely aesthetic aspects are allowed to predominate. (See Context: Layout).

A few examples of pages with text and pictures. Each picture has a legend.

Cartography
The preparation and production of maps is called cartography. The product of a cartographer's efforts is a mathematically defined depiction of a reality based on measurements. Maps describe reality and shed light on a number of conditions, such as terrain, political subdivisions, the prevalence of certain types of soil, minerals etc. The utilization of variations in shape and color creates map symbols which provide a picture of the reality they represent. A carefully processed map contains more information per square inch than any other form of printed information.

Infography
A particular message is sometimes presented through the purposeful integration of text, pictures and graphic design into clearly delineated and structured areas, i.e. a functioning whole. This design, i.e. the execution of verbo-visual information, is sometimes referred to as *infography*. The results of this work is a product called *information graphics, infographics, the "third language"* or just *"graphics"*. This infographic product is often interspersed with text and visuals in an information layout. (However, the terms "graphics" and "third language" are often used as synonyms for infography, leading to confusion).

Literacy

Information graphics are informative and may be entertaining. They aid communication, enable better understanding and comprehension. Information graphics are attention-getters when they appear on a page in a newspaper. They may improve readability and increase retention. In the past, information graphics were produced by hand - a tedious work process. Today many information graphics are produced with computers. Ideas can be tested in less time and good solutions may be found. In the case of newspapers, information graphics can be the key to attract new readers and holding on to old readers.

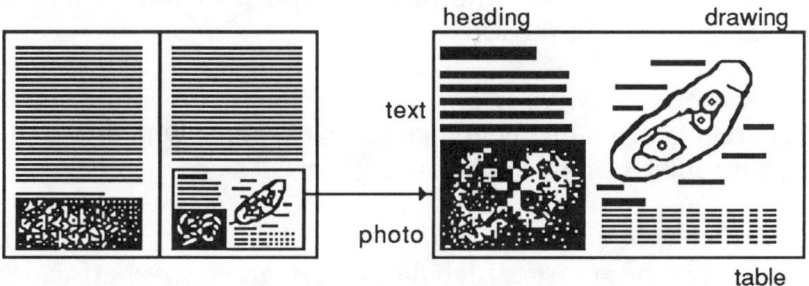

An information graphic is a "functioning whole". It has both text and visual/s. In this example an information graphic is used in a book as an illustration.

Information graphics provide the reader with a rapid and easily grasped overall view of a message and are therefore highly suitable as an introduction to and summary of a subject. However, conventionally illustrated text is better for analysis, discussion and study of details. So information in graphical media can utilize text, pictures, information graphics and graphical design in conveying its message.

We should note that the word "graphics" can be used for completely different concepts.
1. One or more art forms in which copies can be made on paper or the same original.
2. Activity involving the printing of the written word.
3. Integrated presentation of text, pictures and graphical design, in e.g. the daily press, information graphics.
4. The technique of presenting data in the form of figures on a video display screen.

Decorative and *artistic graphics* can also be found in both newspapers and television. Even though informative graphics can be both decorative and aesthetically attractive, the informative function always predominates. So purely decorative and artistic graphics are not information graphics

Objectives
Information graphics can be classified according to different criteria such as objectives, medium, size, and time for production. One specific graphic may very well belong to several of these groups. We can produce information graphics in order to achieve several different objectives.

1. Instruction graphics are used for instructions, e.g. in instruction manuals. Instruction graphics may deal with how to use e.g. a machine or how to prepare e.g. a meal step by step.

2. Presentation graphics depict facts and are often used for different types of statistical tabulations. A graph or chart can be integrated into a symbolic image to heighten impact and identify the subject. Presentation graphics are often used for "business presentations". They are often called *business graphics*.

3. Explanatory graphics depict the ways things were, are or will be, for example the weather. These graphics are ranging from simple drawings to complex combinations of drawings, maps and photographs.

4. News graphics are used to convey all kinds of news that are fit to see rather than to read as a printed story. News graphics are found in e.g. newspapers and some magazines, and also in television. (Also see Time for production, next page.)

5. Signal graphics are small-scale graphics used to add impact and visual relief to a text.

6. Locating graphics are used to give the physical location of an event or of an object. Based on one or more maps, movements of

Literacy

an object can be explained. Maps are often also included in other kinds of graphics.

7. *Expo graphics* are used at exhibitions and trade fairs. A subject matter is presented using verbo-visual technique and the real objects. The graphical information may aid understanding of how the real objects can be used.

Media

We encounter information graphics in many different media. In *graphical media* (books in particular), information graphics are often referred to as *lexivision* or lexi-visual information. In the corresponding manner, *lexigraphy* is a special version of infography for lexi-visual presentation of text, pictures and information graphics in graphical media and computer media. ("Lexigraphy" also encompasses the production of information graphics as a teaching subject at the Danish schools "Den Grafiska Højskole" and "Skolen for Brukskonst"). Graphics are called *reference book graphics* in reference books and *dictionary graphics* in dictionaries, encyclopedias etc. News graphics are found in e.g. newspapers and some magazines, and also in television.

Time for production

The American national daily newspaper USA TODAY has been a pioneer in the field of *news graphics* and has acquired imitators in many different countries. "News graphics" is a summarizing designation for several somewhat differing forms of information graphics. Due to available time for production news graphics can be divided in several groups.

1. Daily graphics is generally produced against tight deadlines. News must be published in the next edition or in the next TV news slot.

2. Planned graphics is the designation for information graphics which the editors of news graphics have a few days to produce. This provides more opportunities for checking facts and more carefully thought-out execution.

3. Feature graphics is a general designation for information graphics which describe more timeless subjects, such as popular science. Here, the producer may have several weeks or even months to create the copy and acquire the photographs.

4. Facts graphics is a general designation for graphics conveying facts.

5. Business graphics are found in computer programs and newspapers (See Computer pictures). Business graphics is a general designation for information graphics which present economic and statistical data, for example: "the production of crude oil over the past five years".

6. Weather graphics are information graphics describing what the weather has been like and how it is likely to be according to available forecasts. The weather graphics in USA TODAY have inspired a large number of dailies to introduce information graphics. Weather graphics are found in TV and newspapers.

Audio-visual representations
Audio-visual representations can consist of "speech and visuals" and "recorded representations".

Speech and visuals
An oral presentation can consist of speech alone, but this is usually not enough to guarantee the best possible communications. One vital basic condition which must be met in all oral communications is that listeners are able to hear what is said without difficulty. So one or more microphones and suitable loudspeakers may be needed when presentations are in a large hall with a large audience. Ensuring that all technical equipment really is working properly is important.

When making an oral presentation, you should use a relaxed voice and an appropriate voice volume, vary your speed and insert pauses at appropriate points. An oral presentation must not be too long. A presentation will often benefit if the speaker can illustrate her/his speech with real objects or employs visuals as aids. Speech and visuals complement and reinforce one another. A summary and detailed information can be supplied as written documentation after an address. Informative words need visuals, and informative visuals need words.

Speech and body language

Speakers always use body language in their oral presentations. This use can be intentional or unintentional. Gestures, mimicry and the method used for presenting material often clearly reflect the speaker's feelings about the subject. Body language should agree with the subject. Otherwise the message's credibility will suffer. A speaker must be visible to her/his audience. The unconscious mannerisms of many speakers irritate audiences. So some speakers hardly recognize themselves on video.

It is important for speakers to adapt their messages to the audience in question and the latter's interests. A message should be conveyed in an active, stimulating manner. The speaker must establish direct contact with the individual members of the audience and ensure that the information is received and understood. A listener cannot back and review the information as when reading a book. So beginning and ending a presentation with a description of the subject is important. This enables the audience to grasp the entire subject in the best possible manner. Leaving time for questions is also a good idea.

Speech and demonstrations

Displaying real objects or e.g. conducting demonstrations in giving audiences a chance to see concrete examples of things mentioned in an oral presentation is almost always useful. Letting listeners even examine or touch objects is even better. The use of authentic sound effects can enhance the mood or sense of reality. Demonstrations attract the audience's interest, reinforce its perceptions and increase its ability to understand a message.

Speech and stills

Pictures should be used when a subject cannot be exemplified with real objects. Stills can be used for supplying structure and an overview, exemplifying, summarizing and reinforcing a message. Stills can consist of text "key words" ("reader slides"), tables, diagrams of various kinds, drawings or photos. Avoid excessive detail. All visuals used should be to the point and readily understood.

In brightly lit rooms, a lecturer can write or draw on the classic (and more often green) *"blackboard"* or *flip chart*. Use of a *flannel board* and flannel pictures requires more preparation but can be very effective, especially when the audience consists of small children.

Overhead transparencies need overhead projectors and a reduced lighting level in the room. Texts must be brief and concise. Letters must be large and distinct (bold face and never less than 5 mm high) for good visibility in a "normal" classroom. Bigger letters are needed in larger rooms. A horizontal format is best. A basic overlay transparency can be successively complemented with one or more overlays.

A dark room is an advantage when showing *slides*, unless equipment for rear projection is available. A slide image should fade in and out of a dark background.

An *episcope* i.e. a projector which projects opaque visuals (e.g. pictures in a book), is sometimes available. *Computer-generated visuals*, displayed with the aid of a TV-projector, are becoming increasingly commonplace. In all projection, the image must not be obscured, and the lights should be turned on as soon as darkness is no longer necessary. In darkness, the audience is unable to see the speaker's body language, and the speaker is unable to see the audience's reactions. This disrupts the communications process.

Speech and moving pictures

A course of events that is hard to depict with stills and demonstrations or that is difficult or dangerous can be exemplified to advantage with the aid of moving pictures, i.e. movies, video, computer animation or TV. A sequence only lasting a minute or so

Literacy 213

may be enough. Video is then an excellent aid. The speaker can insert the moving sequence at the exact right point in the presentation. A sequence can also be repeated if necessary.

Recorded representations

These representations convey information with combinations of audio-visual presentations, i.e. text in the form of e.g. speech and text signs, different kinds of sounds, stills and moving pictures in color or black and white. We can distinguish between two main categories: "linear use" and "interactive use".

Linear use

"Traditional" information and training programs belong to this category. They can be produced with cinema or video techniques and distributed as film prints, video cassettes or video discs in various formats. Material can also be distributed as TV programs, terrestrial or satellite broadcasts and/or via cable systems.

Interactive use

Computer-controlled, interactive programs or databases intended for information and training belong to this category. It is possible to create e.g. "total information material" containing text, sound, visuals, numerical information and opportunities for the user to process information in different ways. (See Picture dimensions.)

CURRENT RESEARCH

In the information society people are being exposed to an increasing volume of "messages" from many different senders. The messages are transmitted from senders to receivers with the aid of different media. In all communications (even in mass-communications), many individuals are the recipients of the messages.

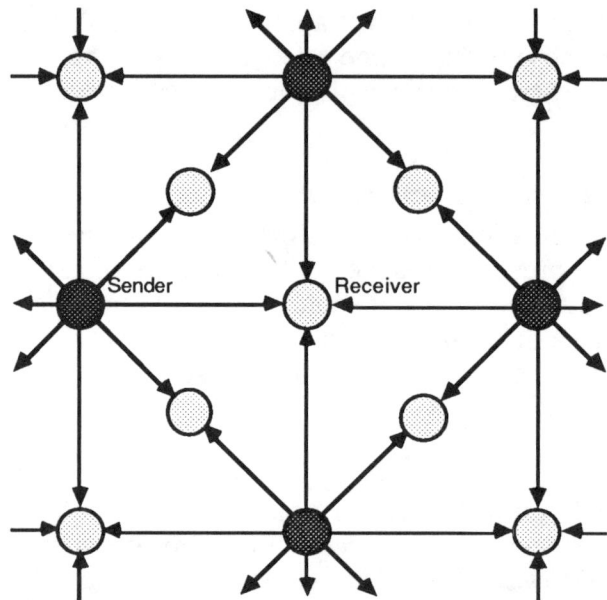
Many individuals are the recipients of messages from many different senders.

How do we receive information about the outside world? We can smell, taste, feel, listen, see and examine our surroundings. We can also ask questions. We ultimately learn to interpret and "read" different coded messages, such as those contained in e.g. text.

Here are some examples of current research issues with the emphasis on *the communications process*
- Interaction of text, pictures and graphical shapes in verbo-visual messages.
- Intended vs. perceived content. How should a presentation be designed for optimum impact?
- Terminology.
- A holistic approach.
- Information bases on new media.
- Text and pictures in databases.

The production of a message commences with an idea occurring to someone or with the need to convey information to a given target group. When an outline is ready, the generation of text, draft sketches, editing, graphical design, the production of origi-

Literacy

nals, masters and, ultimately, a given quantity then begin. The sender produces a representation of reality. A representation is a medium with specific contents, i.e. a message. Other tasks for the sender are stock-keeping, distribution, marketing, advertising, selling, billing, bookkeeping etc.

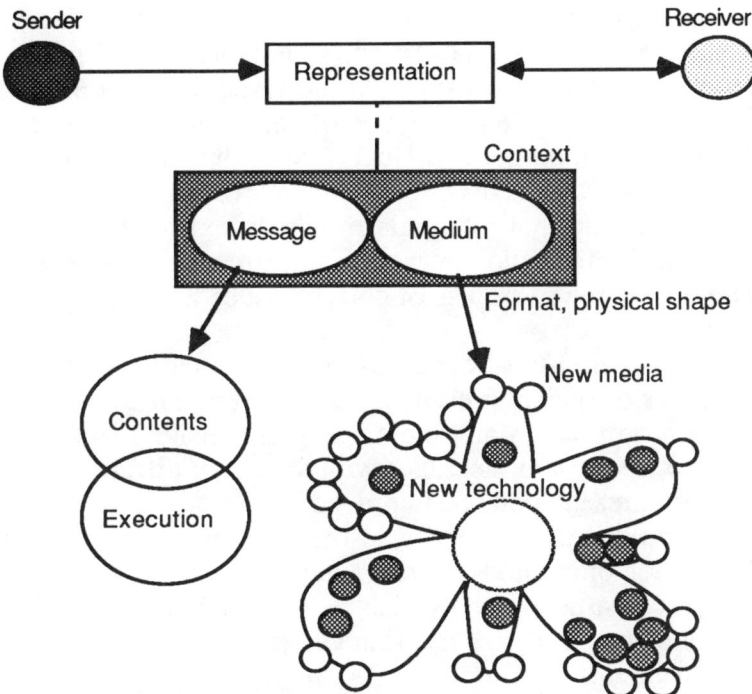

Different media are undergoing comprehensive changes.

Here are some examples of current research issues with the emphasis on *the sender:*
- How are different messages designed?
- Why are messages designed in different ways?
- When are different messages designed?
- The lecturer's perception of her/his lecture.

A message/content with a given design/form is conveyed by the sender to the receiver with the aid of a medium. The various media are undergoing comprehensive (technical) changes, changes in terms of production, duplication, stock-keeping, distribution or presentation of contents. Some of these developments are proceeding in the same direction and working together. Others are on separate paths. Some are even counteracting one another.

Costs and revenue represent both limitations and opportunities. We know that interest in buying and paying for entertainment, education, news and factual information varies. We also know that the development of systems for e.g. DTP (desktop publishing) offers individuals an opportunity to produce graphical products at relatively low cost. At the same time, facilities are being developed for the production of "distributed databases" in the form of small, compact optical discs with a large storage capacity. This option makes it possible to create completely new types of informational materials in which text, pictures, sound and numerical information interact in an extremely flexible way.

Here are some examples of current issues with the emphasis on the message:

- Message/contents - execution/form - medium. Specific properties of typical presentations in different media. How do they conform with Man's biological prerequisites?
- How do we present messages with the aid of different media? How can presentations be improved?
- How should presentations be designed for optimum impact?
- Description of methods for text and picture analysis.
- Analysis of structure and variables in visual language.
- Levels of meaning in visual languages, sub-meanings, complete meanings.
- Use of colors and shapes in symbols and trademarks.
- The perception of the same message in different media.
- Design on video display units.
- Text-picture and picture-text references.
- Laws and regulations, terms of delivery and ethical norms create limitations but even offer some opportunities.

The receiver's perception of a given message is not likely to coincide with the sender's perception of or intention for a given message/ content. A number of studies have shown that there is a very considerable difference between intended and perceived message/ content. In one instance, the differences amounted to 22 units when a scale ranging from 0 to 100 was used.

Literacy

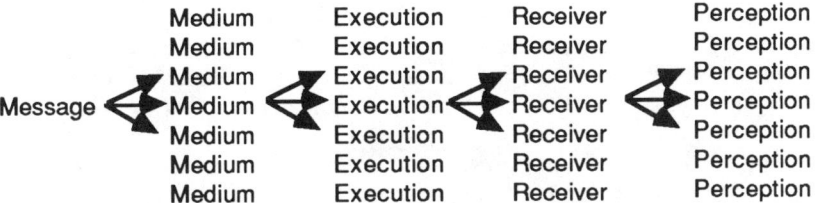

The sender's message and receiver's perception of that message do not always coincide.

We know that both texts and pictures can be interpreted in many different ways. As far as information is concerned, text and pictures should therefore convey the same message/content so as to reduce the number of potential interpretations and increase the learning effect. Captions are needed to "tie down" one of many possible interpretations of text.

Here are some examples of current issues with the emphasis on the receiver:
- Analysis of the receiver's individual perception of variables such as pixels/distance/resolution, movement, captions, readability, "before and after" etc.
- The receiver's perception of different presentations, such as lectures.
- Which factors govern the receiver's interpretation of the message?
- How can we improve coincidence between message intention and perception?
- The receiver's opportunities for interacting with the medium.

As regards various aspects of verbo-visual messages, efforts must be based on a holistic approach with the individual receier at the centre.

REFERENCES

Agrawal, B. C., Deshpanday, N. & Sinha, A. K. (1987). *Visual Symbols in Mass Media: Continuity of Collective Memories*. Paper presented at the Symposium on Verbo Visual Literacy: Research and Theory. Stockholm, June 10-13.

Batley, S. (1988). *Visual Information Retrieval: Browsing strategies in pictorial databases*. In *Online Information 88*. 12th International Online Information Meeting. London 6-8 December. Proceedings Volume 1, 373-381. Oxford and New Jersey: Learned Information (Europe) Ltd.

Berefelt, G. (1976). *AB Se om bildperception*. Liber Läromedel, Lund.

Bertin, J. (1967). *Sémiologie graphique*. Paris and The Hague, Mouton and Gauthiers-Villars.

Braden, R. A., & Beauchamp, D.G. (1986). *Catering to the Visual Audience: A Reverse Design Process*. Presentation at the 18th Annual Conference of the International Visual Literacy Association. Madison, Wisconsin, Oct.30 - Nov.2.

Brun, T. (1974). *The International Dictionary of Sign Language*. Halmstad: Spektra, Swedish translation.

Chomsky, N. (1959). Review of verbal behaviour. In B. F. Skinner, (Ed.). *Language*, 35, 26-58.

Cochran, L.M. (1987). *Visual/Verbal Languaging as Metaphor*. Paper presented at the Symposium on Verbo Visual Literacy: Research and Theory. Stockholm, June 10-13.

Cossette, C. (1982). *How Pictures Speak: A brief introduction to iconics*. Paper presented at the 32nd International Communication Association Conference, Boston May 1-5. Translated from French by Vincent Ross, Quebec.

Dahlstedt, K. H. (1979). *Språk och massmedier*. Presentation at the IVth Nordic Conference for Mass Communication, Umeå University.

Duffy, B. (Ed.) (1983). *One of a kind. A practical guide to learning styles 7-12*. Oklahoma State Department of Education.

Eco, U. (1971). *Den frånvarande strukturen. Introduktion till den semiotiska forskningen*. Lund, Swedish translation.

Ekwall, E. (1977). *Diagnosis and Remediation of the Disabled Reader*. Boston: Allyn and Bacon.

Elkind, D. (1975). We can teach reading better. *Today's Education*, 64, 34-38.

Eriksson, R. (1986). Språkpedagogisk forskning. In F. Marton, (Ed.). *Fackdidaktik. Volym II. Svenska och främmande språk. Samhällsorienterande ämnen*. Lund: Studentlitteratur, 47-74.

Fast, J. (1971). *Body Language*. Stockholm, Swedish translation.

Ferm, R., Kindborg, M., & Kollerbaur, A. (1987). *A Flexible Negotiable Interactive Learning Environment*. Paper presented at HCI'87, Exeter, England. Sept.

Fleming, M.L. (1970). *Perceptual Principles for the Design of Instructional Materials.* Washington, DC: Office of Education Bureau of Research.
Fleming, M. & Levie, W.H. (1978). *Instructional Message Design.* Englewood Cliffs, N.J.: Educational Technology Publications.
Fredriksson, I. (1979). *Konsten spränger ramarna. John Hartfield och det politiska fotomontaget.* Stockholm: Akademilitteratur.
Gazzaniga, M. (1967). The split brain in man. *Scientific American,* 217, 24-29.
Goldberg, A., & Kay, A. (1977). Personal Dynamic Media. *IEEE COMPUTER,* March.
Gunnemark, E., & Kenrick, D. (1985). *A Geolinguistic Handbook.* Kungälv: Goterna.
Haber, R. N., & Myers, B. L. (1982). Memory for pictograms, pictures, and words separately and all mixed up. *Perception,* 11, 57-64.
Kindborg, M., & Kollerbaur, A. (1987). *Visual Languages and Human Computer interaction.* Paper presented at HCI'87, Exeter, England. Sept. 1987.
Kollerbaur, A. (1983). *Final Report from the PRINCESS-Project* (Swedish title: *Slutrapport från PRINCESS-Projektet*). Stockholm: University of Stockholm, Department of Computer Science.
Larssen, A.K., & Skagert, P. (1982). *Hur fungerar annonser?* Aftonbladets Annonstest, Södertälje.
Lawson, L. (1968). *Ophthalmological factors in learning disabilities.* In H. Myklebust, (Ed.). *Progress in Learning Disabilities. (Vol. 1.)* New York, Grune and Stratton.
Lee, D. (1959). *Freedom and culture.* Englewood Cliffs, N.J.: Prentice Hall.
Levie, W.H., & Lentz. R. (1982). Effects of Text Illustrations: A Review of Research. *ECTJ,* 30, 4, 195-232.
Limburg, V. E. (1987). *Visual "Intrusion": A two-way street in Visual Literacy.* Paper presented at the Symposium on Verbo-Visual Literacy: Research and Theory. Stockholm, June 10-13.
Littlewood, W. (1984). *Foreign and second language learning.* Cambridge: Cambridge University Press.
Lodding, K. (1983). Iconic Interfacing. *Computer Graphics and Applications,* 3, 2, 11-20.
Lotman, J. (1973). *Die Struktur des künstlerischen Textes.* Frankfurt am Main.
Melin, L. (1986a). *Text, bild, lexivision. En studie i text-bild-samverkan i en lärobok.* Stockholm: Stockholm University, Department of Nordic Languages.
Melin, L. (1986b). *Termer - Ett kompendium om terminologi och termbildning.* Stockholm: Stockholm University, Department of Nordic Languages.
Paivio, A. (1979). *Imagery and Verbal Processes.* Hillsdale, New Jersey: Lawrence Erlbaum Associates.

Paivio, A. (1983). *The empirical case for dual coding.* In J.C. Yuille. *Imagery, memory and cognition.* Hillsdale, NJ: Erlbaum, 307-332.

Perfetti, C. (1977). *Language comprehension and fast decoding: Some psycholinguistic prerequisites for skilled reading comprehension.* In J. Guthrie, (Ed.), *Cognition, Curriculum, and Comprehension.* Newark, Delaware, International Reading Association.

Peterson, L. (1984). *Seriealbum på myternas marknad.* Stockholm: Liber.

Pettersson, R. (1983a).*Visuals for instruction.* (CLEA-report No. 12). Stockholm: Stockholm University, Department of Computer Science.

Pettersson, R. (1983b).Factors in visual language: Image framing. *Visual Literacy Newsletter,* 9 and 10. Also (CLEA-report No. 11). Stockholm: Stockholm University, Department of Computer Science.

Pettersson, R. (1984a). *Picture legibility, readability and reading value.* In A. D. Walker, R.A. Braden and L.H. Dunker. *Enhancing human potential.* Readings from the 15th Annual Conference of the International Visual Literacy Association. Blacksburg, Virginia, 92-108.

Pettersson, R. (1984b). *Numeric Data, presentation in different formats.* Presentation at the 16th Annual Conference of the International Visual Literacy Association. Baltimore. Nov. 8-11. Published in: N. J. Thayerand S. Clayton-Randolph (1985). *Visual Literacy. Cruising into the Future.* Readings from the 16th Annual Conference of the International Visual Literacy Association. Bloomington: Western Sun Printing Co. Inc., 121-136.

Pettersson, R. (1985). *Intended and Perceived Image Content.* Presentation at the 17th Annual Conference of the International Visual Literacy Association. Claremont. CA. Nov. 1-2.

Pettersson, R. (1985.b) Interplay of Visuals and Legends. *Visual Literacy Newsletter,* 5.

Pettersson, R. (1986a). See, look and read. *Journal of Visual Verbal Languaging.* Spring, 33-39.

Pettersson, R. (1986b). *Image - Word - Image.* Presentation at the 18th Annual Conference of the International Visual Literacy Association. Madison, Wisconsin, Oct.30 - Nov. 2.

Pettersson, R. (1986c). Picture Archives. *EP Journal.* June, 2-3.

Pettersson, R. (1987a). Interpretation of image content. Paper presented at the 19th Annual Conference of the International Visual Literacy Association. Tulsa, Oklahoma, Oct.28 -Nov.1. 1987.

Pettersson, R. (1987b). Picture processing. *EP Journal.* June.

Pettersson, R., Carlsson, J., Isacsson, A., Kollerbauer, A., & Randerz, K. (1984). *Color Information Displays and Reading Efforts.* (CLEA-report No. 18a). Stockholm: Stockholm University, Department of Computer Science.

Postman, N. (1979). *Teaching as a Conserving Activity.* New York, Delacorte Press.

Reynolds Myers, P. (1985). *Visual literacy, higher order reasoning, and high technology.* In N. H. Thayer and S. Clayton-Randolph (Eds.). *Visual*

Literacy, cruising into the future. Readings from the 16th annual conference of the International Visual Literacy Association. Bloomington, Western Sun Printing Co, Inc., 39-50.

Sinatra, R. (1986). *Visual Literacy Connections to Thinking, Reading and Writing.* Springfield. Illinois, Charles C Thomas.

Skinner, B. 1957: *Verbal behaviour.* New York: Appleton - Century - Crofts.

Slobin, D. (1973). *Cognitive prerequisites for the development of grammar.* In C. Ferguson and D. Slobin, (Eds.). *Studies of child language development.* New York: Holt, Rinehart & Winston.

Smith et al. Designing the Star User Interface. *BYTE,* April 1982.

Sperry, R. (1973). *Lateral specialization of cerebral functions in the surgically separated hemispheres.* In F. J. McGuigan and R. A. Schoonever, (Eds.). *The Psychophysiology of Thinking: Studies of Covert Processes.* New York, Academic Press.

Sperry, R. (1982). Some effects of disconnecting the hemisphere. *Science,* 217, 1223-1226.

Trice, R. W. (1986). *Development of a videodisc database.* Presentation at the AECT conference. Las Vegas.

Twyman, M. (1982). The graphic presentation of language. *Information design journal.* 3, 1, 2-22.

Vogel, D.R., Dickson, G.W., & Lehman, J.A. (1986). Driving the Audience Action Response. *Computer Graphics World.* August.

Zimmer, A. & Zimmer, F. (1978). *Visual literacy in communication: Designing for development.* Hulton Educational Publications Ltd., in cooperation with the International Institute for Adult Literacy Methods, Teheran.

Chapter 4

DESIGNING VISUALS FOR INFORMATION

In the designing and production of visuals for information we have to consider the characteristics of visual languages. We need to know how the illustrations will be used. We should consider image variables related to content, graphic execution, context and format. This chapter does not present rules but some guide-lines and advice which might be useful for everyone producing visuals for information.

CONTENT

Before starting designing visuals for information it is very important to define if, why and how the illustrations can be used. The most important factors seem to be informational or educational objectives and user characteristics. Visuals may not always be really necessary but are useful in many situations. However, in some situations pictures may be distracting and not supporting the information. In these cases illustrations should not be used.

In the design and production of visuals for instruction or for education, pictures must obviously contain the information they are intended to convey. The visuals must be relevant to the situation. Without a clear content the visual will not be able to function well.

224   *Visuals for information*

We should carefully define the objective of each visual. What information or knowledge is the visual intended to convey? Who is the sender? Who are the receivers? And in which medium or media is the visual to be distributed? Cues for understanding the message in a visual are different in various cultures as well as in different socio-economic groups. It is very important to consider this in each specific situation. Messages including visuals are preferred by most subjects and attract attention. Generally speaking humans, especially their faces, are the kind of content that will get maximum attention in images. It is also known that objects and pictures of objects are remembered better than their names. Adding illustration to textual material may fail to enhance attitude change. Results depend on how pictures are executed and how they are used. Association is facilitated when items are shown together.

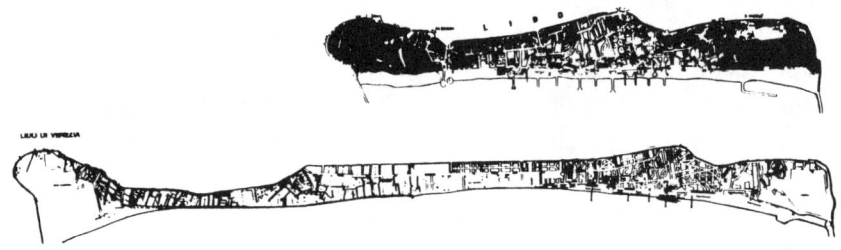

The island Lido is located south-east of Venice. Lido is long and narrow The island is indeed presented very differently in these maps. As well as other pictures, maps must contain the information they are intended to convey.

Structure

A well defined structure of the content facilitates learning. There is a need for structure in a complete material as well as within parts of that material. Normally the structure of the instructional message is built to be continuous, to form a connected whole that presents the message clearly to the learners. The instruction progresses logically step by step. After an initial orientation or instruction, instructional materials should develop at a pace that is suitable for the intended audience. A major factor in instructional effectiveness is repetition. Also summaries will help learners to

Designing visuals for information 225

remember the most important points of the specific subject matter. Background colors, shades, frames, and special use of fonts and type size can be used to achieve unity.

When the learner doesn't see, read or hear what s/he expects to see, or can't find agreement between verbal and visual content, the message is likely to be misunderstood. Since the competition for our attention is very fierce in commercial arts and in advertising, discontinuity is often used intentionally to attract and even to hold attention. The intended message may be hidden within verbal or visual puns, metaphors, satires, parodies or humour. In these cases designers break the traditional rules of instructional design. It might also be possible to use the unexpected to attract attention to instructional material as well.

Realism
A visual should usually possess a moderate and selected degree of realism and be true-to-life. Rather often this means culturally accurate detailed drawings in natural color.

Informative pictures should be "unambiguous", i.e. not too "artistic" and therefore ambiguous. Cartoons, line drawings and photographs represent a continuum of realism in visuals.

Cartoons, line drawings and photographs represent a continuum of realism in visuals.

The more realistic a visual is the closer it is to reality. Too little or too much realism in a visual can interfere with the communication and learning processes. Addition in stimuli over optimum makes it difficult for learners to identify the essential learning cues. Learning is always related to the needs of the learners and to the level of objectives in each specific situation. Low level objectives such as naming of objects need only a limited amount of information. High level objectives such as synthesis and analysis need a lot of information.

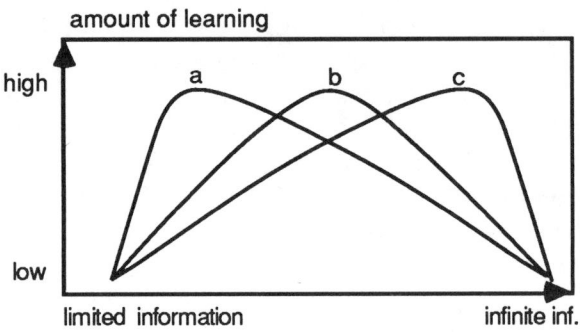

Low (a), medium (b) and high (c) level objectives demand various degrees of realism for high amount of learning.

Degree of detail

A visual should contain the details that are essential in communicating the intended message. Too many details and too much complexity give rise to distracting "interference" and reduces the interest for the content and the impact of the important part of the content in the visual. Thus we should avoid unnecessary elements in the picture. Too few details or too little complexity makes it impossible to understand the picture. For each picture there is an optimal degree of details. (This is depending e.g. on the content, the format, the intended audience and the objectives.)

If necessary, use a series of visuals instead of one visual overloaded with information. E.g. in a slide show "one-message slides" are usually ideal. This is also true for print material designed for children. A depiction of sequence in a series of frames should have a reasonable continuity.

We are able to perceive up to about seven stimuli at the same time. It has been found that 7+/-2 is a reliable measure of human capacity in both vision and audition.

Objects and events perceived as different or as similar in any way will be grouped and organized in our perception. Learning is facilitated when critical cues are apparent. Avoid non-critical cues if possible.

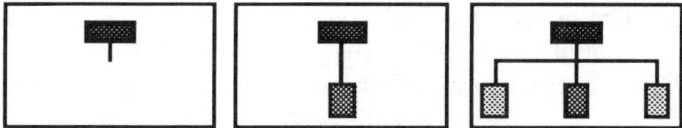

In AV-productions, it is usually a good idea to deliver the message step by step. A sequence of pictures can aid communication.

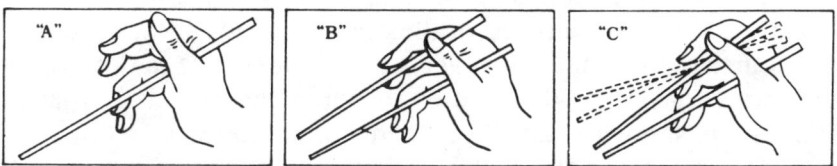

Instructions on how to use chop sticks. The illustrations contain the necessary degree of detail.

Factual content
In instructional message design the content is very often factual. "Realistic" pictures can provide reasonably objective documentation of an object or a product.

Objects
The type of subject should be commonplace, easy to recognize and neither uncommon nor abstract. The visuals should not contain any strange or unknown codes. The more familiar a message is to its audience, the more readily it is perceived. Familiarity with the depicted objects themselves is basic to understanding. Also the purpose of the visual should be obvious to the readers for whom the message is intended. In developing countries pictures of people are most easily understood. Parts of the body like arms, hands, legs and feet are more difficult to recognize. Even more difficult to recognize are tools and objects in the environment. People should, however, be dressed appropriately. Facial resemblance to members of the community is often an advantage.

Select a wide variety of examples as well as non-examples to enhance concept learning. In the examples the criterial attributes should show as little variation and be as obvious and typical as possible. The non-criterial attributes should show much variation and be as non obvious and non-typical as possible.

Objects and pictures of objects are better remembered than their names.

Time
A still picture is a "frozen moment in time". The passage of time is best illustrated with a series of illustrations which shows details in the course of an event. However, nonliterate people in developing countries may have difficulties in understanding that adjacent frames e.g. show the same people in a time sequence.

Picture context and picture composition can illustrate e.g. an age, year, season, time of day etc. Enhance comprehension with the aid of captions! Sometimes a time-scale may be useful.

For AV productions it should be remembered that the perception of time durations and time intervals is relatively inaccurate without a standard or frame of reference. Time that is filled with activity appears to pass more rapidly than time that is not filled with activity. Time is an essential factor in television and film. We can distinguish between objective time (clock time) and subjective time (psychological time).

People seem to prefer programs with fast pace and action. Such programs also result in greater learning efficiency.

Place
The location of objects may be shown in various kinds of scales, graphs and maps. (There is a large literature in cartography and the design of maps. However, these topics are not discussed in this report.)

Statistics
Numeric data are often used to illustrate situations such as relationships between variables and parts of a whole. Data can be

Designing visuals for information

presented in many formats. Graphical formats include comparisons of numbers, lengths, areas, volumes, positions and also comparisons of different combinations of these. Discriminations are most readily learned when the differences between stimuli are maximal. If you wish to be clear, choose clear examples.

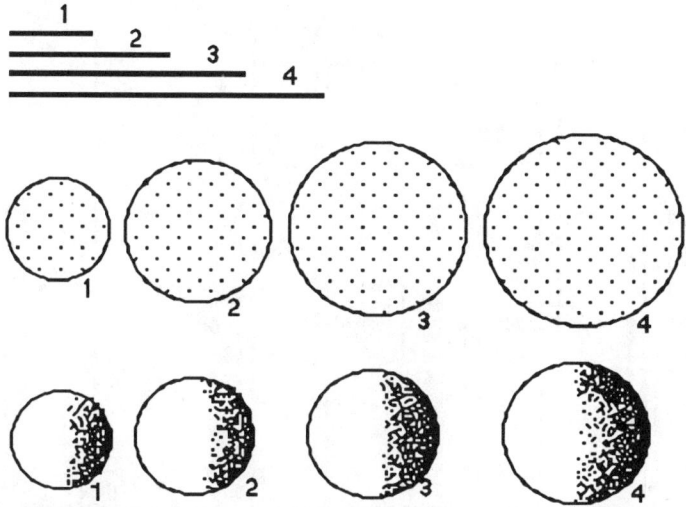

Comparisons of lengths, areas and volumes. In this example using the units 1, 2, 3 and 4. It is easier to distinguish between lines than between areas (grey) or between volumes (white).

It is easier to distinguish between lines than between areas or volumes. In most contexts the difference in the sizes of circles, squares, triangles, ellipses, and several other two-dimensional symbols are underestimated.

It is easier to assess "parts of a whole" than "relationships between variables". When relationships between variables shall be presented comparisons of length give the best results. When parts of a whole shall be presented, pie charts may be used. Don't use too many segments!

Design of graphic elements is important. Patterns should be discrete and not disturbing.

It is far too easy to convey misleading information about statistical relationships by using misleading illustrations or scales that are difficult to understand. Use a scale break only when it is necessary. If a break cannot be avoided, the break must be very distinct and easy to understand. (Also see Screen Communication: Numeric Data.)

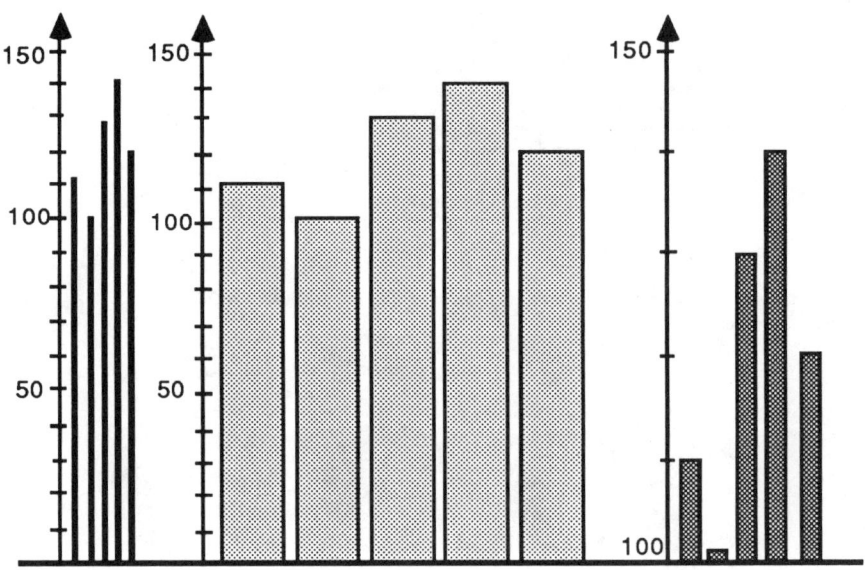

The three bar graphs in this illustration contain the same information, but they give us different impressions.

Events
Several kinds of image contents are related to events. "Action", humour, drama, violence etc., time displacement, parallel action, metaphoric descriptions (symbolic actions) and change are all examples of events that may be the content in visuals.

It is known that pictures showing events usually are more interesting and more effective instructional materials than static pictures. Activity is best shown in film or TV-sequences. However, also a series of stills may be used.

Designing visuals for information 231

Motion
Obviously several types of content benefit from being shown in moving media such as film and TV.

The best way to illustrate motion in a still picture is to depict a natural movement in contrast to a static situation. The impression of motion can be enhanced with graphical motion symbols such as speed lines. The meaning of these symbols has to be learned and is easily learned already by young children.

Motion in a visual attracts attention. The relation of figure to ground is particularly determinative of motion perception, which is highly related to depth perception. Perception of motion is influenced by contextual variables.

Rhythm consists of regular changes between different levels of a variable. This can be illustrated by arraying image elements into distinct groups.

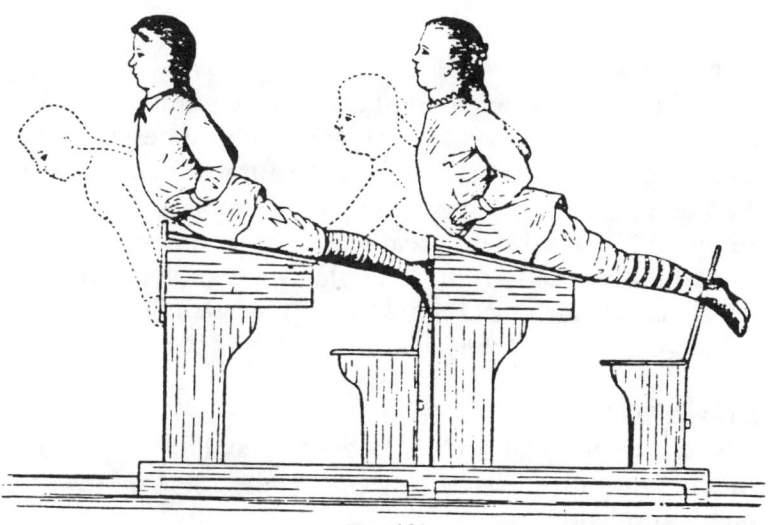

Fig. 164.

An illustration from a physical training textbook. The picture illustrates different positions. (From Liedbeck, C.H., Gymnastiska dagöfningar för folkskolan. Stockholm 1891).

Sound

The impression of sound in a still picture is most readily conveyed with onomatopoetic combinations of letters combined with graphical symbols and legends

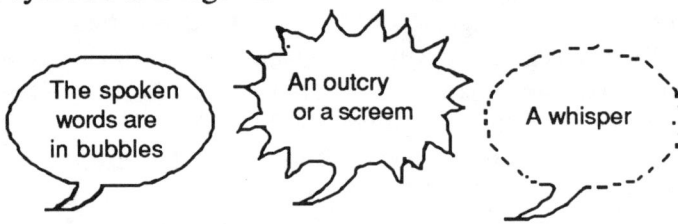

Comic strips enclose the text in different kinds of bubbles.

In AV productions words and sound-effects can enhance perception of the visual stimuli. However, there should be a redundant relationship between these different stimuli.

Humour and satire

Humour and satire are often used in cartoons to point out a special situation, occurence or event. In instructional material humour may sometimes be used as a visual pun to attract attention or dramatize certain portions of a visual (also see Emphasis). However, humour should be used with great care in instructional material. Misuse of humour and "funny people" may ruin the intended message. This is sometimes referred to as the "vampire-effect".

Relationships

Visuals may express relationships between people. For example in various cultures the distance between people tells the viewer a lot about their relationship.

Emotions

A picture is able to express emotions in at least three different ways. It may suggest an image of some emotional concept, i.e. a picture may look the way an emotion feels, e.g. "happy" or "sad". A picture may arouse emotional response in a viewer, i.e. the viewer may feel pleasure, excitement or fright. A picture may also express and reflect the picture creator's feelings about a given subject, such as politics or religion.

Visuals with an emotional content support and extend the attitudes we already have.

Pictures will usually not change our attitudes but they make us more convinced that we already hold the "right" views.

If people like the content in a visual, they like it even more when the visual is presented in color and vice versa.

In the western cultural sphere, people tend to associate colors with emotions or moods in the following way. The red and yellow part of the spectrum is often said to be warm and is felt to be active, exiting, happy and clear. Green to blue are described as cold and are perceived as being passive, comfortable, controlled and peaceful.

Emotions and moods are readily conveyed with onomatopoetic combinations of graphical symbols. However, we have to remember that the meaning of the symbols must be learned by the readers.

Credibility

A visual should depict reality in a manner appropriate to the content and be as relevant and credible as possible. If possible use familiar pictures.

High-credibility sources, like television, new film, and radio, exert a more persuasive influence than low-credibility sources, like newspapers and magazines. However, if attention is assured the degree of credibility does not affect the amount learned.

The most important components of credibility are expertise and trustworthiness. The endorsements of real people are memorable and persuasive.

The use of misleading illustrations in comparisons and statistics reduces the credibility of the message itself.

Pictures basically intended for advertisement or propaganda are very common in our society. Advertisements always speak in favour of someone or something. Propaganda speaks against someone or something.

Viewer completion

Our minds constantly fills in missing details and complete images, most of the time without our realizing that it has happened. The most probable interpretation of the message is created as a meaningful whole. However, the human imagination may be triggered by the design to provide details that will increase viewers' attention and possibly also facilitate learning. In drawings the lines that are missing may be as important as those that actually are there. This is often seen in cartoons.

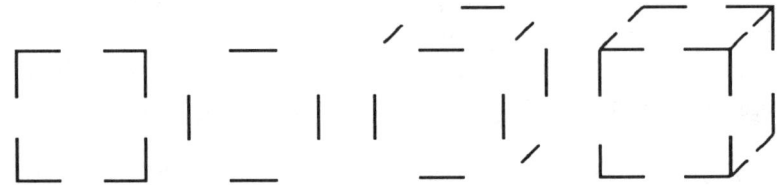

Some lines are more important than others at giving key information. This is clearly shown in these examples of squares and cubes.

Our minds fills in missing details and make the best possible interpretation of a given stimulus. To the left we may see a person with a hat, not just a few lines. To the right we may see an animal face.

Designing visuals for information

EXECUTION

Perception is always organized. We perceptually construct relationships, groupings, objects, events, words and people. We see dots, lines, areas, light, dark etc. in an organized way. One of the most simple perceptual organizations is that of "figure and background". Some elements in a visual are selected as the figure. The remaining elements constitute the background. Our ability to distinguish the boundaries of an image is usually very high.

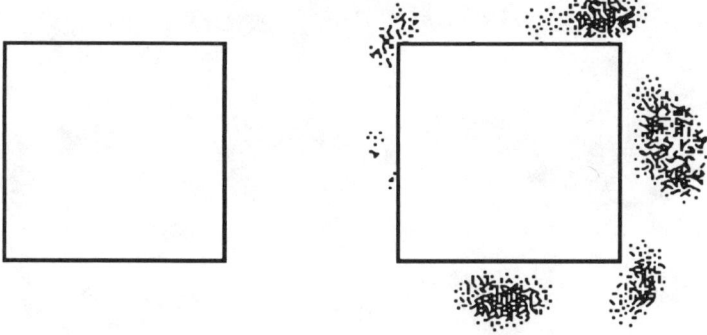

In these two illustrations, we easily recognize two squares as "figures" against the white (left) and also against the dotted background (right).

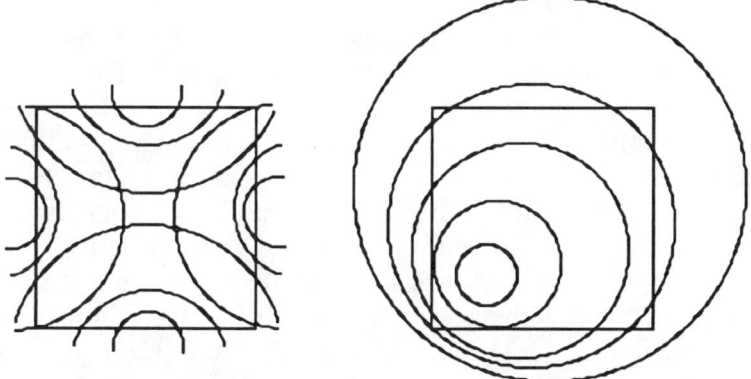

In these two illustrations, the properties of "figure and background" cannot be sharply distinguished. Despite our perceptions, the squares are of the same size with straight sides.

"Good figures", i.e. in the sense of simplicity, regularity and stability, are closed and exhibit a continuous contour. A given contour can belong only to one of the two areas it encloses and shapes. Whichever side, the contour shapes will be perceived as a figure. Necker's cube (See Illusions) can be seen in either of two configurations. Reversible figures lack sufficient cues as to which side of a contour is figure and which is the background. This is often used to create illusions. We have all seen a reversible figure that is peceived as a vase or as two heads facing each other.

In camouflage the intention is to make a figure as much like the background as possible.

An example of camouflage. Two differently painted models of tanks photographed in the same position in a woodland model. Photo by FOA, Swedish National Defence Research Institute.

When lines overlap or compete, emerging figures have good continuation. The most symmetrical and simple figures constructed will be perceived.

The simplest image components should be arrayed so that the picture's message is brought out as clearly as possible. This can be combined with high demands on aesthetic quality, but it is difficult to make any general recommendations on how e.g. various drawing styles should be used. Fine details in the texture of a drawing disappear in the dot screen structure of the printed image. Even more detail is lost in a TV image. To save money pictures could be tailored to the technical limitations of the systems that are used to make originals, masters and print runs in the respective medium/distribution channel.

When visuals are produced for informative purposes, it is always a good idea to start by trying to "visualize" the information to be conveyed. "Visualizing" a message means that you attempt

Designing visuals for information

to materialize it in an effective synthesis of words and pictures. So visualization is always a composite task, never a single act on its own, and requires the collaboration of several different parties. The stages in the production of instructional material from visualization to the finished product are listed below.

A Visualization
- *Synopsis*. Define the message! How can this message be expressed? What are the required characteristics and conditions? A synopsis should be verbal, take a broad view, be concise and to the point.
- *Idea conception*. The idea should be materialized in the form of e.g. a sketch. Ideas for the text, sound and visuals are conceived.
- *Integration*. An interplay is organized between the verbal and pictorial information.
- *Graphical design*. The layout and any last-minute ideas are brought in and a preliminary manuscript is prepared.

B Making the original
- *Text*. The manuscript is edited into its final version.
- *Drawings*. Previous sketches serve as the basis for making the originals.
- *Photography*. Prints suitable for repro, transparency copies or original pictures are produced in accordance with sketches made previously or test shots.

C Making the "master"
- *Text*. Technical production.
- *Drawings*. Technical production.
- *Photography*. Technical production.
- *"Master"*. The text and the visuals are brought together to form a "master" which can be used to print a run.

D Run
- *Copies*. The specified number of copies are made. In principle, the procedure is the same as in the production of graphical products, AV-media, films and TV-programs. Sound is an additional representation in the latter.

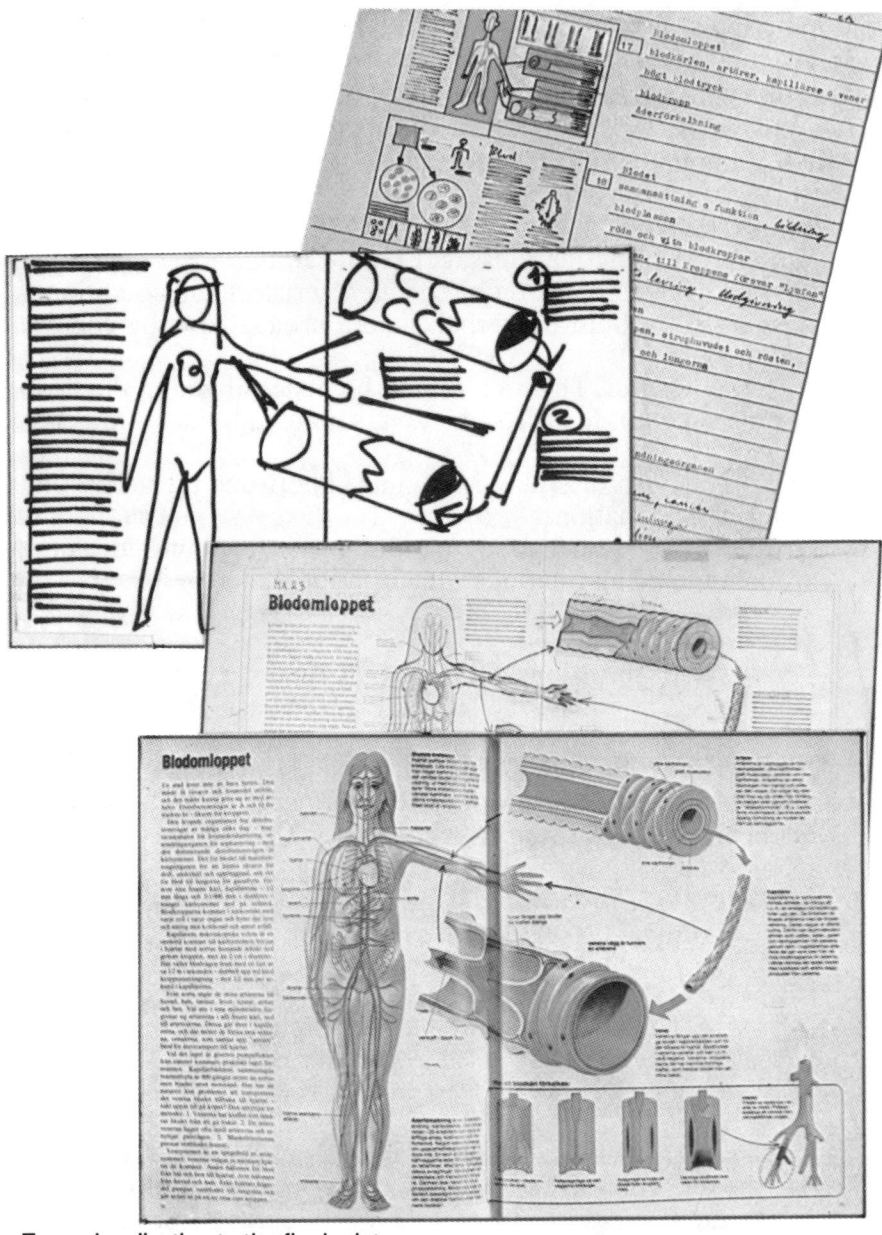

From visualization to the final print.

Graphical elements

Generally, the most simple elements making up a visual are dots, lines and areas which can vary in a great many ways. A dot can vary in size, shape/color, value and grain. Whether a graphic element is defined as a dot or as an area is related to the size and the scale of the visual. Obviously the borders between dots, lines and areas are not at all very distinct. Three-dimensional visuals also have volumes.

In the left figure, black areas illustrate the track left by the domestic cat. In the middle figure, areas with different shading form the track of the marten (Martes foina). In the right figure, lines and areas illustrate a track of the arctic fox (Alopex lagopus).(All illustrations from Pettersson, R. & Staav, R., Djurens spår. Spårstämplar och spårtecken. Stockholm 1973.)

Basic properties of graphic elements .

Dots	Lines	Areas	Volume
size	point of origin	size	size
shape	length	"emptiness"	shape
color	direction	shape	color
value	curvature	color	direction
grain	shape	value	position
position	thickness	grain	weight
	evenness	texture	
	points of changes	shaded	
	printing	non-shaded	
	color	combination of colors	
	value	brightness	
	grain		
	brightness		
	orientation		
	terminus		

A line has one of two functions. It can lead from one place to another or it can be a border between two areas. Since we always perceive graphical elements with respect to the context the meaning of a simple and single line will vary.

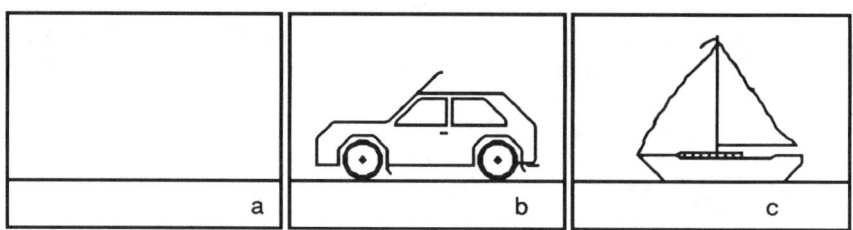

A horizontal line can serve e.g. as a horizon (a), a street (b) or a sea (c).

Vertical and horizontal lines, parallel to the borders of the picture give the impression of calm and stability. Horizontal lines give the impression of depth. Vertical lines often stop eye movement. Diagonal lines give the impression of movement. There is a tendency for curved lines and smooth shapes to stand out more than straight lines and shapes made out of straight lines. Lines that reach out from one point in different directions may be perceived as aggressive or violent.

There are several good reasons for using lines in drawing.
- Line is the natural way to draw. Infants begin with line and adults continue throughout life.
- Line is a quick way to visualize ideas.
- Line needs a minimum use of time and material.
- Line drawing materials are least expensive.
- Line emphasizes the basic structure and composition of a drawing.
- Other drawing techniques may be added.
- Line drawings are the most readily recognizable form of depiction in general.

Designing visuals for information

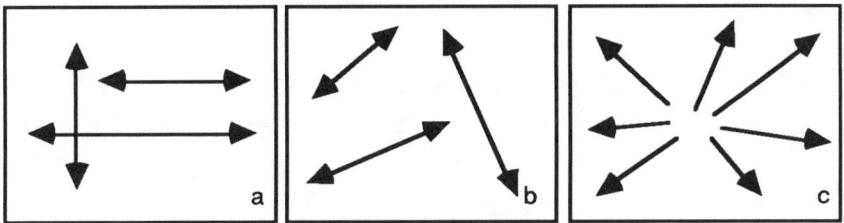

Vertical and horizontal lines (a) are harmonious and flat. Diagonal lines disrupt harmony and add depth to the visual (b), reaching out from one point they may be perceived as violent (c).

An area may have a geometric, an abstract or a representational shape. The size of an individual area is always relative. It depends on our knowledge of its surroundings.

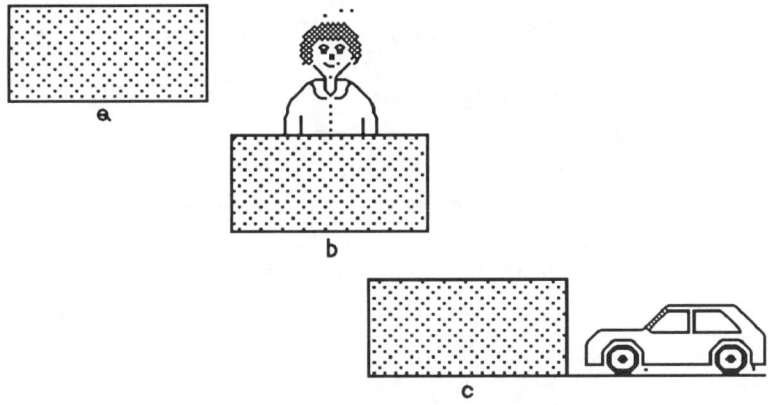

The size of a rectangle (a) means little to us. A person sitting behind the rectangle gives it the size of a desk (b). A car in front of it makes it the size of a building (c).

A volume has got a three-dimensional form. The form may be actual or simulated. In two-dimensional representations of three-dimensional objects shadows are the key cues for simulated volumes (see light). We structure the three-dimensional field into various depth planes, or grounds, a fore-ground, a middle-ground and a back-ground.

In printing technology graphic elements may be defined as types for letters and lines and screen points for visuals. In work with digital images in computerized image processing, graphic elements can be defined in one of two systems. Either mathematically as points and vectors, defined by cartesian coordinates, or in the form of pixels (minute rectangular picture elements) defined by raster coordinates (also see Format).

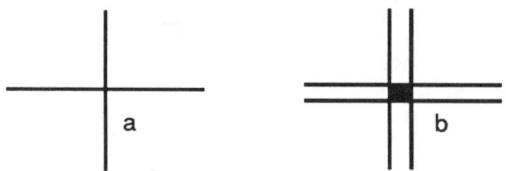

In image processing graphic elements are defined as points and vectors (a) or as pixels (b).

A vector can be assigned basic graphic properties in the same way as attributes in display fountains, but it has as such only mathematical properties. A pixel is in fact a minute area and can vary with respect to color. Lines, areas and symbols, such as letters, are composed of several pixels.

An area may have a geometric, an abstract or a representational shape defined by the lines or by the dots that form it. The size of an individual area is always relative. It depends on our knowledge of its surroundings. A square is an example of a static area. A rectangle is perceived as more active. A volume has got a three-dimensional form. The form may be actual or simulated. In two-dimensional representations of three-dimensional objects shadows are key cues for simulated volumes (see Light). We structure the three-dimensional field into various depth planes, or grounds, a foreground, a middleground and a background.

Study the works of good artists, painters and sculptors. Most artists use many of the possibilities in the visual language. However, some artists have made paintings, drawings etc. using mainly one or two different elements with limited basic properties. Here are just a few examples. Vincent van Gogh only used dots and lines in some paintings. Paul Cezanne used hues in different areas. Pablo Picasso often used areas in different shapes. Henry Moore is a master of lines and volumes in his sculptures.

The most important elements of the visual may be emphasized as to enhance attention and perception (see Emphasis). Design

Designing visuals for information 243

visual material taking into account dots, lines and areas so that the important content will stand out and be easy to perceive.

Type of visual

Look around! In your home, at work and in other places you will see that there are many different types of visuals. You may see drawings, paintings, collages, montages, mosaics, maps, pictures or textiles, lithographs, photographs, pictures in books, magazines, newspapers and television. The visual register is very large and we see a good deal of it every day. Visuals showing the same subject can be executed in many different ways.

Preference for a particular visual format does not necessarily result in increased learning. Yet, in the absence of more substantial data, information based on student preference has a meaningful role to play in affecting learning from instructional texts. All other things being equal, we should provide formats which are preferred by the viewer, thus making the text more attractive, and hopefully more motivating.

Visuals for instruction should be attractive but "unambiguous", i.e. not too "artistic" and therefore ambiguous. Visuals that are attractive and that people like also have greater impact.

Generally speaking it is not possible to rank the different types of visuals. Often the type of visual which should be used must be determined in each individual case with a view to various demands on the picture and the prevailing budget framework. It is often easier to control the production of a drawing than the production of a photograph. So a drawing may be the only realistic alternative in many instances.

Subject

A subject may be presented in several different ways. The part of the subject that is important to the subject must be large and clear, take up a large proportion of the image area and be perceivable as an entirety. Symbolic illustrations are easier to do but they may be more difficult to recognize.

244   *Visuals for information*

For children up to the age of about seven years, the entire subject must be clearly visible. No important part of the subject must be hidden in or missing from the visual. Absent items do not really exist, in the minds of many children. To a large extent this is also true for nonliterate adults in developing countries. The "personal space" between people in a visual is important with different meaning to readers belonging to different cultures.

Light

The word photography has its origin in greek and means "writing with light". Drawers as well as painters and photograpers make use of various lighting conditions, light, shadows and darkness to create perceptions of volume in two-dimensional pictures. A person or an object depicted in hard or soft light will be perceived differently.

The physicist defines light as visible radiant energy. Actually, light is invisible. We can see it only at its source and when reflected. Light has outer as well as inner orientation function.

Examples of different lighting conditions.

Outer orientation functions

Light will articulate our outer orientation with respect to space, texture and time. Without any shadows we can make out the basic contour of an object. Shadows define space. The *attached shadow*

Designing visuals for information

is on the actual object. It helps to reveal the basic form and dimensions of that object.

The *cast shadow* is frequently observed as being independent of the object that caused it. Depending on the angle of the light source the cast shadow may reveal the basic shape and location of the object that caused it. The surface appears to be curved when the light falls off gradually. A highly directional (hard) light produces fast fall-off. Thus a curved surface is emphazised. A highly diffused and nondirectional (soft) light produces slow fall-out. Prominent cast shadows caused by hard light from a low angle emphasize texture. Soft light, on the other hand, de-emphasize texture. Thus both hard and soft light may be used successfully for spatial and tactile orientation, for example in portrait photography. In daylight the background is usually bright. The cast shadows are very pronounced and the fall-off is fast. In a night time scene the background is dark. The lighting from various light sources is highly selective. Shadows are prominent.

Inner orientation functions

As well as light can articulate space, texture and time it can also articulate inner orientation functions. In motion picture and TV-production light, especially combined with music and sound effects, can evoke a great variety of specific feelings and emotions within us. Already minor position changes of principle light sources may have drastic effects on our perception of mood and atmosphere. For example a face lighted from below may appear unusual, ghostly and brutal.

Lighting

The two basic ways of external lighting are chiaroscuro and Notan lighting. The light-dark chiaroscuro method means lighting for volume and emphasizing of three-dimensional qualities. The lighting is specific and hits only parts of the scene. The overall illumination is low-key with high-contrast lighting on figures, persons and objects. The background is usually dark. The shadows are prominent with fast fall-offs. Notan lighting is flat, for simple visibility. The light comes from no specific direction and it is nonselective. Shadows have extremely slow fall-offs. The images have extremely low contrast and the background is usually light.

Shape

For small children (three to six years), color stimuli have greater impact than shape stimuli. However, the reverse is true of older children; i.e., shape becomes more important than color.

Shape constancy is our tendency to judge shapes as the same despite changes in distance, viewing angle and illumination.

External shape

The picture area in drawing, painting and still photography can have any shape and orientation. Still most pictures are cropped and published in square or rectangular formats. However, the visual's external shape should be "free-form", round or oval and not delineated by straight lines. Perception of shape is influenced by contextual variables.

Television as well as film screens are horizontally oriented, since we basically experience the world on a horizontal, rather than a vertical plane. When HDTV was developed it was found that people preferred the aspect ratio of 3 x 5 over the 3 x 4 ratio of the current television system.

Note that different shapes are visually assessed to be of different sizes (see Size).

External contour

The visual's external contour should be blurred and unclear so the visual fades in/out of the background and never clear enough to stand out against the background. It is possible that very distinct framing diverts interest from the actual content in the visuals.

Illustrations in early European books frequently had gently rounded contours. Many artists still frequently draw free-form visuals which are not delineated by straight lines and which fade in/out of the background.

Designing visuals for information 247

In one study typical primary school textbooks from Ghana, Japan and Sweden were compared. Irregularly shaped, oval, or round image shapes were predominant in the Ghanian and Japanese books. In the Swedish book fewer than one-fourth of the illustrations were "free" or rounded images.

Size

It is easier for us to distinguish between lines than between areas or volumes. When we judge the size of objects, e.g. areas, we are apparently most influenced by the length of horizontal lines or horizontal distances (Also see Statistics). In most contexts the differences in the sizes of circles, squares, triangles, ellipses and other two-dimensional symbols are underestimated.

Size constancy is our tendency to judge the size of an object as the same despite changes in distance, viewing angle and illumination.

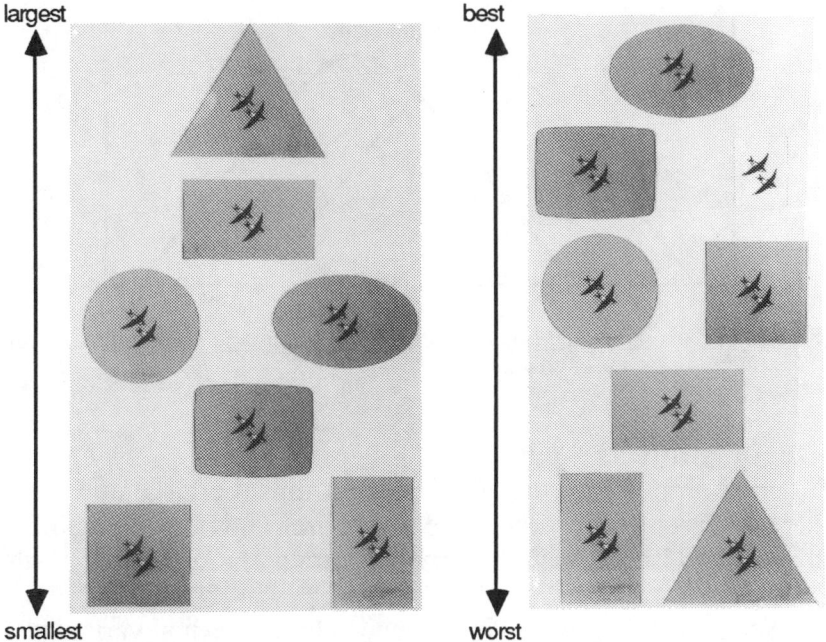

Children's assessment of visuals with equal areas, to the left and children's preferences of image shapes, to the right. (From Rune Pettersson, Bilder barn och massmedia. Stockholm 1981.)

Size of visual

A visual should neither be too small nor too large. However, the size must be large enough for the image to be legible. A visual with a "large content" and many details must be larger than a visual containing a more limited amount of information. If one picture is larger than the others in an array this picture will attract the most attention. "Noise" in the visual results in a need for a larger size. A picture 4 - 5 cm (1 1/2 to 2 inch) wide in a book corresponds to the eye's perception of the width of a TV screen at a normal viewing distance and is adequate in some cases. In TV the spectacle of things is de-emphasized but human actions gain prominence. A large cinemascope image is more overpowering than the small TV image. In film people as well as things attain spectacular dimensions.

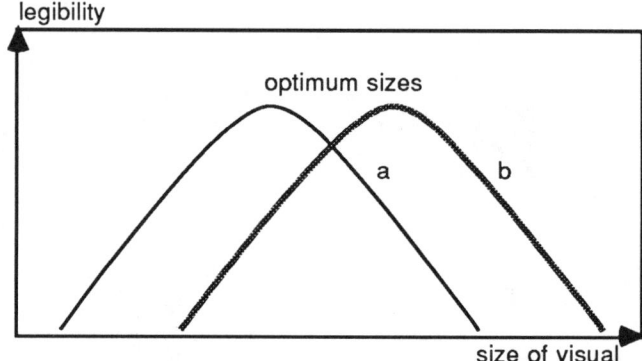

The size of a visual should be large enough for the image to be legible. There is an optimum size for each visual.

Size of subjects

The most important part of the subject must be large and clear, take up a large proportion of the image area and be perceivable as an entirety. Large visual elements attract the attention of the reader.

The perception of size is influenced by contextual variables. It is usually a good idea to include some familiar object to supply the scale for judging the size of an unfamiliar object.

Designing visuals for information

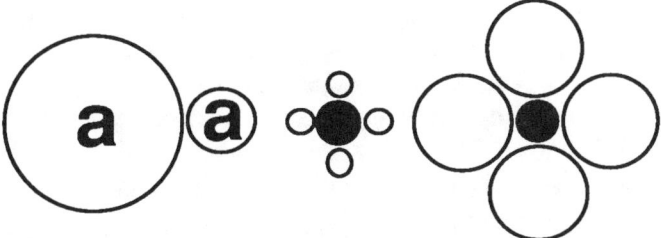

The perceived size of an object is relative to the size of nearby objects. Above, the letter 'a' is equal in both contexts, so is the dark circle in the other pair.

This caricature was produced and published to illustrate opposition to the theories about evolution published by Charles Darwin in his work "On the Origin of Species by means of Natural Selection".

People vary greatly in their ability to perceive proportional relationships. The perceived size of an object is relative to the size of other objects. The size of unfamiliar objects are perceived as relative to the size of familiar objects. Sometimes it is possible to include a scale in the visual. Any simple and distinct part of an image can be visually superimposed to measure proportional relationships of the whole. In caricatures, however, proportions are deliberately wrong. Deliberate distortions create aesthetic tension between the caricature and the normal image of the subject. This induces emotional responses in viewers. Feelings are readily aroused by a departure from what is considered visually correct or normal. Photographers can also produce "caricatures" by using unusual angles and/or distorting lenses. When we need visuals for instruction, caricatures are usually not the best choice.

When the size of an object changes in a story from one page to another or even on the same page, children up to seven years of age often believe that the objects are different.

Size and depth
The perception of size is related to perceived distance and the perception of distance is reciprocally related to perceived size. Regardless of distance there is a constancy in the perception of the size of known objects.

Color
A visual should usually be in color but not in unrealistic colors. It is possible for us to see the difference between several million colors. However, we can only distinguish about 10,000 different colors. Color can be described in technical, physiological, psychological and aesthetic terms. Color is capable of enhancing communication, adding clarity and impact to a message.

Yellow-green (about 555 millimicrons) lies in the region of the eye's greatest sensitivity. Sensitivity decreases markedly toward the red and blue ends of the spectrum. Perception of color is strongly influenced by and dependent on contextual variables such as lighting conditions and other, surrounding colors. (Also see Screen Communication: Color Description Systems.)

Color constancy is our tendency to judge surface colors as the same despite changes in distance, viewing angle and illumination.

Designing visuals for information

People in different cultures and in different socio-economic groups use colors in different ways and with different meanings. In cultures in Africa, Central and South America and Indonesia bright colors and high contrast are common in illustrations.

Color preferences
People prefer surface colors according to this ranking: 1 blue, 2 red, 3 green, 4 violet, 5 orange and 6 yellow,
 Children prefer colors that are light, distinct and shining better than colors that are dark and gloomy. Color intensity should be strong and color contrast should be clear.

Color visibility
Color intensity influences our perception of shapes and objects. When colors of equal intensity are compared the most visible colors are: white, yellow and green in that order. The least visible colors are red, blue and violet.
 In information graphics and statistical presentations the most important elements should have the brightest colors with the best contrasts to the background.
 The most legible combinations of print colors is black or dark brown text on a light yellow background. Other combinations may attract more attention but are less legible and, thus, require bigger letters. (Also see Screen Communication:Text.)

Attentional use of color
Colors are good aids in drawing attention to circumstances that need highlighting. It is hard to recognize an image when it has many colors. It has been found that even if color is not adding any information it is still contributing to a better learning because the interest for the picture increases. There are many ways to use colors to get attention to a certain information.

Affective use of color
Color enhances the perception of a visual message. If people like the content in a picture they like it even more when the visual is presented in color and vice versa. Sometimes color enhances

learning but in many cases black and white would be better. However, from many experiments it is quite clear that people usually prefer color in visuals. Advertising is known to be much more effective when visuals are in color than in black and white.

Tests have indicated that viewers feel they have a better understanding when TV images are displayed in color, although the use of black and white sometimes would be sufficient. However, an improper use of color can produce negative results. It can be distracting, fatiguing and upsetting.

Cognitive use of color
Color is important in a visual when it carries information that is vital for the content in the visual. It is for example easier to learn to distinguish between various species of birds or butterflies when color illustrations are used instead of black and white. It is known that highlighted information tends to be better remembered. Colors can easily be used for highlighting, separating, defining, and associating information. In line drawings or in black and white photos for example the addition of one color may be very efficient. To avoid confusion and misunderstanding it is very important that color be used consistently.

Color coding
Colors are often used for color coding, for example of objects. This is used also in different signs and symbols. The number of color codes should be very limited. As the number of color coded items increase, the value of color as a cue for selecting important information decreases. In videotex for example subjects tend to dislike the use of more than four or five colors at the same time.

Decorative use of color
There are many situations where colors can be used for decoration. However, a decorative use of color should never be mixed with other uses of color. It must always be easy to understand when color is used for decoration and when the use is cognitive.

Color psychology
In spite of the large quantity of research, color perception still only seem to be partially understood. It could be concluded that:
- Colors can be associated with temperature and emotions.
- The human reactions to color stimuli cannot be standardized. Depending on sex, age and culture, the subjective reactions to color are different. People might see colors in the same way. However no two persons experience color in precisely the same way.
- There are likes and dislikes of color, based on general and personal associations.
- Everywhere we find user expectancy to the use of color and their meaning.

Contrast
The contrast i.e. the difference between the brightest and the dimmest parts of a visual should be clear. This is regardless of the color chosen and color-contrast effects. It is known that high contrast between objects attract attention. Children prefer "light" visuals as compared to dark visuals in relation to whiteness-blackness i.e. the grey scale. In the comparison of the darkness of tones on a graphic display, differences in tones will be overestimated.

It is far too common that illustrations e.g. in textbooks do not have good contrast. Instead, it is often a more or less even shade of grey.

Emphasis
Emphasis is used to attract or direct attention or dramatize certain points of a visual. A dark dot in a light field or a jog in a line are examples of emphasis. The contrast of the dark area against the light background draws attention to the dot. The more dots the less the degree of contrast and the less effective the emphasis. Many dots form a pattern of light and dark areas which compete with each other. Neither shade dominates or demands more attention. The more competition for attention the less effective is the

emphasis. Many different elements in a visual can cause emphasis. Light against dark, color against no color, detail against no detail, change in size, arrows, implied motion, circles or ovals around objects, stars, shaded areas, line drawings in photos, words, position or placement of elements, line intersections, or any other unexpected change or variation out of context will create emphasis. (Also see "Symbols".) Furthermore emphasis on the message is achieved by reducing the number of details in the picture to those who are really essential.

Composition

Composition is discussed here mainly within the individual visual. (Also see "Context".)

Organization

The elements in a visual may be arranged in a pattern that is easy for the reader to comprehend. Organization provides a pattern that facilitates learning. By organizing the graphic elements it is possible to direct the eye movements within the picture.

Perceptually, we group things on the basis of similarity and distinguish between things on the basis of disparity. Certain stimuli, such as contour-lines, unusual colors or graphical symbols, are accentuated in perception while others, such as uniform areas, are not.

Horizontal and vertical lines are more intense than other lines, i.e. they evoke more mental activity and they are more easily compared. Organizing a message can make perception much easier and learning more efficient. The visual should have a moderate degree of complexity. Complexity without order produces confusion and order without complexity produces boredom. Differences in texture and grain may help organizing information.

Direction, position and orientation of objects are essential parts in organizing the information. Many confusing results may occur if used improperly. The more informative parts of a visual attract more eye fixations than the less informative parts.

Designing visuals for information 255

Centres of interest
The visual should only have a few centres of interest, preferably only one at or near the visual's optical centre, i.e. just above and to the left of its geometric centre or otherwise in the upper third of the visual. Thus the visual has unity. The most important elements of the visual may be emphasized to enhance perception.

Young children may chose to pay attention either to the whole picture or to specific parts of it. For children until about nine years of age it might be difficult to switch attention between a part and the whole.

41 ●	20
25	14

In the U.S. viewers tend to begin looking at a visual from the left side, particularly the upper left portion (41%). The optical centre is above and to the left of the geometrical centre.

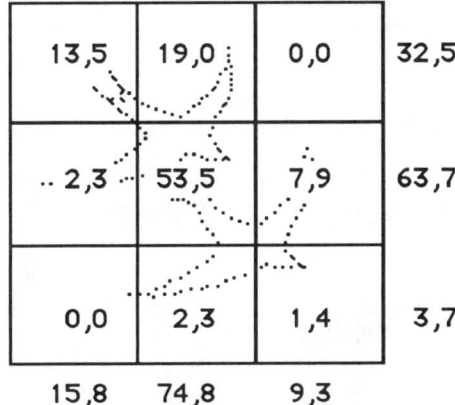

13,5	19,0	0,0	32,5
2,3	53,5	7,9	63,7
0,0	2,3	1,4	3,7
	15,8	74,8	9,3

In one experiment adult subjects looked at a drawing of two flying House Martins. The distribution of fixations (%) within different parts of the image area is shown in this figure. More than half of the 215 fixations made by the seventeen subjects were in the central field. (Also see Image framing.)

According to the "rule of thirds" the centre of interest may be selected at any one of the four points where equidistant vertical and horizontal lines divide a picture in three parts.

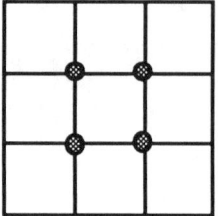

Centres of interest according to "the rule of thirds".

Balance

A visual should display the best possible balance. Elements of the visual should fit together in a harmonious relationship in a manner which is interesting but not distracting.

Imbalance creates an uncomfortable feeling in the reader and should be avoided.

Balance could be formal with total symmetry or informal. Formal balance is felt to be static. Informal balance contributes to a feeling of dynamism.

Perspective

Spatial perception is not the perception of space as such but of the learned meaning of the relationship between different objects seen in space.

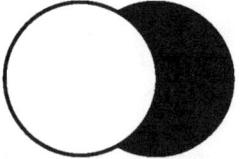 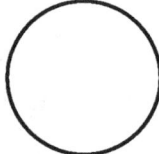 

We see this pattern (left) as a black disc partially occluded by a white disc (the natural way of things). However, the figure may actually represent an incomplete black disc nestled against the white disc, as demonstrated to the right (the discs now separated).

We have to distinguish between an optical and a perceptual reality. Optical reality is only governed by geometry and is only visual. However, perceptual reality is governed by *object constancy* and combines what we already know about the subject with what we can see, hear, smell etc. Central perspective is the graphic equivalent of optical reality and is a rather recent perceptual acquisition developed in the early Renaissance by artists who learned to see form and space in a new way.

In central perspective all perspective lines converge toward common vanishing points. The accurate proportion is established by our intuitive experience. People in some cultures do not see our central perspectives. An orthographic projection is the graphic equivalent of our perceptual reality. A mechanical orthographic drawing shows proportions exactly.

Depth
The perception of depth is related to the relative size of known objects, to illumination and shadows, judicious croppings, linear perspective, texture gradients, upward angular location of grounded objects, overlap inter-position and filled space. Image elements conveying a sense of depth should be clear and easy to comprehend. Depth perception is also based on different color's varying wavelengths. Warmer colors empasize foreground. Colder colors empasize background.

A visual must not incorporate any built-in optical illusions or geometric patterns making it possible to interpret the image in different ways.

In the new visual communication media, like video games and computerized pictures, the use of depth composition is common. The combination of rapid inward-outward movement, distorted depth of field, and forceful direction of visual elements placed on the Z-axis disturbs viewer comprehension and diminishes the aesthetic appreciation of such images.

Visuals in some books for children have differing perspectives at the same time, making it quite confusing for the readers.

Depth of field

Photographs often have well defined foregrounds and backgrounds and parts in between. During photography the depth of field is influenced by the distance to the object and the camera aperture. The depth of field can vary from several meters to a few decimeters.

By making the foreground sharp and background blurred interest is directed to the foreground and vice versa. Obviously, it is also possible for an artist to choose depth of field in her or his drawing.

Uneasy backgrounds should be avoided in visuals for instruction. Instead balance and harmony should be present in any picture. Very often it could be recommended to move in closer on the object and thus avoid uneasy components in the background.

Picture angle

A picture angle corresponding to the angle of normal vision is preferable to wide-angle or telescopic views. However, regardless of the angle there is a constancy in the perception of known objects (*object constancy*).

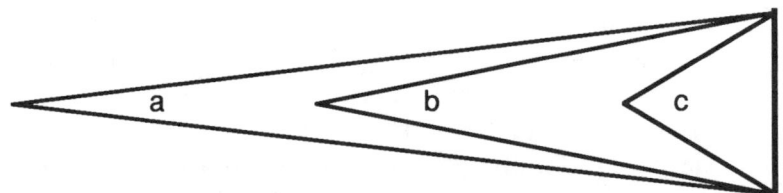

Regardless of the angle (in this example a, b and c) there is a constancy in the perception of known objects.

Picture height

A frontal projection in which the subject is rendered from normal eyelevel is easier to comprehend than other projections and angles.

An unusual view of a person.

Technical quality

Obviously the technical quality of a visual should be "good" and tailored to the medium. A printed picture should be matt and distinct, not blurred overly glossy or dazzling. Resolution should be sufficient for the reproduction of the desired details. Remember that fine details in the texture of a visual disappear in the dot screen structure of the printed image. Even more detail is lost in a TV image (Also see Format: Image morphology).

Poor technical quality is far too common in instructional message design. The result of most of the previous work on visualization and making originals can easily be destroyed by a single error in the making of the master or in the actual production of the copies. Negative text in color is often hard to read due to misalignments in printing.

Symbols and explanatory words, lettering

Explanatory words, numbers or other symbols should be incorporated into the picture as reading aids when this facilitates comprehension and learning. These aids must not then be distracting, large nor ugly. Simple styles and fonts are more easily read than complex ones.

Relationships, moods, sound and movements can be conveyed in a picture with the aid of signs and symbols. However, symbols have to be learned by the readers. Usually they are not naturally understood. Especially in developing countries symbols must be introduced slowly and patiently.

Symbols are of special value and importance in maps.

In audio-visual materials, such as slides and filmstrips, and screen presentations, lettering must be considered carefully. Fifteen to twenty words on a slide are maximum for effective communication. Letters should be medium to medium-bold. Lettering height should be no less than one twenty-fifth the height of the artwork to be transferred. Generally speaking lower-case letters are more legible than capitals.

Symbols of various kinds may be used for emphasis. (See "Emphasis").

Mixing and zoom

Film and TV-production is not discussed in this book. However, even in print media, especially in comics, the use of sequences of pictures often remind of film and television. Comics might in fact be called "graphic films". Content is added to content frame by frame. It is possible to "cut" between scenes and zoom in and out to direct attention.

Picture editing

Modern computerbased graphical systems for picture handling have great built in possibilities for editing of the content.

Selection

Every published visual has been selected, not only once but several times. First the picture creator, the photographer and/or the artist, makes a selection of the subject matter. In any given situation a lot of different pictures may be produced. Then the editor makes a selection among various pictures in a collection or in an archive. Usually several sketches or outlines makes a basis for decisions necessary in the production of the final drawings. A selected photo often need cropping. By cropping distracting and/or uninteresting parts of the image are eliminated.

Changes of image content

The content of an image can be modified and changed in several ways. We can change the scale, change projection, crop or expand, reduce, delete, modify, move, turn, supplement, isolate

Designing visuals for information

or combine various image elements. Pictures can be stored as object oriented descriptions, in bit-mapped form or as a combination of same.

Scale. An image may be scaled up or down. The content remains the same but the chosen scale can influence our perception of it. If the plane of projection is changed the relations between various parts in the picture will be influenced (See Size: Size of visual).

Cropping. An original picture can often be improved by removal of irrelevant or distracting elements. Pictures can be cropped from all sides. The photographer always performs some initial cropping, i.e. when composing or taking a photograph, the photographer sets the boundaries or "frame" of the picture. Changing scale and/or cropping are the most common methods used in picture editing.

Changing projection. The projection plane can be altered through image modification or shrinkage. This distorts size relationships within the picture and affects our perception of image contents.

Expansion. The use of a filler, such as the addition of a tint block, can alter a picture's height-width relationship. The picture can be vertically or horizontally stretched.

Compression. A picture can be "compressed", i.e. squashed from the sides or top and bottom.

Deletion. Distracting or undesirable details in a picture can be removed by painting with an appropriate retouching color or shade. This is also a way to isolate parts of a picture.

Changes. Individual picture elements can be changed so as to improve contrast, acuity, sharpness, grey scale or color scale. The grey scale can sometimes be transformed into optional colors.

Addition. The relation between width and height of the image can be changed by the addition of space. To achieve emphasis it is common to add information such as shadows, contrasts, colors, signs and symbols.

Move. Individual picture elements can be moved within an image for the sake of better balance and harmony. It is also possible to move parts of the picture to other pictures.

Turn. Individual picture elements can be turned and twisted into new appropriate positions.

Supplement. Letters of the alphabet, numerals, other symbols or markings can be added to a picture for the purpose of enhancing image content and links to the legend. The super-imposition of text onto a picture image usually impairs our ability to absorb the contents of both text and picture.

Isolation. An attractive, interesting or amusing detail in a picture can be isolated by, say, peeling and cropping. The detail can then be used independently or as part of other pictures.

Combination. A few thousand "stock" pictures with standard backgrounds and foregrounds, such as landscapes, scenic views, people, vegetation, animals, etc. can be combined to form an infinite number of compositions. For example, clip art programs are available for several personal computers.

The picture in context

Pictures should always be adjusted to fit into their final context (see Context). Image framing makes a clear distinction between image and background (see Image framing). Fading is used to have the image gradually appear on the page (see Shape). Layout is the integration of text and images, i.e. on an opening in a book (see Layout). Legends give the reader necessary guidance in understanding the image content (see Interplay of words and visuals).

Copyright

The rights of copyright holders are protected according to international conventions. In Sweden, for example, a photographer enjoys sole rights to a picture for 25 years after a picture's production. However, pictures with artistic or scientific merit enjoy protection for fifty years after the death of the copyright holder. Drawings belong to this category. In practice, almost all photographers can be said to have some "artistic merit".

When photographs are produced on *commission*, the client usually enjoys all copyright rights, including rights to prints made from originals. The client can freely utilize the commissioned pictures in any way desired.

Publishing rights to archive photographs are usually bought for each publishing occasion. The buyer may not then transfer publishing rights without written permission.

As regards drawn illustrations, the client usually pays for the actual sketching/drawing work, originals and reproduction rights for a particular application. The physical drawings, i.e. the originals, usually remain the artist's property. Thus, the client becomes entitled to compensation, equivalent to the "re-acquisition cost", if an original should be damaged. Unless contractually forbidden, the artist has the right to use a commissioned illustration in other contexts. In contrast to the position for the photographers, artists are unable to sell artistic rights to pictures.

The name of the picture creator or copyright holder must be stated in each printed document containing the pictures, preferably in direct conjunction with the pictures.

After 1st January 1979, no person's name or picture may be used in Swedish advertising without permission.

The development of new technology and new media will result in some infringement of existing legislation. A Swedish committee has been conducting a "Copyright Study" since 1976. The Study is examining the problems related to copyright rules. The Study's directives specified e.g.: "A main task for the Study is to establish a reasonable balance between the copyright holder's wish to maintain control over her/his work and the public need to utilize this work without needless obstacles. However, the object is not to convey improper benefit to people who make commercial use of work under copyright at the expense of the originator. Nor may the artistic rights enjoyed by originators, according to existing legislation, be compromised". No completely new law is likely to be passed in Sweden before the end of the 1980's. However, existing laws may be amended from time to time. Following a legislative change which came into effect on 1st July 1982, Swedish penalties for copyright infringement were increased. Thus, the penalties for "picture plagiarism", deliberate or in consequence of gross negligence, are now a fine or prison for up to two years, i.e. a quadrupling of the previous penalty.

Terms of delivery
Many photographers, most picture agencies and newspaper archives and some museums are members of the Swedish Association of Picture Suppliers (BLF). This organization promotes the interest of picture copyright holders. Its detailed terms of delivery reject every kind of manipulation of picture contents. They note e.g. (p.7 and p.17):"A picture may not be manipulated, without the photographer's/ seller's specific consent, by electronic or other means.

"Nor may the picture nor any part thereof be combined, without said consent, with any other picture so the two pictures appear to be a single work.

"A charge of at least SEK 5000 (appr. US$ 850) will be levied for each such infringement of this ban on manipulation.

"If infringement is deemed offensive to any individual party, legal redress may be sought to the Penal Code."

Nordic Artists (NT) is a joint body for artists' and graphical design organizations in Denmark, Finland, Iceland, Norway and Sweden. It promotes the interests of artists and has drawn up common terms of delivery. They specify (point 3), among other things: "No changes nor any other kind of image processing may be performed without the express consent of the originator."

Thus the contents of a picture may not be changed without the express consent of the picture's copyright holder.

Ethical rules
Ethical rules, drawn up by the Swedish Newspapermen's Professional Association (PK), the Swedish Journalists' Union (SJF), the Swedish Newspaper Publishers' Association (TU) and Swedish Broadcasting Corporation (SR) are available for the press, radio and TV. The object of these rules is to provide the individual members of the public with protection over and above that laid down in law. The rules instruct newspapers to avoid publication of information on a person's private life unless that information is of indisputable public interest. These ethical rules condemn manipulation or counterfeiting of picture contents by cropping, montage or misleading captions. Non-authentic pictures may not be published as authentic, genuine material. The "Ground Rules for Press, Radio and TV" published by the Joint Press Council also point out that people who buy pictures are responsible for ensuring that the pictures are not misused.

A person who feels that she/he has been poorly treated or erroneously described in a newspaper article has the right to demand a correction from the magazine or newspaper. She/he may also turn to the Press Ombudsman of the General Public (AO). This officer will assist the plaintiff by getting in touch with the newspaper in question, procuring a correction or retraction or having the matter brought before the Swedish Press Council (PO), an unofficial "court" on ethical matters. If the PO feels that criticism of a newspaper or magazine is warranted, the newspaper or magazine is obligated to print the PO's verdict. This verdict is often printed in other newspapers such as the Journalist (SJF) and the Press Journal (TU). The criticized magazine/newspaper must also pay a service charge. *Ethical rules are similar in other countries.*

CONTEXT

The context in which a visual message is presented has a major impact on the way the message is perceived. For example, the context may consist of text, speech, music, sound effects or other visuals. Our attention is on either the sound or the image when we view a film or a TV-program. This is even more obvious when we look at a multi image slide and film presentation. As soon as the film starts our attention is directed towards the movement in the film from the surrounding stills. It is just impossible for viewers not to be influenced by the film.

a, A B C   b, 12 13 14

The same pattern is identified as "B" in the first sequence (a) and as "13" in the second sequence (b).

Indirect contexts are the medium in which the visual is presented, the receiver of the message, the society and the culture. Our perception of a stimulus is thus not only determined by the characteristics of the main stimulus but also by those of the context. This is however, not the case with young children. A background which might give extra information to an adult cannot be assumed to fulfil the same function for a child.

Perception of brightness, color, size, shape, pattern, and motion have all been shown to be influenced by contextual variables. One and the same visual can be perceived in different ways in different contexts. A single picture taken from a series of pictures may be hard to decipher but the visual's content becomes easier to comprehend when that picture is returned to its proper sequential context.

A background which might give extra information to an adult reader cannot be assumed to fulfil the same function for a child. It may actually hinder the child from perceiving the picture at all. Thus we should be very careful in selecting context for our messages.

Interplay of words and visuals

As seen earlier pictures may have various functions. For example, pictures are very good at conveying information about what objects really look like. Text, however, is very good to use when e.g. logical relations will be expressed. Visuals used to be a kind of special features in books and still are in far too many situations. The illustrations in the laboriously copied books from the Middle Ages can often be compared to paintings in a museum or windows in a church. The illustrations in the manuscripts even had frames of genuine gold in many cases. For hundreds of years, visuals often remained extra features with a rather limited connection to the text. In the last century, textbook visuals were often placed vertically to provide better use of page space or an already existing illustration, e.g. a wood-cut was sometimes used. It was not unusual that one picture was used to depict e.g. several different persons or several different towns. Visuals were often a kind of "painting" with little or no real interaction with the text. However, visuals have been used in a more intentional way in non-fiction books. As early as the Middle Ages, some secular texts were illustrated.

Medical science demanded a knowledge of herbs. Plant recognition was aided by clear and analytical drawings as early as the 5th Century. Color, when used, was true to life. Each illustration had a text under it giving the characteristics of the herb and its medical use. However, copies made from earlier manuscripts, rather than from living plants, ultimately transformed the illustrations into stylized forms very different from botanical reality.

Visual stories with only brief text occur in many situations. A surprising variety of the frame shapes and juxtapositions is shown. One of the most impressive visual stories was made as a textile. The *Bayeux Tapestry,* 70 m long and 50 cm wide, uses 79 consecutive scenes to depict the story behind the Battle of Hastings in 1066.

In manuscripts it was easy to put words and visuals anywhere on a page. The skills of integrating words with visuals were gradually developed. In Europe, the ability to print images on paper was achieved during the 14th Century. The *block book* contained text that was written by hand and printed images. These printed images invariably included some form of captions or texts. When moveable type was introduced during the 15th Century it was possible to produce books in larger quantities. This was the beginning of a cultural revolution. There followed a dramatic growth in the quantity and quality of books and other printed documents like maps. Informative drawings developed.

However, the new technology impaired the possibilities for integration of words and visuals

In more modern time, the first one to really show how visuals and words could interplay was Johannes Amos Comenius of Moravia (today a part of Czechoslovakia). In his illustrated textbook *Orbis sensualium pictus* (1658) the illustrations had several numbers referred to in the text, in four different languages. His findings were more or less forgotten and "reinvented" only recently. Today, words and text usually interact nicely with visuals in instructional message designs. The systems for desktop publishing make it possible for the author to integrate words and visuals to aid communication.

Substantial research has clearly shown that learning efficiency is much enhanced when words and visuals interact and supply redundant information. The improvement sometimes exceeds sixty percent and averages thirty percent.

Text

The text should be readable, legible and well worth reading. *Readability* in this context can be defined as the degree of linguistic difficulty, i.e. the sum of the linguistic properties of a text which make it more or less accessible to the reader.

The two factors which best designate the linguistic comprehensibility of a text are sentence length and the proportion of long words. An easily comprehensible text is characterized by short sentences, short words and simple sentence structure. Other variables which affect the comprehensibility of text are the vocabulary's degree of abstraction, the number of syllables in words, the commonness of words used, the choice of subject, the subdivision into paragraphs, the prevalence of clauses, headings and sub-headings, line length, inter-line distance, illustrations, the size of letters, the relevance of the text to the reader and the page size. The index of readability (LIX) is calculated as follows:
- Count the number of words in the text.
- Count the number of words with more than six letters.
- Count the number of sentences.

Designing visuals for information

- Divide the number of long words by the number of words and multiply the product by 100. This yields the average word length (WL).
- Divide the number of words by the number of sentences. This yields the average sentence length (SL).
- WL + SL = LIX.

20 - 30	=	simple text, suitable for children's books
30 - 35	=	Swedish literature
35 - 45	=	moderately difficult text, weekly magazines
45 - 50	=	popular science subjects
50 - 55	=	difficult text, trade literature
55 -	=	extremely difficult text

The concept *legibility* refers to a text's external properties. These are properties such as letter size, interline distance, line length, the distance between letters, the number of letter per line, the distance between words, the typographic style, the subdivision into paragraphs, headings, headings in the margin, the layout, color of the printing ink and paper, the paper quality etc. These different external properties have not been found to have a drastic effect on legibility as long as the text is presented with the framework of variation normally found in contemporary books. It is, however, possible to give some general guide-lines to achieve optimum legibility:
- Running text should be in lower case letters. All-capital printing has been shown to markedly reduce the speed of reading.
- Typographic styles with serifs, Roman type, are considered to be easier to read than line type, sans serif, except for small letter sizes.
- Bold face or italics should not be used for continuous text. They may, however, be used for emphasis of small parts.
- The optimum line length seems to be about 40 characters and spaces. This is nine to eleven centimetres with optimum character size, ten to twelve point, at a normal reading distance.
- The maximum line length should not be much more than 60-70 characters and spaces. However costs often force people to use more characters on each line.

- The distance between lines should be one or two points more than the character size.
- Letter size must be adjusted to the visual format and the reading distance. It should be "large enough". Too small or too large lettering impair reading. A text on a poster should be at least five times larger than a corresponding text in a book.
- Text with a generous amount of space within it is rated as "easier" and more interesting than text which has a more solid appearance.
- A larger type size in a single column is preferable to a smaller type size in a double column layout.
- Less skilled readers find unjustified text easier to read than justified text. It makes no difference for advanced readers.
- For text printed in black all paper surfaces are equally legible if they have a reflectance of at least 70 %. The most legible combination is a black text on a light yellow background.
- In a normal reading situation black print on white paper is over 10 % more efficient than white on black. When negative text is used a larger type with open counters and adequate character spacing should be used.
- Legibility is severely impaired when text is printed over a picture.
- Margins have three main functions. They provide space for headings, comments and illustrations. They provide space for fingers to hold the book. They make it possible to do notes.
- The technical quality must be high (Also see Technical quality).

The text should be *well worth reading*. This designates the properties of the content of a text and is very dependent on the reader's degree of interest. Each group of readers selects reading material on the basis of personal preference. Studies of readability have resulted in lists with reading suggestions for various age groups.

Legends
In existing printed materials we may find legends with several different functions. A legend may be just a label. It may convey

factual content, or information about events. It may also evoke emotions. In text-books legends may be instructing and directing the reader on what to study in the picture. Legends may have redundant, relevant, irrelevant or contradictory relationships to the main text and/or to the picture.

People who look at a visual will to a great extent perceive it differently. A visual means different things to us and evokes many different associations depending on our different situations. A vivid example of this can usually easily be demonstrated by showing people a visual and asking them to write legends or just tell you about the content.

Legends are very important in instructional message design. We must tell the reader or viewer what we want her/him to see and learn from the illustration. Thus every visual should always be supplied with a legend which should be brief and easy to understand. In instructional message design the function of the legend is to help the reader select the intended content in the picture.

We can use five different strategies for reading legends and visuals. A few people read only the texts and ignore the visuals. They then use mainly the left half of their brains. Similarly, some people mainly use the right half of their brains, and only pay attention to the visual. Most people utilize both the legend and the visual in a legend-visual, a visual-legend or in an interactive strategy. It is easy to understand that these different strategies result in different learning efficiencies.

Content of legend
The legend and the visual should interact as parts of a whole. A legend should describe image contents and govern the way a picture is read: A picture producer's intentions about what the reader is supposed to see and learn from each illustration should be as clear as possible.

The legend should be redundant in relation to the visual, i.e. the legend should supply the same information as the visual. The relationship between legend and visual might also be relevant but should never be irrelevant or contradictory.

Form of legend
Generally speaking, a legend should be brief and easy to understand. It should be edited to fit different reader categories, such as general readers (children, teenagers, adults...), technical readers and specialist readers.

A general reader knows little, if anything, about the subject matter. The legends and the pictures are kept simple, attractive and informative. They should not be too complicated and, thus, distracting to the reader.

A technical reader will understand technical concepts but may not be familiar with special terminology. Legends may provide detailed explanations of attractive and informative pictures.

A specialist reader has a good understanding of the subject matter. Both the text and illustrations, which may consist of detailed drawings, graphs, technical photographs, ultrasonograms or other realistic pictures or symbols, may be detailed.

The legend should be brief and cogent. An excessively long legend diverts the reader's attention from the main thread in the main text. Just as it is natural for the main text to refer to the legend, it is equally important for the reader to be able to make her/his way with ease from the legend to the main text. Not merely the readers who shift back and forth between the main text and the legend! This also applies to an equal degree to the many readers who begin with the pictures and legends without any intention of reading the entire main text and who are only interested in obtaining detailed information on a particular illustrated section.

Placement of legend
The legend should always be located close to the picture, preferably under, to the right or left or above but never inside the picture frame. Placing the legend inside the picture makes it harder for people to read both the picture and the text. Nor should the legend be located on some other page, as happens far too often in reference books and school books. A legend can have a heading as an additional link between the visual and the legend.

The legend should have a different typographic size or even a different font so it can be easily distinguished from the main text, e.g. on a page in a book. The legends should not be in negative form in a color picture since the slightest misalignment in printing

Designing visuals for information

would make the legends extremely difficult to read. The legend may well have a heading which summarizes picture contents.

Image framing

A frame around an image, or sometimes around an illustration and text, may have different functions. Image framing can be functional and/or attentional. A frame will separate the image from the surrounding context, and draw special attention to information within the frame. E.g. in a newspaper, framing is a way of helping the readers to combine the corresponding text and pictures on the page.

Registrations of eye fixations on an image, in one version with a frame and in another version without a frame, have shown that a frame is not distracting for adult viewers.

Seventeen subjects viewed a drawing of two flying House Martins. The recorded fixations have been plotted on these outlines of the image versions. Eight subjects viewed the frame version and made 98 fixations. Nine subjects viewed the version without a frame and made 117 fixations. (Also see Centres of interest.)

Interplay of visuals

In many situations it is a good idea to use pairs of visuals in which one is true-to-life, such as a photograph, and the other represents an analytical representation, such as a simple line drawing . The analytical visual makes it easier for us to understand the content, and the realistic visual enables us to believe in the content. So the two visuals should be closely linked in a carefully thought-out relationship.

Time scales and charts provide a reference in time and space. Sometimes it is necessary to divide a message content into a series of visuals. The amount of details can be great or the content can include a certain period of time.

Layout

A layout is the result of graphic design. The purpose of this work is to find a suitable presentation for the content with respect to the receiver, the subject matter and the financial situation.

A page or a spread with only text or with one "painting" might be considered to be very beautiful by graphic designers and some readers of fiction in books, magazines and journals.

In this example of a non-fiction layout, the individual visuals compete intensely. They are not explained by legends and can be regarded as a "non-example" of instructional message design.
(From Borrman et al., Nu läser vi E. Uppsala 1977. Reduced in size.)

Designing visuals for information 275

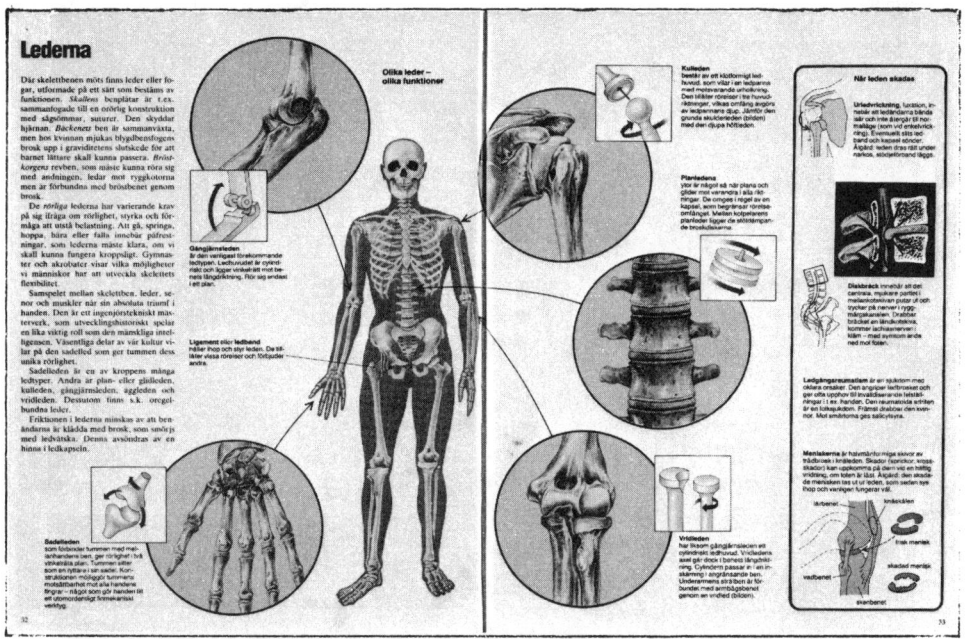

An example of an "informative layout" in a text-book about Man. Here the documentary and analytic drawings and descriptive texts interact in a lexi-visual presentation. We read and view at the same time. We are provided with clear and concrete information.
(From Media Människan. Stockholm 1981. Reduced.)

In *newspaper layout* many different messages have to be communicated. The problem is to communicate a series of disconnected messages of infinitely varying significance within a limited space, time and economy with a recognizably consistent style for each section of the paper. Many readers will only spend time on a limited amount of information in a newspaper. It is known that elements like headlines, photos, drawings and information graphics attract attention and often are entry points into a page. Size and placement of such elements influence how the reader will read a page. It is possible that many readers may jump over too large pictures and never look at them at all.

In *magazine layout* visuals are often very large. The visuals have no or a very limited contact with the text. *Fiction layout* certainly does not work very well in instructional message design.

Even in traditional non-fiction publishing, it is often very hard to access the information.

Picture placement has very often been based on aesthetic rather than instructional characteristics. Visuals should be located in close proximity to the parts of the text in which pictured motifs are discussed. Visuals plus their captions should preferably be inserted into the text between two paragraphs, not in the middle of a paragraph, so they do not disrupt reading rhythm. Legends and visuals are often piled up in different areas and sometimes even on different pages. Here, an effort should really be made to achieve the best possible interplay of words and visuals. Visuals interact with the legends, with other visuals, headings, running text, tables, maps etc. on a page and on a spread in a book, magazine or newspaper. The layout of the whole spread should be attractive. However, the mere use of a lot of pictures is not enough. In an *artistic layout*, the message may be effectively hidden. The message is more effectively conveyed by an *informative layout*. (Also see Linguistic combinations.)

An *infographer*, or a *graphic journalist*, i.e. a person whose occupation is to create verbo-visual information, has several different "tools" or means of expression at her/his disposal.

1. Text: headings, introductions, column text, legends (sometimes with legend headings), text in pictures (occasional words, texts, numbers and signs), verbograms (tables, information boxes, quotation boxes, explanations of words).

2. Visuals: drawings (realistic drawings, schematic drawings, stylized drawings, drawings of animate objects, drawing of inanimate objects, exploded views, X-ray drawing, blueprints, panorama drawings), maps (plotting maps, detailed maps, figurative maps, cartograms), diagrams (bar diagrams, linear diagrams, pie charts, block diagrams, pictograms), scales (time scales, distance scales, size scales), charts (flow charts, organizational charts), serial technics (picture sequences, balloons, graphical symbols for sounds and emotions), photographs (product photos, portraits, situation photos, landscapes etc.), combinations of photos, drawings and symbols (trademarks, logos, traffic signs etc).

3. Graphical markers: we can use frames, lines, arrows, flags, colors etc. to reinforce a method. The graphic journalist needs to work together with subject experts, writers, photographers, page designers and documentalists. S/he also needs access to reference libraries with books, maps, statistical data etc.

Harmony in typography will be achieved when there is good relationship between the individual elements in the design and the "wholeness". A balanced typography gives an impression of quality and credibility. Contrast in typography may be achieved e.g. by using different fonts, styles, sizes and colors.

The basics for instructional message design could be summarized in the following: Select Arrangement, Balance and Color to maximize Dynamism, Emphasis, Fidelity and Graphic Harmony.

FORMAT

An image is a multidimensional representation of an inner or of an external reality, depicting the physical structure of the objects or events it represents. An image can also be described as a more or less complicated sense of vision, i.e. awareness of the stimulation of the eye's vision perception cells, with a specific message/content. An inner image, a visual experience, can originate in thoughts and in dreams. It may be caused by words, e.g. a picture description, without any help of pictures. Every possible visual, every format has got different possibilities to supply any specific message/content. This depends on the choice of material and type of production. At Tsukuba Expo -85 in Japan, it was possible to view an image on Seiko's about four square centimetre bracelet television (1.7 x 2.5 cm) and at the same time see the same image-content on the Sony Jumbotron with a screen one thousand square meters large, that is 2.3 million times larger. Obviously another video signal could also feed TV-monitors of traditional sizes with the same image-content. It is easy to understand that these images will give each viewer different perceptions, even though they all depict the same motif and are created by the same video signals. We should ask ourselves, if these differently sized images have really got the same image contents.

Image morphology

An artist or a painter producing a picture may use lead, crayons, India ink, various kinds of paint, paper, canvas and several other kind of materials in a variety of different combinations. The actual picture is built up of materials and pigments which, according to intentions, can be completely separated or gradually mixed. Except for the printing of line drawings, all other pictures have to be *divided into small elements* in the technical process of duplicating, e.g. in the printing of books or in the broadcasting of television.

Normally these picture elements or *pixels* are very small. At normal reading distance they can hardly be seen. In fact *an image with "good quality" must have a resolution that is better than that of our own vision.* In real life, nature and all kinds of objects have got an infinite number of color nuances and shades of grey. Our perception system can handle enormous quantities of information under very different conditions. At any given moment, the eye may contain 2,500,000 bits of information. However, our eyes are by no means "perfect" optical systems. It is possible for us to see the difference between several million color stimuli at simultaneous viewing. However, if not being seen simultaneously the number we can *identify* is much smaller, maybe 10,000 to 20,000. It is often claimed that we can only identify 64 shades in a grey-scale. There is also a limit to acuity and the eye has got inertia. Acuity is best in the fovea, and considerably worse outside it. Take a close look at a color-TV-image (about arm's length distance). In the very centre of the gaze you are able to clearly see the small red, green and blue dots or bars making up the TV-image. This clear oval or circular area, between a dime and a quarter in size, is falling on your foveas. It will jump around as you move your eyes over the image and make four to six eye fixations per second. At normal television-viewing distance all the small dots blend together and we may perceive the image as "rather good" or "good". More pixels are needed to make a really good TV-image (more below).

The necessary number and size of individual pixels will be defined by:
- the size of the object depicted

Designing visuals for information

- the size of the image
- the viewing distance
- the image content, and also
- the actual material carrying the image (paper, film, glass etc).

Close viewing distances require the images to be divided into many small pixels. For long viewing distances it is enough with fewer and larger pixels. And pixels really vary in size, and they also represent very different parts of reality. Some examples will be given here to illustrate this.

The first American *Landsat-satellite* was sent up in 1972. Landsat-1 registered green, red and two bands near infra-red. Pictures cover 185x185 kilometres on earth. Each pixel represents 80x80 metres, that is 6,400 square metres. Landsat-1 was a great success and was followed by Landsat-2 in January 1975 and by Landsat-3 in March 1978. Since 1982, the Landsat-satellites produce images with a resolution of 30 metres. Each pixel has been reduced to 900 square metres. In February 1986, the European *SPOT-satellite* was launched into orbit. The SPOT-satellite delivers images with 20 metre resolution in color and 10 metre resolution in black and white. Now the pixels were reduced to 400 and 100 square metres respectively. Usually SPOT-pictures depict 60x60 kilometres of the surface of the ground. Such a black and white "scene" has got 6,000 lines with 6,000 pixels each, that is a total of 36 million pixels. At Esrange, the premises of the Swedish Space Corporation in Kiruna, in northern Sweden, a quarter of a million SPOT-pictures are received every year. With pictures like this it is possible to produce several kinds of maps for use e.g in agriculture and forestry. Certain military satellites, "spy-satellites", are suggested to produce pictures with a resolution of a few decimetres. Then it is possible to distinguish individual people for example on board a ship.

When a SPOT-scene and a photographic portrait of a person are printed with the same resolution as full pages in the same book, a pixel in the first image represents a portion of reality that is one million times larger than the area represented by a pixel in the second image.

At the 1980 Olympic summer games in Moscow some 3,000 Russian soldiers holding square *textile fabrics* in different colors produced several different images. The image of Mischa, the Russian bear, became a symbol of the games.

The *Jumbotron*, the largest video-screen in the world was 40x25 metres, equivalent to a ten-storey building. The Jumbotron-image, which could be seen by more than 50,000 people at the same time, consisted of 150,000 picture elements. Each picture element was a 8x4.5 centimetre TRINI-LITE cell with a blue, a green and a red section. A computer system was used to control all the different pixels individually.

For a few thousand years artists have produced *mosaics* as decorations on floors, walls and roofs. Mosaics consist of thousands of small pieces, usually of glass or marble in different colors. Each piece is carefully put into a soft foundation which then hardens. The large mosaics in the cathedral of St. Peter in Rome are seen as actual paintings. You have to get really close to the images to see the individual pieces of glass-pixels.

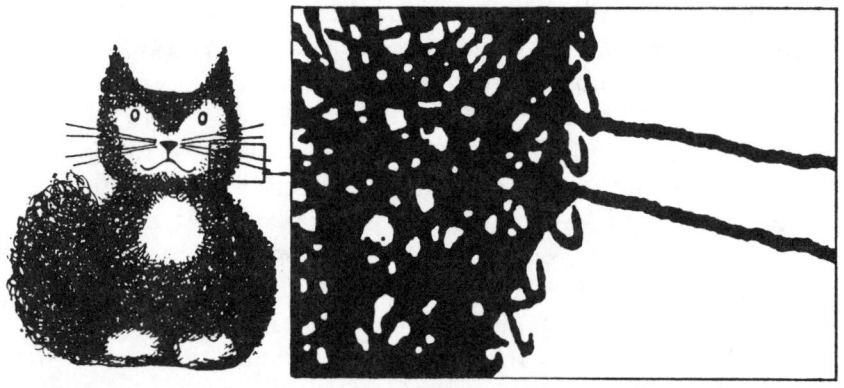

A line drawing, with an enlargement about eleven times of a small part.

In modern printing processes, half-tone pictures are divided into picture elements by using "raster-screens". The printed dots vary in size within the "pixel-area" from nothing or a very small dot to gradually increasing dot-sizes, until the dot covers the complete "pixel-area". Thus it is possible to reproduce photos, drawings and other originals with scales of grey and color. In newspaper production, rasters with a density of 50 lines per inch may be used in the prepress process. For book production,

Designing visuals for information

rasters with a density of 100 lines, or more, per inch may be used. The films that are used to make printing plates may be produced using photo type setting machines, working with resolutions of 600 lines per inch for the newspaper plates and 1,200 lines per inch for the book plates. An image, say a two by two inch portrait, may be printed with 10,000 dots in a newspaper and 40,000 dots in a book. In a newspaper, the printed dots can be seen with the aid of a magnifying glass.

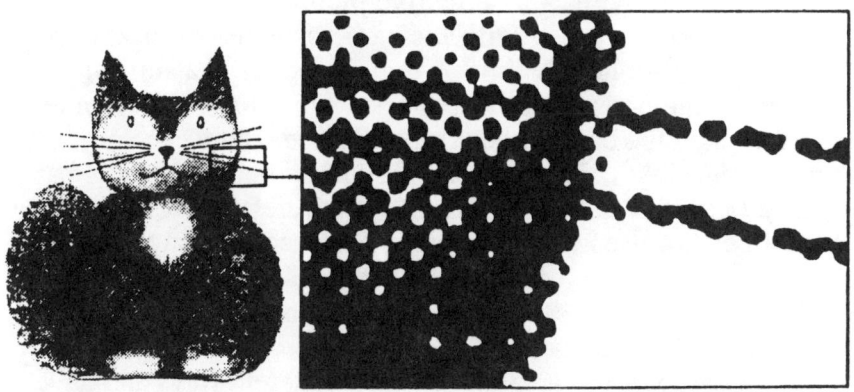

An image with raster. The raster pattern is easy to see in the enlargement.

Images in color are separated into four different half-tone films: blue, yellow, red and black. A printing plate is generated from each film. The picture is then printed in each color. For the printing of black and white pictures, only one film and one plate are needed.

A large outdoor placard printed with low resolution may be at least one thousand times larger than the same advertisement printed with high resolution in a magazine. Both images may have equal number of pixels.

Film pictures, on paper or film, consist of very small grain or pigments, which are developed in chemical-technical processes. It is very unusual that we can see the individual grain or pigments. That is only the case with extreme enlargements. Our perception of a projected slide will be dependent on the quality of the screen as well as the quality of the equipment used and the amount of light in the room.

A *TV-image* is built up by lines or picture elements. The NTSC-system uses 525 lines and the European PAL-system uses 625 lines. In NTSC 30 and in PAL 25 images are created every second (or rather 60 and 50 "half-pictures" respectively). This is in phase with the kind of alternating current being used on the different continents. In both systems some lines are used for synchronizing and "administering" the image information. Usually a black and white television-image is built up by 420 "effective lines" with 560 "effective picture elements" each i.e. some 235,000 pixels, all with the same size and with 256 grey levels. A PAL-color TV-image is built up by 1.2 million red, green and blue phosphorus dots or bars forming 400,000 pixels. For each pixel the balance between the three colors can vary, creating all possible color nuances. However, better systems have already been developed. In HDTV (high definition television) 1,125 lines are used and 30 frames per second, which is about four times the quality of NTSC. HDTV is also wider than the traditional TV-image. The HDTV-screen has an aspect ratio of 3x5 compared to the traditional 3x4.

Computer screens are built in many different ways and have a variety of resolutions. For example the 9" screen of Apple Macintosh has got 512x342 = 175,104 pixels. The Apple 13" Color Monitor has got 640x480 = 307,200 pixels and the Super Mac Color Screen has got 1024x768=786,432 pixels.

During 1983 IMB presented a 50 x 56 cm flat plasma screen with 750 horizontal and 1,000 vertical pipes which makes 750,000 image points. The screen can display 9,920 characters and can be divided into maximum of 16 separate parts. Behind the screen is a microcomputer with a memory of 24,000 characters. Several other companies are also working on improvements of screen quality.

Even better systems are available. The most advanced system is said to consist of 8,000x8,000=6,400,000 pixels. A high image frequency is needed to get a stable image on a computer screen. As an example, an IBM PC has got 50 and a PS/2 70 images per second. The Macintosh II has got 67 images per second. A detailed picture needs to be divided into at least four million picture elements to be satisfactorily presented. Since each single picture element has the ability to change according to the

Designing visuals for information 283

greyscale and color content, no less than one hundred million bits of information is needed. Thus a large computer capacity is needed, especially where film- and TV-images are concerned. Film uses 24 and TV 25 or 30 frames per second. However, computer software is available that only takes account of the parts in the pictures where changes occur. Thus, the necessary number of calculations is limited.

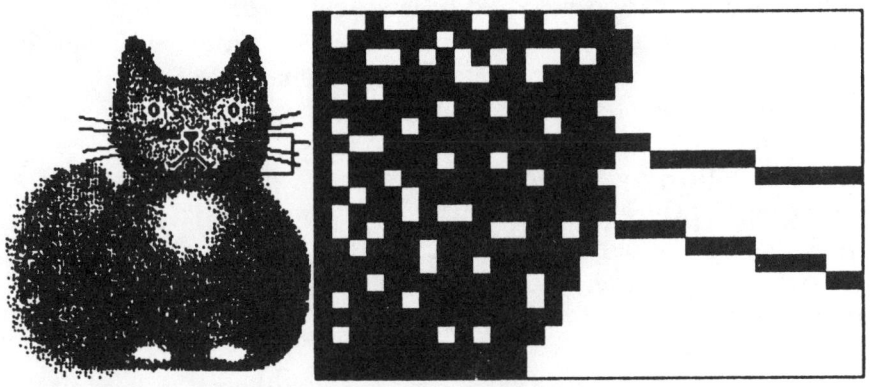

An image created in the computer with a resolution of 72 d.p.i. It is easy to see the individual dots in the enlargement.

Computer printouts vary in quality. A printout can be made using pen plotters, color ribbons, ink jet printing, laser printers, type-setting machines and other systems (Also see Screen Communication: Computer Print-outs). Simple systems have a resolution of 50 lines per inch. Laser printers usually produce 300 lines per inch. Photo type-setting machines produce 1,200, 2,400 or even 3,200 lines per inch. Image Maker is a slide-making system, conveying a computer image to color film with a resolution of 8,000 lines per inch. Regardless of the resolution of the screen, computers can usually work with higher resolution images. To make use of this capacity, however, a high quality output system is needed. Obviously, an image printed with higher resolution will be better perceived than an image printed in low resolution, when the reading distance is the same. However, the better system also costs a lot more.

By using a bit-map-technique, a whole page with text and illustrations can be handled in computer systems. Desk top systems usually work with 300 lines per inch. However with Linotronic 300, a photo type-setting machine, it is possible to work with 2,540 lines per inch. In this case an A4-size page contains 623,7 million pixels.

Analogue and digital coding

Whether information is stored in analogue or digital codes is of major importance. Analogue coding takes up much less space than digital coding. Video data stored in analogue form is suitable, for example, for entertainment when sequential viewing of a program from beginning to end is desired.

The following example illustrates the difference between analogue and digital storage of information: A single page of a book can hold about 2,500 characters (i.e. 50 lines containing 50 characters, including spaces). Storing the same page information in digital form would require 20,000 bits of information (binary ones and/or zeros).

This may seem like a great deal but is still almost negligible compared to the storage and transmission of information in other media. Here are some equivalents: a line drawing is equivalent to five pages of text, one second of FM radio to ten pages of text, one second of digital sound on a compact disc to 35 pages of text, one second of TV to 250 pages of text, one second of HDTV to 1,500 pages of text and one frame (a scene) from the SPOT-satellite is equivalent to no less than 50,000 pages of text.

Thus digitally stored information always take up much more space than information stored in analogue form. Provided that the number of pixels are large enough, digitally stored information offers numerous opportunities for easy and convenient "manipulation" and editing of text, sound or image in different ways. This may be highly important in different kinds of interactive applications, such as systems for education and training.

The editing of a written text can result in the production of a "message" with fewer words. In speech synthesis, i.e. computer-generated speech, the amount of transmitted information can sometimes be reduced by 99% with no loss of message comprehension, even if the aesthetic quality of the speech may decline. In a similar manner, the number of pixels in an image can be reduced

Designing visuals for information 285

without any major impact on the image's message. Thus it is possible to more effectively make use of computer memory capacity.

A bit-mapped image, created and stored in a computer may be scaled. However, no new information is added when the image is enlarged and important information is lost when the image is reduced. Thus it is normally best to create an image in the correct size.

Perception of pixels

Pixels are always small in relation to the screen on which they are displayed. The greater the number of pixels used by a system for image formation in a given area, the greater the system's sharpness and resolution. When resolution is good, a black or white pixel cannot be distinguished from other adjacent black or white pixels. This applies both to monitor screens and copies on paper, plastic or film. However, an individual white (black) pixel is highly visible when surrounded by black (white) pixels. When black and white pixels are evenly distributed in an image, individual pixels become indistinguishable. The image then assumes a gray appearance. Thus our perception of an individual pixel is always heavily influenced by the context in which the pixel appears. The relative distribution of black and white pixels, or the "sum" of each pixel's context, is decisive to our perception of image content. Purely random distribution of pixels produces a gray, uninteresting pattern. A controlled, *intentional* distribution of pixels can result in different patterns or depictions. Moving or changing the pixels in a picture enables us to create thousands of new images. Computers process each such variation as a different picture. But a human viewer may regard these images as functionally identical or equivalent. Analogously, a text can be presented in many different ways, with different typefaces and pitches etc. with no major effect on perception of the text's content.

Normally speaking, an individual pixel is non-significant from a visual language point of view. A surprisingly large number of pixels can be e.g. deleted from an image. When performing image analysis, a computer is usually incapable of deciding whether or not an individual pixel is significant to the image. One exception is the GOP computer developed in Linköping, Sweden. It can decide whether an individual pixel is e.g. part of a demarcation line separating one structure from another. A pixel may be an important feature of a basic graphic image element (a dot, a line or an area) or of a simple shape, thereby contributing to a visual sub-meaning or syntagm. So we can delete, add or shift information in an image without drastically affecting perception of image contents. The pixels which form borders/edges between different shapes are more important to picture perception than other pixels. Since the brain fills in missing information and always strives to make the best possible interpretation of a given stimulus, the deletion of even some meaningful parts of a picture is also possible. In cartoons, absent lines can be as important as the lines actually present. The ability to utilize the "right" amount of graphic image elements and finding the "right" balance in a picture are characteristics of experienced and skilled artists, photographers and graphic designers. Too little information results in an inadequate picture. Too much information results in a picture which is hard to decipher and comprehend. There is an ideal trade-off for every type of picture content and for every application.

Image format categories

An important difference between main categories of pictures is the use of light. All pictures printed in books, magazines, papers and other printed matter are seen in the normal directed lighting. In TV- and computer screens the light comes through the image. Films, slides and overhead transparencies are usually projected on a screen. The difference in nature of these groups of pictures is important to study.

It might be possible to organize or classify pictures according to their format. The following is such a suggested scheme. (In all groups images can be displayed in color as well as in black and white.)

Designing visuals for information 287

1. **Two-dimensional pictures**
   1.1 Passive, finished, pictures
   　　1.1.1 Still pictures
   　　　　handicrafted pictures: drawings, paintings, mosaics, textiles etc. on different materials such as paper, canvas, glass, stone etc.
   　　　　technically crafted pictures: such as 1, lasting images with examples such as photo prints, printed pictures and 2, projected images such as slides, overhead transparencies, microfiche, video still images (Mavica) and simple computer images

   　　1.1.2 Moving pictures
   　　　　film: in several different formats (8, S8, 16, 35 mm, widescreen) and types of programmes
   　　　　TV: several means of distribution (air, video-cassettes, video-discs) and types of programmes

   1.2 Active, dynamic, pictures
   　　1.2.1 Still pictures
   　　　　overhead transparencies with overlays, different computer pictures (larger than the screen)

   　　1.2.2 Moving pictures
   　　　　animated film and TV, PiP (S-8) and Bezeler (16), animated computer images, video teleconferencing, interactive television, overhead transparencies with movement

2. **Three-dimensional pictures**
   2.1 Passive, finished, pictures
   　　2.1.1 Still pictures
   　　　　objects such as sculptures and different articles, holograms, stereo-images such as viewmaster, autostereo, chromatic stereo, polarized light

   　　2.1.2 Moving pictures
   　　　　moving holograms, stereo film such as chromatic stereo film, polarized light film, stereo TV

   2.2 Active, dynamic, pictures
   　　2.2.1 Still pictures
   　　　　stereo-overhead transparencies with overlays

   　　2.2.2 Moving pictures
   　　　　inner images, live images such as body language, sign languages, theatre, dance and models

REFERENCES

Content
Culbertson, H. M. (1974). Words vs. pictures. Perceived impact and connotative meaning. *Journalism Quarterly*, 51, 226–237.
Fleming, M., & Levie, W.H. (1978). *Instructional Message Design*. Englewood Cliffs, N.J.: Educational Technology Publications.
Haber, R. N., & Hershenson, M. (1973). *The Psychology of Visual Perception*. New York: Holt, Rinehart, and Winston.
Pettersson, R. (1981). *Bilder Barn och Massmedia*, Stockholm: Akademilitteratur.
Pettersson, R. (1982). International Review Cultural Differences in the Perception of Image and Color in Pictures. *ECTJ*, 30, 1, 43–53.
Vernon, M. D. (1962). *The Psychology of Perception*, Baltimore, Maryland: Penguin Books.
Zimmer, A., & Zimmer, F. (1978). *Visual literacy in communication: Designing for development*. Hulton Educational Publications, Ltd., in cooperation with the International Institute for Adult Methods, Teheran.

Structure
Fleming, M., & Levie, W.H. (1978). *Instructional Message Design*. Englewood Cliffs, N. J.: Educational Technology Publications.
Heinich, R., Molenda, M., & Russell, J. D. (1982). *Instructional media and the new technologies of instruction*. New York: John Wiley and Sons.

Realism
Allen, W. (1960). *Audio-visual communication*. In C. W. Harris, (Ed.). *Encyclopedia of Educational research* (3rd ed.). New York: Macmillan, 115–137.
Attneave, F. (1959). *Application of information theory to psychology*. New York: Henry Holt.
Black, H. B. (1962). *Improving the programming of complex pictorial materials: Discrimination learning as affected by prior exposure to and relevance of components of the figural discriminanda*. Final report NDEA Titel VI, Project 688, Wahington D. C.: U. S. Office of Education.
Borg, W. R., & Sculler, C. I. F. (1979). Detail and Background in Audiovisual Lessons and their Effect on Learners. *ECTJ*, 26, 1, 31–38.
Dwyer, F. M. (1972). *A guide for improving visualized instruction*. University Park, PA: Learning Services.
Dwyer, F. M. (1978). *Strategies for Improving Visual Learning*. State College, PA: Learning Services.

Fuglesang, A. (1973). *Applied communications in developing countries, ideas and observations.* Uppsala: Dag Hammarskjöld Foundation.
Gibson, J. J. (1966). *The senses considered as perceptual systems.* Boston: Houghton-Mifflin.
Heinich, R., Molenda, M., & Russell, J. D. (1982). *Instructional media and the new technologies of instruction.* New York: John Wiley and Sons.
Katzmann, N., & Nyenhuis, J. (1972). Color vs black and white effects on learning, opinion and attention. *AV Communication Review,* 20, 16–28.
Levie, W.H. (1973). *Pictorial research: An overview.* Viewpoints, Bloomington: Indiana University.
Lindgren-Fridell, M. (1977). *Barns reaktioner inför bild, särskilt barnboksbild.* In M. Lindgren-Fridell (Ed). *Bilder i barnboken.* Göteborg.
Lindsten, C. (1975). *Hembygdskunskap i årskurs 3. Att inhämta, bearbeta och redovisa kunskaper.* Lund: Liber Läromedel.
Lindsten, C. (1976). *Aktiviteter i hembygdskunskap: Elevpreferenser i årskurs 3. En faktoranalytisk studie. (Activities in Science and Social Studies: Pupils preferences in grade 3. A factorial study.)* Pedagogiskpsykologiska problem. (Malmö, Sweden: School of Education), Nr. 310.
Lindsten, C. (1977). *Bilder i hembygdsboken: Elevpreferenser i årskurs 3. En faktoranalytisk studie. (Activities in Science and Social Studies: Pupils preferences in grade 3. A factorial study.)* Pedagogisk-psykologiska problem (Malmö, Sweden: School of Education), Nr. 312.
Myatt, B., & Carter, J. M. (1979). Picture Preferences of Children and young Adults. *ECTJ,* 27, 1, 45–53.
Patty, C. R., & Vredenberg, H. L. (1970). *Electric signs: Contribution to the communication spectrum.* Fort Collins: Colorado State University.
Rydin, I. (1979). *Hur barn förstår TV II, Från frö till telefonstolpe. Med rörlig bild eller stillbild? Stockholm:* SR/PUB, Projekt Nr. 747073.
Spaudling, S. (1955). Research on pictorial illustrations. *AV Communication Review,* 34–35.
Travers, R. M. W. (1969). *A study of the advantages and disadvantages of using simplified visual presentations in instructional materials.* Final Report, Grant N. OEG-1-71070144-5235, Washington, D. C.: U.S. Office of Education, ED 031951.
Valentine, E. W. (1962). *The experimental psychology of beauty.* London: Methuen.
Wicker, F. W. (1970). Photographs, drawings, and nouns as stimuli in paired-associate learning. *Psychonomic Science,* 18, 205–206.

Degree of detail
Anderson, R. C., & Faust, G. W. (1973). *Educational Psychology, The science of instruction and learning.* New York: Dodd, Mead & Co.
Ball, J., Byrnes, F. C., Eds. (1960). *Research, Principles and Practice in Visual Communication.* Washington, D. C.: National Educational Association.

Berelson, B., & Steiner, G. A. (1964). *Human Behavior: An Inventory of Scientific Findings.* New York: Harcourt, Brace, and World.

Black, H. B. (1962). *Improving the programming of complex pictorial materials. Discrimination learning as affected by prior exposure to and relevance of components of the figural discriminanda.* Final report NDEA Titel VI, Project 688, Washington D.C.: U.S. Office of Education.

Brody, P. J. (1982). *Affecting Instructional Textbooks Through Pictures.* In D.H. Jonasson. The Technology of Text. Englewood Cliffs N.J.: Educational Technology Publications, 301–316.

Borg, W. R., & Sculler, C. I. F. (1979). Detail and Background in Audiovisual Lessons and their Effect on Learners. *ECTJ*, 26 1, 31–38.

Dwyer, F. M. (1972). *A guide for improving visualized instruction.* University Park, Pa: Learning Services.

Fuglesang, A. (1973). *Applied communications in developing countries, ideas and observations.* Uppsala: Dag Hammarskjöld Foundation.

Haber, R. N., & Hershenson, M. (1973). *The Psychology of Visual perception.* New York: Holt, Rinehart, and Winston.

Lindsten, C. (1975). *Hembygdskunskap i årskurs 3. Att inhämta, bearbeta och redovisa kunskaper.* Lund: Liber Läromedel.

Lindsten, C. (1976). *Aktiviteter i hembygdskunskap: Elevpreferenser i årskurs 3. En faktoranalytisk studie. (Activities in Science and Social Studies: Pupils preferences in grade 3. A factorial study.)* Pedagogisk-psykologiska problem. (Malmö, Sweden: School of Education), Nr. 310.

Miller, G. A. (1968). *The magical number seven, plus or minus two: Some limits on our capacity for processing information.* In R. N. Haber (Ed.). *Contemporary Theory and Research in Visual Perception.* New York: Holt, Rinehart, and Winston, Inc.

Murch, G. M. (1973). *Visual and Auditory Perception.* Indianapolis: The Bobbs-Merrill Co.

Rock, I. (1975). *An Introduction to Perception.* New York: Macmillan Publishing Co.

Rydin, I. (1979). *Hur barn förstår TV II, Från frö till telefonstolpe. Med rörlig bild eller stillbild? Stockholm:* SR/PUB, Projekt Nr. 747073.

Travers, R. M. W. (1969). *A study of the advantages and disadvantages of using simplified visual presentations in instructional materials.* Final Report, Grant N. OEG-1-71070144-5235, Washington, D. C.: U.S. Office of Education, ED 031951.

Wohlwill, J. F. (1975). Childrens responses to meaningful pictures varying in diversity: Exploration time vs. preference. *Journal of Experimental Child Psychology*, 20, 341–355.

Objects
Belson, W. A. (1978). *Television Violence and the Adolecent Boy.* London: Saxon House.

Clark, D. C. (1971). Teaching concepts in the classroom: A set of teaching prescriptions derived from experimental research. *Journal of Educational Psychology, Monograph,* 62, 253–264.
Cook, B. L. (1981). *Understanding Pictures in Papua New Guinea.* David C. Cook Foundation, Elgin, Illinois.
DeCecco, J. P. (1968). *The Psychology of Learning and Instruction: Educational Psychology.* Englewood Cliffs: Prentice-Hall.
Fuglesang, A. (1973). *Applied communications in developing countries, ideas and observations.* Uppsala: Dag Hammarskjöld Foundation.
Haber, R. N., & Hershenson, M. (1973). *The Psychology of Visual Perception.* New York: Holt, Rinehart and Winston.
Kowalski, K. (1977). *Barn och bildskapande. Hur man stimulerar barns föreställningsförmåga, fantasi och idéer.* Stockholm: W&W.
McBean, G., Kaggwa, N., & Bugembe J. (Ed.) (1980). *Illustrations for development.* Afrolit Society. Kenya.
Richards, J. P. (1976). Stimulating high-level comprehension by interspersing questions in text passages. *Educational Technology,* 16 (11), 13–17.
Sheppard, A. N. (1971). *Changing Learner Conceptual Behavior Through the Selective Use of Positive and Negative Examples.* Ed. D. thesis, Indiana University.
Thiagarajan, S. (1971). *Instantial and Contrastive Teacher Names and Students Conceptual Behavior.* Ph. D. thesis, Indiana University.
Travers, R. M. W., & Awarado, V. (1970). The design of pictures for teaching children in the elementary school. *AV Communication Review,* 18, 47–64.
Vernon, M. D. (1962). *The Psychology of Perception.* Baltimore, Maryland: Penguin Books.

Time
Cook, B. L. (1981). *Understanding Pictures in Papua New Guinea.* David C. Cook Foundation, Elgin, Illinois.
Fairbanks, G., Guttman, N., & Murray, S. Miron, 1957: Effects of Time Compression Upon the Comprehension of Connected Speech. *Journal of Speech and Hearing Disorders,* 22, 10–19.
Forgus, R. H. (1966). *Perception.* New York: McGraw-Hill Book Company.
LaBarbara, P., & MacLachlan, J. (1979). Time-Compressed Speech in Radio Advertising. *Journal of Marketing,* 43, 30–36.
MacLachlan, J. (1979). *What people really think of fast talkers.* Psychology today, 113–117.
McLachlan, J & LaBarbara, P. (1978). Time-Compressed TV Commercials. *Journal of Advertising Research,* 18, 11–15.
Murch, G. M. (1973). *Visual and Auditory Perception.* Indianapolis: The Bobbs-Merrill Co.

Statistics

Ackmann, D. (1984). *Advanced Business Graphics Forms.* CAMP/ 84. Computer Graphics Applications for Management And Productivity. Berlin Sept 25–28. Proceedings: AMK Berlin. 79–81.

Chaprakani, T. K., & Ehrenberg, A. S. C. (1976). *Numerical information processing.* London: London Business School.

Croxton, F. E., & Stein, H. (1932). Graphic comparison by bars, squares, circles and cubes. *Journal of the American Statistical Association,* 27, 54–60.

Culbertson, H. M., & Powers, R. D. (1959). A study of graph comprehension difficulties. *AV Communication Review,* 7, 97–100.

Culbertson, H. M., Flores, T., Powers, R., & Sarbaugh, L. E. (1959). *Using graphs more effectively for economic information.* Bulletin 29. University of Wisconsin: Department of Agricultural Journalism.

Ehrenberg, A. S. C. (1975). *Data reduction,* New York: Wiley.

Feliciano, G. D., Powers, R. D., and Kearl, B. E. (1962). *Text table or graphs for communicating statistical information.* Bulletin 32. University of Wisconsin: Department of Agricultural Journalism.

Feliciano, G. D., Powers, R. D., & Kearl, B. E. (1963). The presentation of statistical information. *AV Communication Review,* II, 32–39.

Hayashi, K. (1982). Research and Development on High Definition Television. *SMPTE Journal,* 3, 178–186.

ISSCO, (1981). *Choosing the right chart. A comprehensive Guide for Computer Graphics Users.* San Diego.

Lanners, E. (1973). *Illusionen.* Lucerne: Verlag C.J. Bucker.

Lax, L., & Olsson M. (1983). NAPLPS Standard Graphics and the Microcomputer. *Byte,* 8, 7, 82–92.

Legatt, A. L. S. (1983). *Financial Information on Teletext.* London: The City University, Centre for Information Science, M. Sc. Thesis.

Mac Donald-Ross, M. (1977). How numbers are shown. A review of research on the presentation of quantitative data in texts. *AVCR,* 25, 4, 359–409.

Miller, G. A. (1968). *The magical number seven, plus or minus two: Some limits on our capacity for processing information.* In R. N. Haber (Ed.). *Contemporary Theory and Research in Visual Perception.* New York: Holt, Rinehart, and Winston, Inc.

Myers, E. (1981). Boom in business graphics. *Datamation,* april, 33–35.

Pettersson, R. (1984). *Numeric Data, presentation in different formats.* Presentation at the 16th Annual Conference of the International Visual Literacy Association, Baltimore, Nov. 8–11.

Pettersson, R., Carlsson, J., Isacsson, A., Kollerbaur, A., & Randerz, K. (1984). *Attitudes to variables on visual displays.* CLEA-report, No 24. Stockholm: University of Stockholm, Dept. of Computer Science.

Reidhaar, J. W. (1984). An overview of nontabular methods for statistical presentation of data before this century. *Information design journal,* 4, 1, 25–35.

Washburne, J. N. (1927a). An experimental study of various graphic, tabular and textual methods of presenting quantitative material. Part 1. *Journal of Educational Psychology*, 18, 361–376.
Washburne, J. N. (1927b). An experimental study of various graphic, tabular and textual methods of presenting quantitative material. Part II: Numerals and written numbers. *Journal of Educational Psychology*, 18, 465–476.
Vinberg, A. (1981). *Designing a good graph*. San Diego: Integrated software systems corporation.

Motion
Allander, B. (1974). *TV-rutans verklighet*. In B. Allander, S.S. Bergström, and C.Frey. *Se men också höra*. Stockholm.
Bergström, S. S. (1974). *Rörelse*. Stockholm.
Engqvist, A. (1966). *Några principer för konstruktion och användning av undervisningsfilmer*. Uppsala: Uppsala University, Education Department.
Filipson, L. , & Schyller, I. (1980). *Barnens tittande, 3–8-åringars TV tittande 2. 18 May 1979*. Stockholm: SR/PUB 2.
Fleming, M., & Levie, W.H. (1978). *Instructional Message Design*. Englewood Cliffs, N. J.: Educational Technology Publications.
Forgus, R. H. (1966). *Perception*. New York: McGraw-Hill Book Company.
Heurling, B. (1975). *Att se på film. Lärobok i film och TV kunskap*. Stockholm. Pogo Print.
Johansson, G. (1958). Rigidity, stability, and motion in perceptual space. *Acta Psychologica*, 14, 359–370.
Lanners, E. (1973). Illusionen. Lucerne: Verlag C. J. Bucher.
Lindsten, C. (1976). *Aktiviteter i hembygdskunskap: Elevpreferenser i årskurs 3. En faktoranalytisk studie. (Activities in Science and Social Studies: Pupils preferences in grade 3. A factorial study.)* Pedagogiskpsykologiska problem. (Malmö, Sweden: School of Education), Nr. 310.
Madsen, R. P. (1969). *Animated Film: Concepts, Method, Uses*. New York: Interland Publishing Inc.
Madsen, R. P. (1973). *The Impact of Film*. New York: Macmillan Publishing Co. Inc.
Morgan, C. T. (1956). *Introduction to Psychology*. New York: McGraw-Hill.
Murch, G. M. (1973). *Visual and Auditory Perception*. Indianapolis: The Bobbs-Merrill Co.
Pettersson, R. (1984). *Factors in Visual Languages: Motion*. CLEA-report, No. 17. Stockholm: University of Stockholm, Dept. of Computer Science.
Rydin, I. (1979). *Hur barn förstår TV II. Från frö till telefonstolpe. Med rörlig bild eller stillbild?* Stockholm: SR/PUB, Projekt Nr. 747073.
Schyller, I., and Filipson, L. (1979). *1000 och en siffra om barns läggvanor – biovanor – tv-tittarsituation – rädsla vid tv-program – sagoläsning* v.51. Stockholm: SR/PUB 16.

Travers, R. M. W. (1969). *A study of the advantages and disadvantages of using simplified visual presentations in instructional materials.* Final Report, Grant N. OEG-1-71070144-5235, Washington, D. C.: U.S. Office of Education, ED 031951.

Sound
Allander, B. (1974). *TV-rutans verklighet.* In B. Allander, S.S. Bergström, and C.Frey. *Se men också höra.* Stockholm.
Berefelt, G. (1976). *AB Se om Bildperception.* Lund.
Fleming, M., & Levie, W.H. (1978). *Instructional Message Design.* Englewood Cliffs, N.J.: Educational Technology Publications.

Humour and satire
Colwell, C., Mangano, N. and Hortin, J. A. (1984). *Humour and Visual Literacy: Keys to Effective Learning.* Readings from the 15th Annual Conference of the International Visual Association. Ed. A.D. Walker, R.A. Braden, and L.H. Dunker. Published at Virginia Polytechnic Institute and State University, Blacksburg. VA. 313–320.
Thayer, N. (1984). *Verbal-Visual Mis-literacy: Creative Discontinuity.* Presentation at the 16th Annual Conference of the International Visual Literacy Association, Baltimore, Nov. 8–11.

Emotions
Belson, W. A. (1978). *Television Violence and the Adolescent Boy.* London: Saxon House.
Birren, F. (1950). *Color Psychology and Color Therapy.* New York: Mc-Graw-Hill.
Birren, F. (1969). *Light, color and environment.* New York: Van Nostrand Reinhold.
Birren, F. (1973). Color preferences as a clue to personality. *Art Psychotherapy,* 1, 13–16.
Booth, G. D., & Miller, H. R. (1974). Effectiveness of monochrome and color presentations in facilitating affective learning. *AV Communication Review,* 22, 409–422.
Gardener, B. C., & Cohen, Y. A. (1966). ROP color and its effects on newspaper advertising. *Journal of Maketing Research,* 3, 365–371.
Gattengo, D. (1963). *Teacher's Guide: Words in Color.* Chicago: Encyclopedia Brittanica Press.
Karowski, T. F., & Odbert, H. S. (1938). Color Music. *Psychol. Monogr.,* 50, 2.
Lindgren-Fridell, M., *Barns reaktioner inför bild, särskilt barnboksbild,* In M. Lindgren-Fridell, (Ed.). *Bilder i barnboken.* Göteborg.

Lindsten, C. (1977). *Bilder i hembygdsboken: Elevpreferenser i årskurs 3. En faktoranalytisk studie. (Activities in Science and Social Studies: Pupils preferences in grade 3. A factorial study.)* Pedagogisk-psykologiska problem (Malmö, Sweden: School of Education), Nr. 312.
Linné, O. (1964). *Barn och etermedia.* Stockholm: SR/PUB 6/64.
Lucus, D. B., & Butt, S. H. (1950). *Advertising Psychology and Research.* New York: McGraw-Hill.
Petterson, R. (1984). Factors in Visual Language: Emotional content. *Visual Literacy Newsletter*, 13, 3. and 13, 4.
Plack, J. J., & Shick, J. (1974). The effect of color on human behavior. *Journal of the Association for the Study of Perception*, 9(1), 4–16.
Prawitz, M. (1977). *Varför förstår du inte vad jag säger, när jag hoppar, skuttar och målar?* In G. Berefelt. *Barn och bild.* Stockholm: AWE/Gebers..
Roman, K., & Maas, J. (1976). *How to Advertise. A professional guide for the advertiser. What works, what doesn't. And Why.* New York: St. Martins Press.
Scanlon, T. J. (1970). Viewer perceptions on color, black and white TV: an experiment. *Journalism Quarterly*, 47, 366–368.
Schramm, W., Lyle, J., & Paker, E. B. (1961). *Television in the Lives of our Children.* Stanford.
Schyller, I., and Filipson, L. (1979). *1000 och en siffra om barns läggvanor – biovanor – tv-tittarsituation – rädsla vid tv-program – sagoläsning v.51.* Stockholm: SR/PUB 16.
Starch, D. (1966). *Measuring Advertising Readership and Results.* New York: McGraw-Hill.
Winn, W., & Everett, R. J. (1978). *Differences in the affective meaning of color and black and white pictures.* Paper presented at the annual meeting of the Association for Educational Communication and Technology. Kansas City, Missouri, April, 23 pp. Document ED 160 067.
Winn, W., & Everett, R. J. (1979). Affective rating of color and black-and-white pictures. *ECTJ*, 27, 2, 148–156.

Credibility
Duck, S. W., & Baggaley, J. (1975). Audience reaction and its effect on perceived expertise. *Communication Research*, 2, 79–85.
Mc Guire, W. J. (1969). *Nature of attitudes and attitude change.* In G. Lindzey and E. Aronson (Eds.). *Handbook of Social Psychology.* (2nd ed., 3), Reading Mass.: Addison-Wesley.
Rogers, E. M., & Shoemaker, F. F. (1971). *Communication of Innovations.* New York: The Free Press.
Ryan, M. (1975). The impact of television news film on perceived media credibility. *Journal of Applied Communications Research*, 3, 69–75.
Singletary, M. W. (1976). Components of credibility of a favorable news source. *Journalism Quarterly*, 53, 316–319.

Triandis, H. C. (1971). *Attitude and attitude change.* New York: John Wiley and Sons, Inc.

Viewer Completion
Kince, E. (1982). *Visual Puns in design.* New York: Watson-Guptill Publication.
Thayer, N. (1984). *Verbal-Visual Mis-literacy: Creative Discontinuity.* Presentation at the 16th Annual Conference of the International Visual Literacy Association, Baltimore, Nov. 8–11.

Execution
Alm, T., (1979). *Signaler och signalpositioner i annonser. En metodstudie.* Göteborg: Göteborgs Universitet, Konstindustriskolan. Rapport Nr. 1. Forsknings- och utvecklingsarbete om fysisk/estetisk utformning av retoriska framställningar.
Attneave, F. (1959). *Application of information theory to psychology.* New York: Henry Holt.
Cosette, C. (1982). *How Pictures Speak: A brief introduction to iconics.* Paper presented at the 32nd International Communication Association Conference. Boston, May 1–5. Translated from French by Vincent Ross. Quebeck.
Dodwell, P.C. (1975). *Pattern and object perception.* In E. C. Carterette and M. P. Friedman (Eds.). *Handbook of Perception (Vol. 5).* New York: Academic Press.
Fleming, M. L. (1970). *Perceptual Principles for the Design of Instructional Materials,* Washington, DC: Office of Education Bureau of Research.
Forgus, R. H. (1966). *Perception.* New York: McGraw-Hill Book Company.
Hochberg, J. E. (1966). *Perception,* Englewood Cliffs, N.J.: Prentice-Hall, Inc.
Murch, G. M. (1973). *Visual and Auditory Perception.* Indianapolis: The Bobbs-Merrill Co.
Rock, I. (1975). *An Introduction to Perception.* New York: Macmillan Publishing Co.

Type of Visual
Feilitzen, C., Filipson, L. & Schyller, I. (1978). *Blunda inte för barnens tittande. Om barn, tv och radio nu och i framtiden.* Stockholm: Sveriges Radios Förlag.
Fleming, M., & Levie, W.H. (1978). *Instructional Message Design.* Englewood Cliffs, N.J.: Educational Technology Publications.
Heider, F. (1946). Attitudes and cognitive organization. *Journal of Psychology,* 21, 107–112.

Petterson, R. (1981). *Bilder Barn och Massmedia.* Stockholm. Akademilitteratur.

Subject
Higgins, L. C. (1975). *Children's inference drawing behaviour: Its psychological nature and responsiveness to educational intervention.* Unpublished doctoral thesis, University of Sydney.
Higgins, L. C. (1980). Literalism in the Young Child's Interpretation of Pictures. *ECTJ*, 28, 2, 99–119.
Miller, G. A. (1968). *The magical number seven, plus or minus two: Some limits on our capacity for processing information.* In R. N. Haber (Ed.). *Contemporary Theory and Research in Visual Perception.* New York: Holt, Rinehart, and Winston, Inc.
Murch, G. M. (1973). *Visual and Auditory Perception.* Indianapolis: The Bobbs-Merrill Co.
Zimmer, A., & Zimmer, F. (1978). *Visual literacy in communication: Designing for development.* Hulton Educational Publications Ltd., in cooperation with the International Institute for Adult Methods, Teheran.

Light
Hering, A. (1925). *Grundzuge der Lehre vom Lichtsinn. Handbuch der gesamten Augenheilkunde.* (2:nd edition, 3:rd volume.) Berlin.

External shape
Allport, G. W., & Pettigraw, T. F. (1957). Cultural influence on the perception of movement: The Trapezoidal illusion among Zulus. *Journal of Abnormal and Social Psychology,* 55, 104–113.
Annis, R. C., & Frost, B. (1973). Human visual ecology and orientation anistropics in acuity. *Science,* 182 (4113), 729–731.
Herbener, G. F., Van Tubergen, G. N., & Whitlow, S. S. (1979). Dynamics of the Frame in Visual Composition. *ECTJ,* 27, 2, 83–88.
Lanners, E. (1973). *Illusionen.* Lucern: Verlag C. J. Bucher.
Macbeth, D. R. (1974). *Classificational preference in young children: Form or Color.* Chicago: National Association for Research in Science Teaching, ED 092362.
Modreski. R. A, & Gross, A. E. (1972). Young childrens names for and matches to form - color stimuli. *Journal of Genetic Psychology,* 121 (2), 283–293.
Otto, W., & Askov, E. (1968). The role of color in learning and instruction. *Journal of Special Education,* 2, 155–165.
Pettersson, R. (1979). *Bildkreativitet, en pilotstudie.* Stockholm.
Pettersson, R. (1982). International Review Cultural Differences in the Perception of Image and Color in Pictures. *ECTJ,* 30, 1, 43–53.

Pettersson, R. (1982). Factors in Visual Languages: Shape. *Visual Literacy Newsletter,* 11, and 10.
Segall, M. H., Cambell, D. T., & Herskovits, M. J. (1966). *The influence of culture on visual perception, an advanced study in psychology and anthropology.* Indianapolis: Bobbs-Merrill.
Sporrstedt, B. (1980). Kring en bildvärld. *Synpunkt, populär tidskrift för konst,* 5, 6–7.
Ward, W. C., & Naus, M. J. (1973). *The encoding of pictorial information in children and adults.* Princeton, N. J.: Educational Testing Service, (ERIC Document Reproduction Service ED 085073).
Yarbus, A. L. (1967). *Eye movements and vision.* New York: Plenum Press.

External Contour
Arnheim, R. (1954). *Art and visual perception.* Berkely: University of California Press.
Gibson, J. J. (1966). *The senses considered as perceptual systems.* Boston: Houghton-Mifflin.
Pettersson, R. (1981). *Bilder Barn och Massmedia.* Stockholm: Akademilitteratur.
Pettersson, R. (1982). Factors in Visual Languages: Shape. *Visual Literacy Newsletter,* 11, and 10.
Yarbus, A. L. (1967). *Eye movements and vision.* New York: Plenum Press.
Weismann, D. L. (1974). *The visual arts as a human experience.* Englewood Cliffs, N. J.: Prentice-Hall.
Zettl, H. (1973). *Sight. Sound. Motion,* Belmont, Calif.: Wadsworth.

Size
Dwyer, F. M.,(1970). The effect of image size on visual learning. *The Journal of Experimental Education,* 39, 36–41.
Falk-Björkman, S. (1978). LMN – är det något för mig? In K. Wearn. *Mot en ekologisk världsbild – En ny väg för naturvetenskaplig undervisning.* Malmö: Liber Läromedel, 71–81.
Forgus, R. H. (1966). *Perception.* New York: McGraw-Hill Book Company.
Hayashi, K. (1982). Research and Development on High Definition Television. *SMPTE Journal,* 3, 178–186.
Holliday, W. G. (1973). Critical analysis of pictorial research related to science education. *Science Education,* 57 (2): 201–214.
Kosslyn, S. M. (1975). Information representation in visual images. *Cognitive Psychology,* 7, 341–370.
Lindsten, C. (1975). *Hembygdskunskap i årskurs 3. Att inhämta, bearbeta och redovisa kunskaper.* Lund: Liber Läromedel.
Lindsten, C. (1976). *Aktiviteter i hembygdskunskap: Elevpreferenser i årskurs 3. En faktoranalytisk studie. (Activities in Science and Social*

Studies: Pupils preferences in grade 3. A factorial study.) Pedagogiskpsykologiska problem. (Malmö, Sweden: School of Education), Nr. 310.
Mac Donald-Ross, M. (1977). How numbers are shown. A review of research on the presentation of quantitative data in texts. *AVCR,* 25, 4, 359–409.
Miller, G. A. (1968). *The magical number seven, plus or minus two: Some limits on our capacity for processing information.* In R. N. Haber (Ed.). *Contemporary Theory and Research in Visual Perception.* New York: Holt, Rinehart, and Winston, Inc.
Moore, D. M., & Sasse. E. B. (1971). Effect of size and type of still projected pictures on inmediate recall of content. *AV Communication Review,* 19, 437–450
Murch, G. M. (1973). *Visual and Auditory Perception.* Indianapolis: The Bobbs-Merrill Co.
Noble, G. (1975). *Children in front of the small screen.* Beverly Hills: California Sage.
Pettersson, R. (1981). *Bilder Barn och Massmedia.* Stockholm: Akademilitteratur
Pettersson, R. (1983). Factors in visual language: Size. CLEA-report, No 13. Stockholm: University of Stockholm, Dept. of Computer Science.
Pick, H. L., & Ryan, S. M. (1971). *Perception.* In P-H. Mussen and M. R. Rosenzweig (Eds.). *Annual Review of Psychology, (Vol. 22).* Palo Alto: Annual Reviews, Inc.
Rock, I. (1975). *An Introduction to Perception.* New York: Macmillan Publishing Co.
Vernon, M. D. (1962). *The Psychology of Perception,* Baltimore, Maryland: Penguin Books.

Color
Berglund, B. (1975). *Gambia.* Uppsala: Nordiska Afrikainstitutet.
Bergström, S. S. (1974). *Varseblivning av Färg.* In B. Allander, S.S. Bergström, and C. Frey. *Om Du skall göra en riktigt dålig bild, då räcker det inte med svartvitt, då måste du ha färg.* Stockholm.
Berlyne, D. E. (1960). *Conflict, Arousal and Curiosity.* New York: McGraw-Hill.
Berlyne, D. E. (1966). Curiosity and Exploartion. *Science,* 153, 25–33.
Englund, E. & Svenström, Y. (1974). *Indianernas När, Var, Hur.* Lund: Forum.
Evans, R. M. (1965). *An Introduction to Color.* New York: Wiley.
Evans, R. M. (1974). *The Perception of Color.* New York: Wiley.
Fleming, M., & Levie, W.H. (1978). *Instructional Message Design.* Englewood Cliffs, N.J.: Educational Technology Publications.
Heider, E. R. (1972). Universals in Color Naming and Memory. *Journal of Experimental Psychology,* 93, 10–12.
Heiss, R., & Schaie, K. W. (1964). *Color and Personality.* Bern: Huber.

Hultén, C-O. (1978). *Modern Konst i Afrika – En översikt.* In *Modern Konst i Afrika.* Lund, 11-60.
Itten, J. (1971). *Färg och färgupplevelse.* Stockholm: Norstedts.
Jacobson-Widding, A. (1979). Vitt, Svart och Rött. *Form,* 7-8, 7-9.
Jacobson-Widding, A. (1980). Färger avspeglar världsbilden. *Forskning och Framsteg,* 6/80, 1-7.
Kowalski, K. (1977). *Barn och bildskapande. Hur man stimulerar barns föreställningsförmåga, fantasi och idéer.* Stockholm: W&W.
Levie, H. (1973). *Pictorial Research: An Overview.* Viewpoints, Bloomington: Indiana University.
Murch, G. M. (1983). Perceptual Considerations of Color. *Computer Graphics World,* 6, 7, 32-40.
Prawitz, M. (1977). *Varför förstår du inte vad jag säger, när jag hoppar, skuttar och målar?* In G. Berefelt. *Barn och bild.* Stockholm: AWE/Gebers.
Segall, M. H., Cambell, D. T. & Herskovits, M. J. (1966). *The influence of culture on visual preception. An advanced study in psychology and anthropology.* Indianapolis: Bobbs-Merrill.
Valentine, E. W. (1962). *The experimental psychology of beauty.* London: Methuen.

Color Preferences
Berlyne, D. E. (1960). *Conflict, Arousal and Curiosity.* New York: McGraw-Hill.
Birren, F. 1950: Color preferences as a clue to personality art. *Psychotherapy,* 1, 13-16.
Bourgeois-Bailetti, A. M., & Cerbus, G. (1977). Color associations to mood stories in first-grade boys. *Perceptual and Motor Skills,* 45, 1051-1056.
Choungourian, A. (1972). Extraversion, Neuroticism, and Color Preferences. *Perceptional and Motor Skills,* 34, 724-726.
Eysenck, H. J. (1941). A critical and experimental study of color preferences. *American Journal of Psychology,* 54, 385- 394.
Fleming, M., & Levie, W.H. (1978). *Instructional Message Design.* Englewood Cliffs, N.J.: Educational Technology Publications.
Gotz, K. O., & Gotz, K, (1974). Color Preferences of Art Students. *Perceptual and Motor Skills,* 39, 1103-1109.
Ibison, R. A. (1952). *Differential effect on the recall of textual materials associated with the inclusion of colored and uncolored illustrations.* Unpublished Doctoral Dissertation, Indiana University, Bloomington.
Kaar, H. (1976). The Color preferences of a young girl in pre-puberty, puberty, and adolescence: Observations over an eight-year period with luscher color test. *British Journal of Projective Psychology and Personality Study,* 21, 21-30.
Krishna, K. P. (1972). Color preference as a function of age and sex. *Journal of the Indian Academy of Applied Psychology,* 9, 10-13.

Lamwers, L. L., Small, Y., & Goss, A. E. (1977). Relational discrimination of hue by young children. *Journal of General Psychology*, 247–254.
Lindsten, C. (1975). *Hembygdskunskap i årskurs 3. Att inhämta, bearbeta och redovisa kunskaper.* Lund: Liber Läromedel.
Lindsten, C. (1976). *Aktiviteter i hembygdskunskap: Elevpreferenser i årskurs 3. En faktoranalytisk studie. (Activities in Science and Social Studies: Pupils preferences in grade 3. A factorial study.)* Pedagogisk-psykologiska problem. (Malmö, Sweden: School of Education), Nr. 310.
Lindsten, C. (1977). *Bilder i hembygdsboken: Elevpreferenser i årskurs 3. En faktoranalytisk studie. (Activities in Science and Social Studies: Pupils preferences in grade 3. A factorial study.)* Pedagogisk-psykologiska problem (Malmö, Sweden: School of Education), Nr. 312.
MacLean, W. P. (1930). A comparison of coloured and uncoloured pictures. *Educational Screen*, 9, 196–199.
Mather, J., Stare, C., & Beinin, S. (1971). Color preferences in a geriatric population. *Gerontologist*, 11, 311–313.
Myatt, B & Carter, J. M. (1979). Picture preferences of children and young adults. *ECTJ*, 27, 1, 45–53.
Pettersson, R. (1979). *Three-dimensional pictures.* ESSELTE Memorandum, Stockholm.
Pettersson, R. (1982). International review cultural differences in the perception of image and color in pictures. *ECTJ*, 30, 1, 43–53.
Pettersson, R. (1985). *Presentation of information on visual displays.* Presented at AECT National Conference. Jan. 17–22. Anaheim, California.
Plack, J. J., & Shick, J. (1974). The effect of color on human behavior. *Journal of the Association for the Study of Perception*, 9, 1, 4–16.
Rudisill, M. (1952). Children's preference for color versus other qualities in illustrations. *Elementary School Journal*, 52, 444–451.
Simon, W. E. (1972). Investigation of the "blue 7 phenomenon" in elementary and junior high school children. *Psychological Reports*, 31, 128–130.
Sivik, L., 1970 (1979): *Om färgers betydelse.* Skandinaviska Färginstitutet, Stockholm.
Valentine, E. W. (1962). *The experimental psychology of beauty.* London: Methuen.
Welsh, G. S. (1970). Color preferences of gifted adolescents. *Sciences del'Art*, 55–61.
Vernon, M. D. (1962). *The psychology of perception.* Baltimore, Maryland: Penguin Books.

Color Visibility
Eysenck, H. J. (1941). A critical and experimental study of color preferences. *American Journal of Psychology*, 54, 385-394.
Kokuhirwa, H. (1977). *Some experiences with the radio study group for the literacy campaign in rural Tanzania: A personal account.* Unpublished

Mimeograph. Reference in J. Mangan. *Cultural Conversations of Pictorial Representation: Iconic Literacy and Education. ECTJ*, 26, 3, 245–267, 1977.

Lamwers, L. L., Small, Y., & Goss, A. E. (1977). Relational discrimination of hue by young children. *Journal of General Psychology*, 96, 247–254.

Lynch., M.P. (1980). Designing effective visual images. *Visual Literacy Newsletter*, 4.

Morris, L. L. (1974). The effects of ball color and background color upon the catching performance of second, fourth, and sixth grade youngsters. *Dissertation Abstracts International*, 35, 6-a 3556.

Morris, G. S. (1976). Effects of ball and background color upon the catching performance of elementary school children. *Research Quarterly*, 47, 409–416.

Murch, G. M. (1973). *Visual and Auditory Perception*. Indianapolis: The Bobbs-Merrill Co.

Attentional use of color

Cater, F. C., Vredenberg, H. L., & Patty, C. R. (1967). *A historical, economic and statistical study of the electric sign industry*. Fort Collins: Colorado State University.

Dwyer, F. M. (1971). Color as an instructional variable. *AV Communication Review*, 19, 399–413.

Holmberg, Å. (1981). *Subtitling of television programmes. New method for the hard-of-hearing*. Stockholm: Sveriges Television.

Ibison, R. A. (1952). *Differential effect on the recall of textual materials associated with the inclusion of colored and uncolored illustrations*. Unpublished Doctoral Dissertation, Indiana University, Bloomington.

MacLean, W. P. (1930). A comparison of coloured and uncoloured pictures. *Educational Screen*, 9, 196–199.

Montén, R. (1981). *"Text-Tv" – Ett nytt etermedium. Resultat från Sveriges Radios "Text-Tv"-försök med hörselhandikappad publik 1979–80*. Stockholm: SR Publik- och programforskning, 5.

Patty, C. R. & Vredenberg, H. L. (1970). *Electric signs: Contribution to the Communication Spectrum*. Fort Collins: Colorado State University.

Rudisill, M. (1952). Children's preference for color versus other qualities in illustrations. *Elementary School Journal*, 52, 444–451.

Spangenberg, R. (1976). Which is better for learning? Color or Black and White? *Audio-visual Instruction*, 21(4), 55.

Affective use of color

Samit, M. L. (1983). The color interface, marking the most of color. *Computer Graphics World*, 7, 42–50.

Winn, W. & Everett, R. J. (1978). *Differences in the affective meaning of color and black and white pictures*. Paper presented at the Annual Meeting

of the Association for Educational Communication and Technology, Kansas City, Missouri, April, 23 pp, Document ED 160 067.
Winn, W., & Everett, R. J. (1979). Affective rating of color and black-and-white pictures. *ECTJ*, 27, 148–156.

Cognitive use of color

Adams, H. F. (1920). *Advertising and its mental laws*. New York: Macmillan
Allander, B. (1974). *TV-rutans verklighet*. In B. Allander, S.S. Bergström, and C.Frey. *Se men också höra*. Stockholm.
Berlin, B., & Kay, P. (1969). *Basic color terms*. Berkeley: University of California Press.
Booth, G. D., & Miller, H. R. (1974). Effectiveness of monochrome and color presentations in facilitating affective learning. *AV Communication Review*, 1974, 22, 409–422.
Dwyer, F. M., & Lamberski, R. J. (1983). A review of the research on the effects of the use of color in the teaching-learning process. *Int'l J. Instructional Media*, 10, 4.
Frey, C. (1974). *Effekten av färg-tv på inlärningen*. In B., Allander, S.S. Bergström, and C. Frey. *Om du skall göra en riktigt dålig bild, då räcker det inte med svartvitt, då måste du ha färg*. Stockholm.
Gardener, B. C., & Cohen, Y. A. (1966). Rop color and its effects on newspaper advertising. *Journal of Maketing Research*, 3, 365–371.
Gattengo, D. (1963). *Teacher's guide: Words in color*. Chicago: Encyclopedia Brittanica Press.
Ibison, R. A. (1952). *Differential effect on the recall of textual materials associated with the inclusion of colored and uncolored illustrations*. Unpublished Doctoral Dissertation, Indiana University, Bloomington.
Kanner, J. (1968). *The instructional effectiveness of color in television: A Review of the Evidence*. Stanford, California, Stanford University, ED 015 675.
Kanner, J., & Rosenstein, A. (1960). Television in army training: Color vs Black and White. *AV Communication Review*, 8, 243–252.
Katzmann, N., & Nyenhuis, J. (1972). Color vs Black and White Effects on Learning, Opinion and Attention. *AV Communication Review*, 20, 16–28.
Lamberski, R. J. (1982). *The Instructional Effect of Color in Immediate and Delayed Retention*. Paper presented as part of a symposium at the Annual Convention of the Association for Educational Communications and Technology, Dallas, Texas, ED 223 201, IR 010 452.
Lamberski, J. R., & Dwyer, F. M. (1983). The Instructional Effect of Coding (Color and Black and White) on Information Acquisition and Retrieval. *ECTJ*, 31, 1, 9–12.
Lucus, D. B., & Butt, S. H. (1950). *Advertising psychology and research*. New York: McGraw-Hill.

May, B. (1978). Color preferences for black and white in infants and young children. *Experimental Psychology,* 38, 6198.
MacLean, W. P. (1930). A comparison of coloured and uncoloured pictures. *Educational Screen,* 9, 196–199.
Murch, G. M., (1983). Perceptual Considerations of color. *Computer Graphics World,* 6, 7, 32–40.
Scanlon, T. J. (1970). Viewer perceptions on color, black and white tv: An experiment. *Journalism Quarterly,* 47, 366–368.
Starch, D. (1966). *Measuring advertising readership and results.* New York: McGraw-Hill.
Tullis, T. (1981). An evaluation of alphanumerics, graphic, and color information displays. *Human Factors,* 23(5), 541–550.
Valentine, E. W. (1962). *The experimental psychology of beauty.* London: Methuen, 1962.
Winn, W. (1976). The structure of multiple free associations to words, Black and White pictures, and color pictures. *AVCR,* 24, 3, 273–293.

Color coding
Fleming, M., & Levie, W.H. (1978). *Instructional Message Design,* Englewood Cliffs, N.J: Educational Technology Publications.
Hartley, J. (1978). *Designing Instructional Text.* New York: Nichols.
Hershberger, W. A., & Terry, D. F. (1965). Typographical cueing in conventional and programmed texts. *Journal of Applied Psychology,* 49, 55–60.
Legatt, A. L. S. (1983). *Financial Information on Teletext.* London: The City University, Centre for Information Science, M. Sc. Thesis.
Nilsson, L-G., Ohlsson, K., & Rönnberg, J. (1981). Psychological experiments with datavision. *Tele,* 33, 29–35.
Ohlsson, K., Nilsson, L-G., & Rönnberg, J. (1981). Speed and accuracy in scanning as a function of combinations of text and background colors. *Int. J. Man-machine Studies,* 14, 215–222.

Decorative use of color
Dwyer, F. M., & Lamberski, R. J. (1983). A review of the research on the effects of the use of color in the teaching-learning process. *Int'L J. Instructional Media,* 10, 4.
Ehlers, H-J. (1982). *How color can help visualize information.* Online Review 6th Int, 'Online Information' Meeting held 7–9 dec. in London, 185–200, Abingdom, Oxon: Learned Information (Europe) Ltd, 491 pp (pm 8621).
Pettersson, R. (1981). *Bilder barn och massmedia.* Stockholm: Akademilitteratur.
Valentine, E. W. (1962). *The experimental psychology of beauty.* London: Methuen.

Color psychology

Birren, F. (1950). *Color psychology and color therapy.* New York: McGraw-Hill.
Bourgeois-Bailetti, A. M., & Cerbus, G. (1977). Color associations to mood stories in first-grade boys. *Perceptual and Motor Skills,* 45, 1051–1056.
Ehlers, H-J. (1982). *How color can help visualize information.* Online Review 6th Int, 'Online Information' Meeting held 7–9 Dec. In London, 185–200, Abingdon, Oxon: Learned Information (Europe) Ltd, 491 pp (pm 8621).
Hartley, J. (1978). *Designing instructional text.* New York: Nichols.

Contrast

Eysenck, H. J. (1941). A critical and experimental study of color preferences. *American Journal Of Psychology,* 54, 385– 394.
Heider, E. R. (1972). Universals in color naming and memory. *Journal of Experimental Psychology,* 93, 10–12.
Kokuhirwa, H. (1977). *Some experiences with the radio study group for the literacy campaign in rural Tanzania: A personal account.* Unpublished Mimeograph. Reference in J. Mangan. Cultural Conventions of Pictorial Representation: Iconic Literacy and Education. *ECTJ,* 26, 3, 245–267.
Kowalski, K. (1977). *Barn och bildskapande. Hur man stimulerar barns föreställningsförmåga, fantasi och idéer.* Stockholm: W&W.
Lynch., M. P. (1980). Designing effective visual images. *Visual Literacy Newsletter,* 4.
Mangan, J. (1978). Cultural conversations of pictorial representation: Iconic Literacy and Education. *ECTJ,* 26, 3, 245–267.
Valentine, E. W. (1962). *The experimental psychology of beauty.* London: Methuen.

Emphasis

Pett, D., & Burbank, L. (1984). *Designing visual presentations.* Presentation at the 16th Annual Conference of the International Visual Literacy Association, Baltimore, Nov. 8–11.

Composision

Alm, T., (1979). *Signaler och signalpositioner i annonser. En metodstudie.* Göteborg: Göteborgs Universitet, Konstindustriskolan. Rapport Nr. 1. Forsknings- och utvecklingsarbete om fysisk/estetisk utformning av retoriska framställningar.
Arnheim, R. (1954). *Art and visual perception.* Berkely: University of California Press.

Ball, J., & Byrnes, F. C., Eds. (1960). *Research, Principles and Practice in visual communication.* Washington, D. C.: National Educational Association.
Berefelt, G. (1976). *AB Se om bildperception.* Lund: Liber Läromedel.
Fabri, R. (1970). *Artist's guide to composition.* New York: Watson-Guptill.
Fleming, M. L. (1970). *Percetual principals for the design of instructional materials.* Washington, DC: Office of Education Bureau of Research.
Graham, C. (1965). *Vision and visual perception.* New York: Wiley.
Gregory, R. L. (1973). *Eye and brain, the psychology of seeing.* New York: McGraw-Hill.
Herbener, G. F., Van Tubergen, G. N., & Whitlow, S. S. (1979). Dynamics of the frame in visual composition. *ECTJ,* 27, 2, 83–88.
Leibowitz, H. W., & Harvey, L. O. (1973). *Perception,* In P. H. Mussen & M. R. Rosenzweig (Eds.). *Annual Review of Psychology, (Vol. 24).* Palo Alto: Annual Reviews, Inc.
Posner, M. I. (1973). *Cognition: An introduction,* Glenview, Ill .: Scott, Foresman and Co.
Taylor, J. F. A. (1964). *Design and Expression in Visual Arts.* New York: Dover
Weismann, D. L. (1974). *The visual arts as a human experience.* Englewood Cliffs, N.J.: Prentice-Hall.
Zettl, H. (1973). *Sight, Sound. Motion,* Belmont, Calif.: Wadsworth.

Perspective
Cook, B. L. (1981). *Understanding Pictures in Papua New Guinea.* David C. Cook Foundation, Elgin, Illinois.
Forgus, R. H. (1966). *Perception.* New York: McGraw-Hill Book Company.
Fuglesang, A. (1973). *Applied communications in developing countries, ideas and observations.* Uppsala: Dag Hammarskjöld Foundation.
Lanners, E. (1973). *Illusionen.* Lucern: Verlag C. J. Bucher.
Murch, G. M. (1973). *Visual and auditory perception.* Indianapolis: The Bobbs-Merrill Co.
Rock, I. (1975). *An introduction to perception.* New York: Macmillan Publishing Co.
Zimmer, A., & Zimmer, F. (1978). *Visual literacy in communication: Designing for development.* Hulton Educational Publications, Ltd., in cooperation with the International Institute for Adult Methods, Teheran.

Technical quality
Pettersson, R. (1981). *Bilder Barn och Massmedia.* Stockholm: Akademilitteratur.

Symbols and explanatory words, lettering
Fleming, M., & Levie, W.H. (1978). *Instructional Message Design.* Englewood Cliffs, N.J.: Educational Technology Publications.
Lidman, S., & Lund, A-M. (1972). *Berätta med bilder.* Stockholm: Bonniers.
Pett, D., & Burbank, L. (1984). *Designing Visual Presentations.* Presentation at the 16th Annual Conference of the International Visual Literacy Association, Baltimore, Nov. 8–11.
Zettl, H. (1973). *Sight. Sound. Motion.*Belmont, Calif.: Wadsworth.

Context
Forgus, R. H. (1966). *Perception.* New York: McGraw-Hill Book Company.
Helson, H. (1974). *Current trends and issues in adaption-level theory.* In P. A. Fried (Ed). *Readings in perception: Principle and practice.* Lexington, Mass.: D. C. Heath and Co..
Murch, G. M, (1973). *Visual and auditory perception.* Indianapolis: The Bobbs-Merrill Co..
Zimmer, A., & Zimmer, F. (1978). *Visual literacy in communication: Designing for Development.* Hulton Educational Publications Ltd., in cooperation with the International Institute for Adult Methods, Teheran.

Interplay of words and visuals
Holliday, W. G., Brunner, L. L., & Donais, E. L. (1977). Differential cognitive and affective responses to flow diagrams in science. *Journal of Reasearch in Science Teaching,* 14, 2, 129–138.
Ibison, R. A. (1952). *Differential effect on the recall of textual materials associated with the inclusion of colored and uncolored illustrations.* Unpublished Doctoral Dissertation, Indiana University, Bloomington.
Jahoda, G., Cheyne, W. M., Deregowski, J. B., Sinha, D., & Collingbourne, R. (1976). Utilization of pictorial information in class-room learning: A cross cultural study. *AVCR,* 24, 3d, 295–315.
Lidman, S., & Lund, A.-M. (1972). *Berätta med bilder.* Stockholm: Bonniers.
Lindsten, C. (1975). *Hembygdskunskap i årskurs 3. Att inhämta, bearbeta och redovisa kunskaper.* Lund: Liber Läromedel.
Magne, D., & Parknäs, L. (1962). The learning effects of pictures. *British Journal of Educational Psychology,* 33, 265–275.
Samuels, S. J. (1970). Effects of pictures on learning to read, comprehension and attitudes. *Review of Educational Research,* 40, 397–407.
Samuels, S. J., Biesbrock, E., & Terry, P. R. (1974). The effects of pictures on children's attitudes towards presented stories. *Journal of Educational Research,* 67, 243–246.
Weitzman, K. (1970). *Illustrations in roll and context.* Princeton: Princeton University Press.

Text
Brody, P. J. (1982). *Affecting instructional textbooks through pictures.* In D.H. Jonasson. *The technology of text.* Englewood Cliffs N.J.: Educational Technology Publications, 301–316.
Björnsson, C. H. (1972). *Läsbarhetsprövade skolböcker 3.* Stockholm.
Hartley, J. (1978). *Designing instructional text.* New York: Nichols.
Kopstein, F. E., & Roshal, S. M. (1954). Learning foreign vocabulary from pictures versus words. *American Psychologist,* 9, 407– 408.
Levin, J. R., & Lesgold, A. M. (1978). On pictures in prose. *ECTJ,* 26, 233–243.
Lotman, J. (1973). *Die struktur des kunstlerischen textes.* Frankfurt am Main.
Pettersson, R. (1984). *Presentation på bildskärm.* Stockholm: Dokumentation Datalär 84. CLEA, FRN, STU och SÖ, 77–86.
Pettersson, R. (1985). *Presentation of Information on Visual Displays.* Presented at AECT National Conference. Jan 17–22. Anaheim, California.
Reynolds, L. (1984). *The Legibility of printed scientific and technical information.* In R. Easterby and H. Swaga. *Information Design.* John Wiley & Sons Ltd, 187-208..
Sampson, J. R. (1970). Free recall of verbal and non-verbal stimuli. *Quarterly,* 48, 134–136.
Spencer, H. (1969). *The visible word: Problems of legibility.* London: Lund Humphries.
Tinker, M. A. (1963). *Legibility of Print.* Ames: Iowa State Univ. Press.
Zachrisson, B. (1965). *Studies in the Legibility of Printed Text.* Stockholm: Almqvist and Wiksell.

Legends
Brody, P. J. (1982). *Affecting instructional textbooks through pictures.* In D.H. Jonasson. *The technology of text.* Englewood Cliffs N.J.: Educational Technology Publications, 301–316.
Gombrich, E. H. (1972). The visual image. *Scientific American,* 227, 82–96.
Holliday, W. G., Brunner, L. L., & Donais, E. L. (1977). Differential cognitive and affective responses to flow diagrams in science. *Journal of Reasearch in Science Teaching,* 14, 2, 129–138.
Jahoda, G., Cheyne, W. M., Deregowski, J. B., Sinha, D., & Collingbourne, R. (1976). Utilization of pictorial information in classroom learning: A cross cultural study. *AVCR,* 24, 3, 295– 315.
Lidman, S., & Lund, A.-M. (1972). *Berätta med bilder.* Stockholm: Bonniers.
Lindsten, C. (1975). *Hembygdskunskap i årskurs 3. Att inhämta, bearbeta och redovisa kunskaper.* Lund: Liber Läromedel.
Magne, D., & Parknäs, L. (1962). The learning effects of pictures. *British Journal of Educational Psychology.* 33, 265–275.

Pettersson, R. (1984). *Interplay of visuals and legends.* Presentation at the Information Design Conference. Dec. 17–19.
Samuels, S. J., Biesbrock, E., & Terry, P. R. (1974). The effects of pictures on children's attitudes towards presented stories. *Journal of Educational Research,* 67, 243–246.

Image framing
Arnheim, R., 1954: *Art and visual perception.* Berkely: University of California Press.
Egidius, H. (1969). *Praktisk Psykologi.* Stockholm: Läromedelsförlagen
Pettersson, R. (1983). Factors in visual language: Image framing. *Visual Literacy Newsletter,* 12, 9 and, 12,10.
Sporrstedt, B. (1980). Kring en bildvärld. *Synpunkt, populär tidskrift för konst,* 5, 6–7.
Weismann, D. L. (1974). *The visual arts as a human experience.* Englewood Cliffs, N.J.: Prentice-Hall.
Zettl, H. (1973). *Sight. Sound. Motion,* Belmont, Calif.: Wadsworth.

Layout
Dahlbak, H., & Öystein, K. (1982). *Bildet i Journalistikken.* Fredrikstad: Institutt for Journalistikk.
Evans, H. (1973). *Editing and Design. Book five. Newspaper Design.* London: Heinemann.
Evans, H. (1978). *Editing and Design. Book four. Pictures on a page.* London: Heinemann.
Taylor, J. F. A. (1964). *Design and expression in visual arts.* New York: Dover.

SUBJECT INDEX

addition 261
aesthetic value 166
alphabets 135
areas 147; 239
assess image contents 81
audial language 202
audiotex 29
audio-visual 203
audio-visual representations 210
auditory modality 99

balance 256
basic elements 83; 147
body language 130
books of the Dead 34
brain 75; 90; 94
broadcast media 18
business graphics 210

cable TV 29
camouflage 236
cartography 206
CD-I 31
CD-ROM v; 31; 37
changes 261

character size 139
classification 174
cognitive level 90; 94
color 51; 108; 250
color blindness 73
color coding 252
color description systems 47
color perception 253
color preferences 251
color ribbons 56
color stimuli 69
color visibility 251
combination 262
communication 1
complete a story 83
composition 254
compression 261
computer media 22
computer print-outs 55
concept learning 101
content 227
context 265
continuity law 71
contour 246
contradictory relationship 7
contrast 253

copyright 263
communications process 214
complete meanings 148
computer art 181
computer distributed pictures 183
computer generated pictures 181
computer pictures 180
computer processed pictures 180
connotations 158; 160
content 153
context 153
create images 82
credibility 233
cropping 261
CRT 46; 47

daily graphics 209
decoration 252
deletion 261
denotation 158; 160
depth 250; 257
describe image contents 80
describing picture context 85
desktop publishing vi
details 226
design pictures 182
development 108
dimensions 199
dots 147; 239
dual-code memory 103
DVI 31

econic memory 102
edutainment 15
electronic publishing 24; 35
electronic revolution 24
electrophotography 57
emotions 232
emphasis 253

ENIAC v
entertainment graphics 182
ethical rules 265
expansion 261
execution 153
explanatory graphics 208
expo graphics 209
events 230
EXPO 85 vi
eye fixations 65
eye movements 64; 68; 93

facts graphics 210
fax 183
feature graphics 210
figure and background 235
film media 17
fonts 139
format 153; 277
framing 273
functional properties 160
functions 142

gestalt laws 89
graphemes 153
graphical media 20
graphic element 239
graphic journalist 276
graphics 206
group communication 16
Gutenberg 34

hand-crafted visual 176
HDTV 282
hear-listen 93
hearing 61
humour 232
hyper-medium 31

iconeme 153
illusions 113
illustrate a story 84

Index

image contents 90
image data bases 183
image factors 154
image interpretations 90
indexing systems 80;187
infocation 15
infographics 84;206
infography 206
infology x
informatics viii
information ergonomic x
information graphics 84; 181; 206
information layout 206
information processing viii
information society 33
information technology ix
information theory viii
inner image 107
inner reality 107
instruction graphics 84; 208
infographer 276
informative layout. 276
infotainment 15
ink jet printing 56
irrelevant relationship 7
isolation 262

Jumbotron 280

kinesthetic modality 99

Landsat 279
language 127
laser printing 56
learning 98; 106; 113; 198
legends 270
legibility 50; 166; 170; 269
levels of meaning 146
lexi-visual 203
lexi-visual representations 204
light 63; 244

lighting 245
linear perspective 89
lines 147; 239
live media 16
locating graphics 208
long-range changes 40
long-term memory 102
luminance 46

manipulation 195
mass-media consumption 10; 11
masscommunications 5
measurement pictures 181
measuring picture properties 167
media 215
media market 12
media-industry mapping 14
mediateques 31
medium 6
memory 4; 101
mental development 109
message 216
message design 213
mixed modality 99
modality 99; 112
models and exhibitions 19
morpheme 133
motion 231
move 262
movie comprehension 111
murals 142
Müller-Lyer's illusion 115

name image contents 79
Natural Color System 48
natural law 71
NCS 49
Necker cube 114
need for information 10
new media 22; 40

news graphics 208
NTSC 282
numeric data 53; 229

objects 227
oral-visual 203
organization 254
originators viewpoints 43

PAL 282
pen plotters 56
percept 89
perception 3; 70
perceptual system 70
personal communication 16
perspective 256
phonemes 133
pictograms 135
pictorial capability 87
pictorial superiority effect 105
picture analysis 172
picture angle 258
picture archives 183
picture comprehension 111
picture databases 186
picture dimensions 191
picture editing 260
picture height 258
picture perception 78; 89
picture quality 165
picture readability 155; 162; 171
place 228
planned graphics 209
Ponzo's illusion 115
pre-understanding 131
presentation graphics 208
principle learning 101
printed word 134
problem solving 101
producer's viewpoints 41
producer/publisher 36

projection plane 261
properties 157
prose memory 106
proximity 70; 71
psychological information theory ix
publishers 37
publishing 25

radiance 46
rank and rate images 81
ratings of variables 155
readability 166; 268
reading speed 68
reading value 166; 167; 170; 270
realistic 143; 160
realism 225
receiver 2; 84; 217
recorded representations 213
redundant relationship 6
regular patterns 117
relationship 6; 232
relevant relationship 7
representation 5; 6; 131; 143
rhythm 231
rock inscriptions 142
rounded images 247

satire 232
scale 261
schematic 143
screen communication 43
see - look - read 93
semantic differential scales 174
semantic information theory ix
semiotics 89
sender 2; 84; 215
Sesame Street 112
shape 108; 148; 246
shadows 244

Index

short-term memory 102
sign languages 130
signal graphics 208
similarity law 71
size 247
social information x
sound 61; 63; 232
sound media 17
Soviet TV 112
speech and body language 211
speech and demonstrations 211
speech and moving pictures 212
speech and stills 212
speech and visuals 210
spoken language 202
Spoken languages 132
spoken word 134
SPOT 279
statistics 229
structure 224
structure of visual language 153
subject 243
sub-meanings 148
suggestive 143
suggestive impact 96
suggestive properties 160
supplement 262
symbol 143; 178; 259
syntagms 133; 148

technical quality 259
technically crafted visuals 176
telecommunications 27
telecommunications media 22
teletext 26
Telstar v
text 50
text and graphic design 204
text and pictures 205

the picture circle 174
the "total teaching aid" 31
time 228
Tsukuba vi
turn 262
TV 12; 110
type-setting machine 57

user's viewpoints 40

verbal language 140; 202
verbo-audio-visual 203
video v; 19; 25
videotex 27; 183
viewer completion 234
vision 63
visualization 237
visual displays 45
visual language factors 155
visual languages 141; 200
visual literacy 146
visual modality 99; 112
visual synonyms 161
volume 239

weather graphics 210
wrist-watch TV vi
write legends 81
written language 202
written language 135
Wundt's illusion 116

zoom 260

CIRCULATION COLLECTION
ROCKVILLE

MONTGOMERY COLLEGE LIBRARIES

0 0000 00503442 6

DATE DUE